Jewish Radical Ultra-Orthodoxy Confronts Modernity, Zionism and Women's Equality

In *Jewish Radical Ultra-Orthodoxy Confronts Modernity, Zionism and Women's Equality*, Professor Motti Inbari undertakes a study of the culture and leadership of Jewish radical ultra-Orthodoxy in Hungary, Jerusalem, and New York. He reviews the history, ideology, and gender relations of prominent ultra-Orthodox leaders Amram Blau (1894–1974), founder of the anti-Zionist Jerusalemite Neturei Karta, and Yoel Teitelbaum (1887–1979), head of the Satmar Hasidic movement in New York. Focusing on the rabbis' biographies, the author analyzes their enclave building methods, their attitude to women and modesty, and their eschatological perspectives. The research is based on newly discovered archival materials, covering many unique and remarkable findings. The author concludes with a discussion of contemporary trends in Jewish religious radicalization. Inbari highlights the resilience of the current generations' sense of community cohesion and their capacity to adapt and overcome challenges such as rehabilitation into potentially hostile secular societies.

Motti Inbari is an associate professor of religion at the University of North Carolina, Pembroke. He is a leading expert on Jewish fundamentalism and has won such prestigious awards as the Adolph L. Dial Award for Scholarship in 2014.

Jewish Radical Ultra-Orthodoxy Confronts Modernity, Zionism and Women's Equality

MOTTI INBARI

University of North Carolina, Pembroke

Translated by Shaul Vardi

CAMBRIDGE
UNIVERSITY PRESS

CAMBRIDGE
UNIVERSITY PRESS

32 Avenue of the Americas, New York, NY 10013–2473, USA

Cambridge University Press is part of the University of Cambridge.

It furthers the University's mission by disseminating knowledge in the pursuit of education, learning, and research at the highest international levels of excellence.

www.cambridge.org
Information on this title: www.cambridge.org/9781107088108

© Motti Inbari 2016

First published 2016

Printed in the United States of America by Sheridan Books, Inc.

A catalog record for this publication is available from the British Library.

ISBN 978-1-107-08810-8 Hardback

To Aliza with love

Contents

Acknowledgments

While I was a postdoctoral fellow at the Schusterman Center for Israel Studies at Brandies in 2008, I received an e-mail one morning from my academic supervisor, Dr. Ilan Troen, informing me that Boston University recently acquired Rabbi Amram Blau's personal archive. As a scholar of Jewish Orthodoxy in Israel, the news was interesting, but still I had many hesitations. At that point, I was engaged in writing another book so I was very busy, and my field of expertise was religious Zionism, not ultra-Orthodox anti-Zionism. Still, I decided to visit the Gottleib Archival Research Center in Boston University, where the personal archive is stored, and I am glad I did that. Blau's archive provided a rich and interesting outlook on Neturei Karta, the movement he established, and its relationship with the greater haredi (ultra-Orthodox) community, and I also found fascinating information about his personal life. From the archival materials I discovered, I composed two chapters, and I wanted to continue my research thus deciding to further investigate other ultra-Orthodox anti-Zionist leaders: Rabbi Yoel Teitelbaum, the Satmar Rebbe, and Rabbi Chaim Elazar Shapira, the Munkacser Rebbe. The book you are holding right now is the product of that research.

I have friends and colleagues who helped me along the way, to whom I owe my gratitude. I want to thank Ilan Troen, the director of the Schusterman Center for Israel Studies at Brandeis. The fellowship he provided me in 2007–2009 was essential for my success as an academic. I remain in deep gratitude to Dr. Troen, who has always been a big supporter of my work. I am also fortunate to have Yaakov Ariel as a friend and a mentor. Dr. Ariel has supported me since my doctoral studies for more than a decade now, and I have learned from him so much. His wisdom and kindness are an inspiration to me.

I am fortunate to have such wonderful colleagues at the University of North Carolina at Pembroke. I want to thank David Nikkel, Chair of the Department of Philosophy and Religion, for being so supportive and making sure I will find the time to conduct my research. I am also grateful to Merrill Miller, Jeffery Geller, Ray Sutherland, Melinda Rosenberg, and Sharon Mattila, my associates at the department, who read sections of the manuscript and offered important comments. I am also very thankful to the Teaching and Learning Center at the University of North Carolina at Pembroke for granting me the HOPES Mid-Career Faculty Support Grant (2013) and the Faculty Research and Development Grant (2014). Their financial assistance was crucial for the success of this project. I am pleased to thank the librarians at UNC Pembroke for their assistance and support.

During the last couple of years, I have had the fortune to get to know Menachem Keren-Kratz, one of the most knowledgeable scholars on the history of ultra-Orthodoxy. Dr. Keren-Kratz has read major sections of the draft manuscript and has offered precious comments. I thank him deeply for his collegiality and friendship. I am also very thankful to Menachem Butler, who read sections of the manuscript and offered excellent comments. I also extend my warm thanks to Robert Eisen, John Collins, and Lorenzo DiTommaso for their comments on Chapter 7.

I thank my dear colleagues and friends for their ongoing support: Marty Slann, Shalom Goldman, Arieh Saposnik, Jody Myers, Eric Fliesch, Joel Rappel, Eliyahu Schleifer, and Baxter Miller. Their friendship means so much to me.

This work could never have been done without the wonderful website hebrewbooks.org. The website is an amazing online library with a collection of over 50,000 scanned rabbinical books, free for use for the general public. I found many of my sources in this library.

Shaul Vardi is my translator and editor for more than a decade. This is the third book he translated for me, and I thank him very much for his work.

Last, I thank my wife Aliza. My academic work has taken us out of Jerusalem into several places around the United States, and the ride wasn't always easy. Still, Aliza went with me without complaints, while raising our two daughters Shani and Shir, allowing me to advance my career. Thank you, Aliza, for being such a wonderful partner. This book is dedicated to you with love.

Sections of Chapter 2 are reprinted with the permission of the Hebrew Union College Annual, originally published as "Rabbi Amram Blau Founder of Neturi Karta Movement: An Abridged Biography." *Hebrew Union College Annual* 81 (2010) 193–232. Sections of Chapter 3 are reprinted with the permission of Indiana University Press, originally published as "The Modesty Campaigns of Rabbi Amram Blau and the Neturei Karta Movement, 1938–1974." *Israel Studies* 17(1), (2012) 105–29. Sections of Chapter 6 are reprinted with the permission of Oxford University Press, originally published as "Messianism as a Political Power in Contemporary Judaism – A Comparison: Radical Ultra Orthodoxy and Messianic Religious Zionism." In: John, Collins (ed.), *Oxford Handbook of Apocalyptic Literature*. New York: Oxford University Press, 2014, 391–406.

Introduction

In May 2006, the campaign against the State of Israel waged by the anti-Zionist ultra-Orthodox (Haredi) public reached a new level when a delegation from Neturei Karta attended an international conference held in Teheran "to reexamine the Holocaust story." The Neturei Karta representatives at the conference called for the destruction of the State of Israel "in peaceful ways."[1] The hostility of this movement toward the State of Israel seems to have pushed it into the arms of Holocaust deniers: a paradoxical development given that Neturei Karta does not question the historical authenticity of the Holocaust.[2] This incongruence may help explain the fact that the delegates' participation in the conference met with an unsympathetic response in the Haredi world and even within their own communities.[3]

The participation of radical ultra-Orthodox Jews in a Holocaust denial conference marked one of the peaks of their anti-Israeli campaign. In the

---

[1] Assaf Uni, "Neturei Karta Delegate to Iranian Holocaust Conference: 'I Pray for Israel's Destruction 'in Peaceful Ways,'" *Ha'aretz*, January 24, 2007 (accessed September 1, 2013). www.haaretz.com/hasen/spages/810100.html.

[2] Rabbi Yoel Teitelbaum, the spiritual leader of the anti-Zionist Haredi movement, is himself a Holocaust survivor. His book *Vayoel Moshe* devotes considerable space to explaining the meaning of the Holocaust. See: Yoel Teitelbaum, *Sefer Vayoel Moshe: Kolel Shelosha Maamarim*. Brooklyn. NY: Bet Mishar Yerushalayim, 1981 (in Hebrew).

[3] The Satmar Rebbe, Yekutiel Yehuda Teitelbaum, even issued a "Torah opinion" stating that the representatives who visited Teheran were "committing an act of insanity" that weakened the community and its zealous struggle. See: www.yoel-ab.com/data/upload_ images/docs/4581bc19075add6b.jpg (accessed September 1, 2013). One of the participants in the delegation was assaulted by other Haredim. See: http://tsofar.com/zofar/ see_article.asp?id=4720 (accessed April 8, 2014).

past, Neturei Karta enjoyed symbolic representation in the governing body of the Palestinian Liberation Organization (PLO), while members of the Satmar Hasidic movement regularly protested against Israel in the United States.

What are the roots of this resentment toward the State of Israel? Why do some Haredi circles engage in what may seem to an outside observer to be an obsessive campaign against Zionism? Are they motivate solely by anti-Israeli sentiments or are less overt motives also involved? This book attempts to answer these questions through an examination of the history of the two main anti-Zionist ultra-Orthodox streams: Neturei Karta and the Satmar Hasidic dynasty. Our narrative focuses on their leaders: Rabbi Amram Blau (1894–1974), head of the Jerusalem-based anti-Zionist Neturei Karta ("Guardians of the City,") and Yoel Teitelbaum (1887–1979), founder of the Satmar Hasidic movement in New York. This historical study highlights the course taken by these leaders in order not only to withstand rising secularism but also to survive the Holocaust, as in the case of Yoel Teitelbaum, and to emerge as important players in contemporary Judaism.

The opposition of Teitelbaum and Blau to the State of Israel must be understood as part of their broader struggle against modern culture in all its manifestations. They embody a unique type of fundamentalist leadership: one that is enclave based and defensive yet engages in constant protest, albeit with only limited use of violence.

This book examines a Haredi subculture that originated in the middle of the nineteenth century in Hungary as a counterresponse to the trends of Enlightenment and Reform. A similar trend also emerged in Jerusalem in the 1920s in response to the rise of the Zionist movement. This subculture was able to survive the Second World War. Rabbi Yoel Teitelbaum, himself a Holocaust survivor, immigrated to Williamsburg, New York in 1946 and reestablished the Satmar Hasidic court. Against all odds, the movement has rebuilt itself and is now one of the strongest Hasidic movements in America and around the world, with an estimated one hundred thousand followers in the United States alone.

Ultra-Orthodoxy is a fast-growing movement in Israel and the United States, primarily due to its very high natural growth rate.[4] This book discusses two movements that stand at the far right of ultra-Orthodoxy and serve, I will argue, as a benchmark for Haredi society as a whole in

---

[4] www.jpost.com/Opinion/Columnists/The-impending-haredi-implosion (accessed April 8, 2014).

terms of religious radicalization. An understanding of these two movements can therefore inform our understanding of religious radicalization in contemporary Judaism.

HISTORICAL PERSPECTIVES ON JEWISH ORTHODOXY

Jacob Katz, a leading scholar of modern Judaism, argues that Orthodox Judaism is a product of the late eighteenth century, when Jewish society on the threshold of modernity underwent a loosening of the bonds of tradition leading to the emergence of non-Orthodox tendencies and trends. According to Katz, the difference between Orthodoxy and earlier traditional Jewish society is that in modern times loyalty to tradition is the product of a conscious decision. Awareness of other Jews' rejection of tradition, an option that was not available in most cases in premodern times, is therefore an essential and universal characteristic of all forms and variations of Orthodoxy. This term became the label for those who persisted in their traditionalist behavior once different kinds of Jew appeared on the scene – *maskilim* (exponents of the Jewish enlightenment) or reformers who deviated from traditional norms while continuing to affirm their affiliation to the community.[5]

However, Orthodoxy is not just the guardian of pure Judaism, as its followers tend to argue. According to Katz, "Orthodoxy was a method of confronting deviant trends, and of responding to the very same stimuli which produced those trends, albeit with conscious effort to deny such extrinsic motivations."[6]

From the eighteenth century onward, Central and Western European Jewry witnessed the rise of the Haskalah movement and various forms of Reform Judaism. The latter part of the nineteenth century saw the

---

[5] Jacob Katz, "Orthodoxy in Historical Perspective." In: Peter Medding (ed.), *Studies in Contemporary Jewry* 2: *The Challenge of Modernity and Jewish Orthodoxy*. Bloomington: Indiana University Press, 1986, pp. 3–4.

[6] *Ibid.*, 5. David Sorotzkin offers a somewhat different analysis, arguing that Orthodoxy and modernity should be seen not as contrasting movements but as two symbiotic sides of the same historical development. As such, one should not see Orthodoxy as merely responding to heterodoxy; these two movements actually interacted with one another. Sorotzkin bases his argument on S.N. Eisentadt's idea of "multiple modernities," according to which secularity and fundamentalism are manifestations of the same modern phenomenon. David Sorotzkin, *Orthodoxy and Modern Disciplination: The Production of Jewish Tradition in Europe in Modern Times.* Tel Aviv: HaKibbutz HaMeuhad, 2011, pp. 3–16 (in Hebrew).

emergence of Jewish secularism,[7] Zionism, and the Bund (Jewish Social-
ism) in Eastern Europe. These ideological movements attracted people
searching for new forms of Jewish identity. For the most part, the traditional rabbinical and communal leadership responded with resolute
opposition. However, they understood that they must create new struc-
tures and organizations in order to compete for the souls of the Jewish
population.[8]

The existence of Jews who deviate from normative Halakhic (Jewish
religious law) practice is by no means an exclusively modern phenomenon. In premodern Jewish societies, however, there was no question that
normative Judaism was defined by allegiance to the law. The autonomous
Jewish communities had the power to expel, fine, or excommunicate the
deviants. The emancipation of the Jews in the nineteenth and twentieth
centuries eliminated the coercive power of the organized community. The
growing number of Jews who preferred a less observant lifestyle created
a dramatic change in the Jewish world as observant Jews became a small
minority among the Jewish masses of Europe.

Moshe Samet proposed the following four characteristics of ultra-
Orthodoxy:

1. A departure from the time-honored principle of *Klal Yisrael*, the
    perception of a unified Jewish community encompassing both the
    observant and the "backsliders." In locations where it was unable
    to control the Jewish community as a whole, Orthodoxy tended to
    separate itself from the larger community and to create its own
    institutions and congregations. In effect, Orthodoxy formed a soci-
    ety within a society.
2. Orthodoxy viewed modern culture with the utmost suspicion. As a
    rule, it rejected modern schooling, even when Jewishly sponsored
    and directed, in favor of an autonomous and conservative Ortho-
    dox educational system. This system adopted a highly selective
    position toward "secular" studies.
3. Orthodox Jews adopted an extremely strict standard of observance
    with respect to the Halakhah. It could be argued that a stringent
    standard of observance previously associated with an elite now

---

[7] Shmuel Feiner, *The Origins of Jewish Secularization in 18th Century Europe*. Philadelphia
and Oxford: University of Pennsylvania Press, 2011.
[8] Adam Ferziger, *Exclusion and Hierarchy: Orthodoxy, Nonobservance, and the Emergence of Modern Jewish Identity*. Philadelphia: University of Pennsylvania Press, 2005,
p. 2.

became the common norm. Likewise, there developed within Orthodoxy a belief in the ability of the pious Halakhic ruler to discern "Halakhic truth."

4. Under Orthodox inspiration, yeshivot were established for advanced religious studies. The students studied Talmud as a means of developing their religiosity and traditionalism and as a sign of piety. Later, in Israel, men studied in these institutions for years on end, regardless of the economic difficulties this created.[9]

According to Adam Ferziger, one of the most important Orthodox responses was the development of a sense of superiority. Many groups within Orthodoxy did not simplistically seek to exclude all other non-observant Jews. They maintained a commitment to a collective bond uniting all Jews, yet at the same time embarked on a constant process of setting boundaries between the members of this collective. Following Mary Douglas's model, Ferziger argues for a distinction between a "hierarchical" and an "enclavist" response. According to Douglas, "Hierarchy is essentially based on grading, so that it must tolerate the idea of a recognized bottom level and make provisions for it [. . .] Enclavists have reasons to avoid grading their members altogether: their habit is outcasting rather than downgrading: their exclusions all work on the outer boundary, the difference between belonging and not belonging. Their virulent hatred of the outsider is shocking to the other cultures [. . .]The religion of an enclave tends to be that of a dissident minority, so sectarian."[10]

Ferziger argues that German Orthodoxy adopted the hierarchical model, allowing it to contain the deviants, who at that point already constituted the majority of the Jewish community, within the boundaries of the Jewish collective. A perception evolved within Orthodoxy that all Jews were part of a greater whole, yet an internal distinction was forged between those who adhered to traditional beliefs and those who deviated from these tenets. The practical result of this process was the stratification of the community into "first-class" and "second-class" Jews. This construction reflected a realization that in a world in which deviance had become normative, an absolutely exclusionary approach was untenable. Room had to be made for those who identified

[9] Moshe Samet, "The Beginnings of Orthodoxy," *Modern Judaism* 8(3), (1988), 249–69.
[10] Mary Douglas, *In the Wilderness: The Doctrine of Defilement in the Book of Numbers.* Sheffield: Sheffield Academic Press, 1993, pp. 45–6.

as Jews despite having abandoned traditional Jewish practice, without legitimizing their actions.[11]

Streams within Hungarian Orthodoxy, which I define as radical ultra-Orthodoxy, developed enclavist tendencies. They labeled as illegitimate any type of Jewish lifestyle that accepts on an ideological level even minor or tactical adjustments to modern innovations and stigmatized those who followed such a course as outcasts. The enclavists developed a pseudo-sectarian approach. Although they did not always attain the level of separateness generally associated with a sect, they demonized all of their enemies, even those from within the Orthodox world, as emissaries of Satanic powers of the *Sitra Ahra* (the "other side") (see Chapter 6). According to Menachem Keren-Kratz, if one of the basic characteristics of Orthodoxy is its conscious seclusion from the non-Orthodox world, radical ultra-Orthodoxy adds a second level of segregation. These groups disassociate themselves not only from non-Orthodox society, but also from mainstream Orthodoxy. These radical groups refrain from participating in Orthodox organizations such as Agudat Yisrael; indeed, their leaders relentlessly and harshly attack these bodies and their members.[12] As Michael Silber has noted, the main campaign waged by radical ultra-Orthodoxy was not directed against the *maskilim* or the reformers but against more moderate exponents of Orthodoxy.[13]

Three different types of Orthodoxy developed in Europe: The first type, neo-Orthodoxy, became the dominant approach among German Jews. Convinced of the inner significance of every detail of the Law, they observed it scrupulously while at the same time remaining open to the influence of the non-Jewish environment, to which they belonged by virtue of civic emancipation.[14]

The second type emerged in Eastern Europe and was willing to adapt to change on various levels. The followers of this philosophy reject modernism and its works on the principled level, even if they have to accommodate themselves to it in practice. The political and cultural developments in Eastern Europe did not include the adoption of modern education and political emancipation, and Jewish social structure was

---

[11] Ferziger, *Exclusion*, pp. 11–5.

[12] Menachem Keren-Kratz, "Marmaros – The Cradle of Extreme Orthodoxy," Modern Judaism 35(2),147–74.

[13] Michael Silber, "The Emergence of Ultra-Orthodoxy: The Invention of Tradition." In: Jack Wertheimer (ed.), *The Uses of Tradition: Jewish Continuity in the Modern Era*. New York: JTS, 1992, pp. 23–84.

[14] Katz, "Orthodoxy," p. 5.

more diverse. The Hasidic communities generally functioned as fortresses against modern life style. However, some Hasidic rabbis adopted a pragmatic approach to the changing times, seeking to promote Torah study while accepting changes that did not threaten the core of their traditional values. An example of this was the Gerrer Rebbe, Avraham Mordechai Alter (1866–1948), who was one of the most prominent leaders of Orthodox Judaism in Poland. Alter supported the use of new mechanisms, such as political parties and limited modern education, in order to preserve the foundations of Orthodoxy (I will discuss this aspect in greater detail in Chapter 4).[15] The response in the Lithuanian Orthodox movement (non-Hasidic) was complex and uneven. One of its leaders, for example, Rabbi Israel Meir HaCohen (the "Hafetz Haim," 1888–1933), developed a multitiered response to deviation that strongly condemned secularity but was on occasions open to a more lenient approach to the Halakhah. As a rule, all of the Eastern European Jewish authorities opposed the idea of a formal schism within the Jewish community between secular and Orthodox.[16]

The third type of response is that of organized and total resistance to change – the radical ultra-Orthodox response that emerged in Hungary, and on which this study focuses. After various religious reforms were introduced in the Arad community under the leadership of Rabbi Aharon Horin (1766–1844) in the early nineteenth century, the traditionalists, under the leadership of Rabbi Moshe Sofer (1762–1839) (known as the "Hatam Sofer,") and Rabbi Moshe Teitelbaum (1758–1841),[17] went onto the offensive. In an effort to safeguard their community, the rabbis adopted an intellectual and institutional strategy that rejected all

---

[15] Gershon Bacon, *The Politics of Tradition: Agudat Yisrael in Poland, 1916–1939.* Jerusalem: Magnes Press, 1996.

[16] Binyamin Brown, "As Swords to the Earth's Body:" Opposition among Eastern European Rabbis to the Idea of Congregational Schism." In: Yossi Goldstein (ed.), *Yosef Daat.* Beersheva: Ben Gurion University Press, 5770 – 2010, pp. 215–44 (in Hebrew); *idem*, "The Spectrum of Orthodox Responses: Ashkenazim and Sephardim." In: Aviezer Ravitzky (ed.), *Shas: Cultural and Ideological Aspects.* Tel Aviv: Am Oved, 2006, pp. 41–96 (in Hebrew).

[17] Moshe Teitelbaum, the great-grandfather of Yoel Teitelbaum, exerted a profound spiritual influence over the Satmar Hasidic movement. Relatively little research has been conducted concerning Moshe Teitelbaum. The first scholar to examine both Teitelbaum Senior and Junior is Keren-Kratz, "Marmaros"; see also: Jacob Katz, *A House Divided: Orthodoxy and Schism in Nineteenth-century Central European Jewry.* Hanover, NH: Brandeis University Press, 1998, pp. 77–85; David Myers, "'Commanded War:' Three Chapters in the 'Military' History of Satmar Hasidism," *Journal of the American Academy of Religion* 81(2) (2013) 1–46.

innovations; indeed, the Hatam Sofer coined the adage that "Anything new is forbidden according to the Torah." He argued that the integrity of the Jewish community depends on the strict adherence of its members to the Orthodox way of life; deviators automatically forfeit the right to be called Jews.[18]

The clash between traditionalists and innovators gained intensity during the decades following the death of the Hatam Sofer. The state authorities also became embroiled in the conflict after the government proposed the establishment of a modern rabbinical seminary, a suggestion that was accepted by the reformers but rejected by the Orthodox. In 1868, following the emancipation of the Jews in Hungary, the government asked the Jews to form a national representative body along the lines of other recognized denominations. The Orthodox minority refused to join such a body, and a schism took place, after which Orthodoxy developed its own institutions. This was the first instance in European Jewish history of an officially recognized Orthodox subgroup.[19]

The attempt to retrace the genealogy and ideological development of radical ultra-Orthodoxy leads to Marmaros County, situated in the northeast of Hungary to the south of Galicia (after the First World War, the area formed part of Romania and later Czechoslovakia). According to Menachem Keren-Kratz, for a period of almost a hundred years, Marmaros and some of the adjacent Hungarian counties served as the arena for the consolidation of ultra-Orthodox ideology. During this period the region became a bastion of religious zealotry, influencing the whole Jewish world by marking the limits of resistance to all modern ideas. It is hardly surprising, therefore, that Rabbi Yoel Teitelbaum emerged from this region.[20]

As Keren-Kratz noted, radical ultra-Orthodoxy developed within two streams of Orthodox Judaism: Ashkenazi (non-Hasidic, often known as Lithuanian) and Hasidic.[21] Neturei Karta developed from both these streams; Amram Blau was not a Hasid, but the movement in the United States was dominated mainly by Hasidic circles. Another form of Jewish Orthodoxy, Religious Zionism, is not relevant to our current discussion though it will be mentioned by way of comparison in Chapter 7.

---

[18] Katz, "Orthodoxy," pp. 6–7.
[19] For more details on the schism see: Katz, *A House Divided.*
[20] Menachem Keren-Kratz, *Marmaros-Sziget: "Extreme Orthodoxy" and Secular Jewish Culture at the Foothills of the Carpathian Mountains.* Jerusalem: Carmel, 2013 (in Hebrew).
[21] *Ibid.*

ULTRA-ORTHODOXY AND ZIONISM

Jewish nationalist ideas began to crystallize in the 1880s with the founding of the Hibbat Zion ("Love of Zion") movement. The movement was not initially associated with a secular worldview, although it included clearly secular elements. Important rabbis also joined the movement, one of whose leaders was Rabbi Shmuel Mohilever, who advocated cooperation between Jews holding different worldviews in order to promote a common national cause.[22]

Although the movement did not arouse strong opposition, certain circles reacted with suspicion. The Mahzikei HaDat ("Adherents of Religion") society was founded by Rabbi Shimon Sofer of Krakow and the Admor (spiritual Hasidic leader, ofter referred to as "Rebbe") Yehoshua of Belz in 1878/9. The purpose of the society was to oppose the Enlightenment that was gaining strength among the Jews of Galicia. The movement founded a newspaper – *Kol Mahzikei HaDat* ("Voice of the Adherents of Religion") – that openly attacked the nationalist ideas promoted by the supporters of the Hibbat Zion movement.[23] The newspaper initially expressed mild disapproval, highlighting the secular tendencies of the movement's leaders. Writers in the newspaper suggested changes to the educational approach of Hibbat Zion and called for its supervision by the Old Yishuv, the community of Torah students living in Palestine who settled the land for spiritual purposes. Toward the end of the 1890s, however, the tone of its opposition intensified considerably. Writers in the newspaper claimed that Jewish nationalism was merely a replication of the process of assimilation on the national level. Indeed, they argued that since Zionism employed the Jewish emblems of language and land, it actually presented a greater threat than Reform or the Enlightenment.[24]

Mahzikei HaDat served as the most prominent body coordinating opposition to Zionism until the formation of the "Black Bureau" in Kovne (now Kaunas) after the First Zionist Congress in 1900. The Black Bureau was established in direct opposition to Herzl's book *The Jewish State*, and was particularly opposed to his demand at the Second Zionist

---

[22] Ehud Luz, "The Limits of Toleration: The Challenge of Cooperation between the Observant and the Nonobservant during the Hibbat Zion period, 1882–1895." In: Shmuel Almog, Jehuda Reinharz, and Anita Shapira (eds.), *Zionism and Religion*. Hanover, NH: Brandeis University Press, 1998, pp. 44–54.

[23] Yosef Salmon, *Religion and Zionism – Early Conflicts*. Jerusalem: The Zionist Library, 5750 – 1990, p. 222(in Hebrew).

[24] *Ibid.*, p. 223.

Congress that the movement seek to secure leadership positions in the Jewish community and to establish Zionist educational institutions – steps that were interpreted as a direct challenge to the hegemony of the traditional Jewish community in Russia. In response, the Musar ("Morality") movement worked under the inspiration of the Black Bureau to establish groups in the major yeshivot and to encourage anti-Zionist and anti-modernist activities. The Musar movement harassed youths from traditional homes who became involved in Zionist activities. These actions were the first organized steps to oppose Zionist supporters.[25]

Cooperation between Hasidim and Mitnagdim (non-Hasidic Orthodox Jews) in the struggle against Zionism began when Shalom Dover Schneerson, the fifth *Admor* of the Lubavitch dynasty, expressed his support for the Black Bureau. Schneerson's antimodernist approach included strong opposition to Zionism. He claimed that at this time there was no commandment to live in the Land of Israel, and indeed he urged Jews living in the Land of Israel to leave. On the theological level he rejected the concept of natural redemption, which argued that the Jews could win their salvation through human actions, and demanded that Jews rely solely on miraculous redemption.[26]

In the spring of 1900 the Black Bureau published a book entitled *Or Liyesharim* ("Light for the Righteous") in an attempt to bring together the main anti-Zionist positions of Haredi Jews in Russia. The contributors to the book included leading figures from traditionalist circles: The leader of Russian Jewry, Rabbi Chaim Soloveitchik, as well as rabbis with modern education such as David Friedman and the British Chief Rabbi Naftali Adler. The Old Yishuv was also represented in an article by Yisrael Dov Frumkin, editor of the newspaper *HaHavatzelet*.[27]

Or Liyesharim was the first book to present a structured argument against the Zionist idea. It presented a theological argument that sanctified Jewish passivity and opposition to activities to expedite the messianic End. The book also emphasized opposition to the antireligious tendencies of Zionism. In practical terms, the authors argued that Zionism was impractical due to economic reasons and that its supporters were few in numbers.[28]

[25] *Ibid.*, pp. 227–9.
[26] Shalom Ratzbi, "Anti-Zionism and Messianic Tension in the Thought of Rabbi Shalom Dover," *HaTziyonut* 20 (5756 – 1996), 77–101 (in Hebrew).
[27] Dalya Levi, "'Or Liyesharim' – An Anti-Zionist Manifesto – and Several Responses," *HaTziyonut* 19 (1998), 31–65 (in Hebrew).
[28] Shlomo Z. Landau and Yosef Rabinowitz, *Or Liyesharim*, Warsaw: R. Meir Yechiel Alter Publications, 1900, pp. 38–43 (in Hebrew).

According to Yosef Salmon, the publication of this book resolved the question of the attitude toward Zionism in traditional circles. During the eight years preceding its publication, traditionalist Jews had shown considerable doubts regarding the new movement. Over this period the response changed from a broadly supportive one to forthright opposition.[29] The publication showed that the efforts made by the Zionist movement, particularly at the Third Zionist Congress, to promote a reconciliation with traditionalist circles had had little practical impact.[30]

After Zionism gained a dominant presence among the Jewish people during the twentieth century, radical ultra-Orthodoxy turned much of its energy to its struggle against the movement. Aviezer Ravitzky has shown that the leaders of radical ultra-Orthodoxy developed a demonological theory according to which the spiritual essence of the Land of Israel intensifies both holiness and impurity and constitutes a battleground between these two polar powers. Since the Land of Israel intensifies impurity, settling the Land should be confined to zealous fearers of God who are capable of withstanding evil. Ravitzky argues that the rejection of Zionism by Chaim Elazar Shapira (1871–1937), the Munkacser Rebbe and one of the prominent leaders of the Hungarian branch of radical ultra-Orthodoxy before the Second World War, developed into nothing less than an existential religious terror that focused on the Land's awesome powers. Yoel Teitelbaum continued to develop this demonological theory by drawing a comparison between the Holocaust and the establishment of the State of Israel. He saw both these events as part of the final eruption of the forces of evil as a prelude to redemption. Teitelbaum argued that the Zionist rebellion against divine authority, and its activities to settle the Land of Israel in violation of God's clear commands not to do so before the coming of the messiah, resulted in the Holocaust as a form of divine punishment. Teitelbaum explained the successes of Zionism, including the establishment of the state and its military victories, as the rise of Satanic powers ahead of the final war of the End Times.[31]

Ravitzky argued that the radical circles developed an antimessianic theory and warned against the false messianism associated with the

---

[29] Another source of anti-Zionism was the newspaper *HaPeles*.
[30] Salmon, *Religion and Zionism*, p. 294.
[31] Aviezer Ravitzky, *Messianism, Zionism, and Religious Radicalism*. Chicago and London: University of Chicago Press, 1993, pp. 40–78; Menachem Keren-Kratz, "Hast Thou Escaped, and also Taken Possession? The Satmar Rebbe – Rabbi Yoel Teitelbaum and his Followers' Response to Criticism of his Conduct During and After the Holocaust," *Dapim: Studies on the Holocaust* 28(2), 97–120.

Zionists' acts. He stressed that radical ultra-Orthodoxy advocated passivity: "It is the Jews' patient expectation for complete, utopian redemption ... that capture the fundamental essence of Judaism itself: acknowledgment of Divine rule."[32] I do not entirely share Ravitzky's view. While radical ultra-Orthodox theology indeed sanctified passivity, the purpose of this approach was intended to hasten redemption, as illustrated by many examples I provide later here. Accordingly, this theology should not be viewed as antimessianic, but rather as an alternative path for active messianism. Passivity is merely a different course of action to channel immanent messianic expectations.

FUNDAMENTALISM

Fundamentalism is a pattern of religious militancy whereby self-styled "true believers" attempt to arrest the erosion of religious identity, fortify the borders of the religious community, and create viable alternatives to secular institutions and behavior. All fundamentalist movements interact with the outside world: some retreat from society in order to avoid the influence of secularity, while others attempt to overthrow the secular regime. The study *Strong Religion* (Almond, Appleby, and Sivan 2003) attempts to define fundamentalists' interactions with the world in four categories: world conqueror, world transformer, world creator, and world renouncer. Religious movements are not frozen and may move from one category to another.[33]

A situation can emerge in which patriotism and complete identification with the secular state become an integral part of the religious identity of certain fundamentalist movements. This pattern is particularly evident in the case of American Christian fundamentalism. A long-standing tradition of the separation of religion and state, alongside encouragement for freedom of religion, led to the emergence of a cultural climate of religious and ethnic pluralism, ensuring the independent and autonomous presence of religious expression and competition for the souls of the believers. Against this background, American evangelical Christianity could develop social and organizational networks that separate it from the liberal streams of Christianity without implying hostility to the

---

[32] Ravitzky, *Messianism*, p. 62.

[33] Gabriel A. Almond, Scott R. Appleby and Emmanuel Sivan, *Strong Religion – The Rise of Fundamentalism around the World*. Chicago: University of Chicago Press, 2003, pp. 145–90.

government or revolutionary aspirations, thus defined as world trans-
formers.[34] By contrast, a world conquering pattern of fundamentalism
that emerged in the Islamic world has sought to replace secular government through an act of revolution. Many Islamic movements have preferred to distance themselves from secular society by creating enclaves
that will allow them to gain strength and support their revolutionary
aspirations. The Shiites in Iran are an example of this approach. Severe
government persecution of religious leaders in Iran, combined with massive agrarian reforms at the expense of the religious establishment, pushed
the Ulama into the 1979 revolution.[35]

The world creator and world renouncer displace the world conquering
mode. They both focus on building and safeguarding the enclave;
however, they leave it to God to conquer the world, and thus adopt a
defensive rather than an offensive stance. The world creator is intention-
ally in competition with the secular world; his strategy is to present
ideological and institutional alternatives and to enlarge the enclave by
bringing in converts. The enclave focuses on preserving purity and
avoiding the corruption that comes from intermingling with outsiders.
For all his defensiveness, the world creator may one day find himself
strong enough to become a world conqueror or world transformer.[36]

The world renouncer, a relative rare type of fundamentalist, seeks
purity and self-preservation rather than hegemony over fallen outsiders.
The movement's energies are directed inward to the preservation of the
enclave through education, domestic life, and religious rituals. The leadership often defines itself and the movement in contrast to the more
lenient and compromising leadership of the general enclave, which it sees
as jeopardizing the integrity of the religious tradition. The ideology is
counteracculturative and antimodern, and the movement is not seeking
to transform outsiders, who are anyway condemned. The world renouncer is a separatist par excellence.[37]

This division between world creator and world renouncer and the
examples given may help explain the place of the mainstream Haredi
circles in Israel and the United States represented by Agudat Yisrael and

---

[34] Joel Carpenter, *Revive Us Again: The Reawakening of American Fundamentalism*. New York: Oxford University Press, 1997; Paul Boyer, *When Time Shall Be No More*. Cambridge: Harvard University Press, 1992, pp. 225–53.
[35] Masoud Kazemzadeh, *Islamic Fundamentalism, Feminism, and Gender Inequality in Iran Under Khomeini*. Lanham, MD: University Press of America, 2002.
[36] Almond, Appleby, and Sivan, *Strong Religion*, 150, pp. 179–80.
[37] *Ibid.*, pp. 150, 185.

their difference from Neturei Karta or Satmar. The Haredi public attempts to keep itself separate from the secular population; it lives in enclaves and isolates itself in geographical terms, as well as through external appearance (distinctive clothing) and language (their unique jargon[38] and to some extent the use of Yiddish). As a rule, the Haredi public creates its own executive frameworks and attempts to avoid reliance on state mechanisms in order to manage its community. This entails a form of physical withdrawal, especially in Israel. This withdrawal is not total, however, and the Haredi public continues to maintain a symbiotic relationship with the secular State of Israel, including full participation in the political system and an effort to shape the character of the state. This involvement is utilitarian in nature and intended to secure financial support to enable the Torah students and the community to maintain their way of life. They operate within the secular world in order to secure political goals and to increase their ranks through institutions that encourage outsiders to join the Haredi world. Their influence on Israel's politics, and hence on Israel's identity, puts them in the categories of both world creator and world transformer.

By contrast, Neturei Karta and Satmar (as well as other similar factions, such as HaEdah HaHaredit and the Toldot Aharon Hasidic movement) view themselves as purist and strongly separatist communities that seek to avoid any contact or cooperation with the secular world and struggle actively against any matter that they perceive as blasphemous. As a generalization,[39] these movements are not willing to compromise their world view, even if this entails a heavy price such as scorn and humiliation. They isolate themselves from any contact with the secular world, oppose any form of compromise or leniency, and engage in frequent public protests bordering on physical violence. In many cases, their protests against the State of Israel expose the weakness of the more moderate leadership of other Haredi groups, who are obliged in practice to accept the radicals' goals. The difference between Neturei Karta and general Haredi society in Israel is also reflected in the realization on the part of the majority of the Haredi public that this way of life is economically unviable and can only be maintained by a small and distinct group that lives among the general public and enjoys its support. The unique

---

[38] Sarah Bunin Benor, *Becoming Frum: How Newcomers Learn the Language and Culture of Orthodox Judaism*. New Brunswick, NJ: Rutgers University Press, 2012.
[39] In Chapter 4 I discuss an exception to this rule in the form of the acceptance by the Satmar court in New York of compromises regarding women's modesty and education.

character of Neturei Karta and Satmar as world-renouncer movements is further manifested in the fact that these groups do not expound revolutionary positions that seek to change the general character of the regime, as do revolutionary Muslims. They hold passive political views and oppose any Jewish political activism until the coming of Messiah.[40]

METHODOLOGY AND STRUCTURE

This book focuses on four main themes: A biographical description of Teitelbaum and Blau; discussion of their enclave-building methods, their attitude to women and modesty, and their eschatological perspectives.

The study of Rabbi Blau's life is based mostly on his personal archive, which recently reached Boston University by a circuitous route. Having access to the personal archive of a fundamentalist leader is a unique opportunity, and particularly so in the case of the study of Neturei Karta. Research on Amram Blau and Neturei Karta has hitherto been hampered by the movement's fierce opposition to the secular world and its refusal to allow scholars to study their archives.[41]

Due to Yoel Teitelbaum's importance in contemporary Judaism, scholarship have been published on his anti-Zionist ideology,[42] though almost none of them discussed his biography.[43] In order to reconstruct Rabbi Teitelbaum's biography, I had to draw on different sources: the

---

[40] Aviezer Ravitzky, "'Forcing the End:' Zionism and the State of Israel as Antimessianic Undertakings." In: Jonathan Frankel (ed.), *Studies in Contemporary Jewry 7: Jews and Messianism in the Modern Era: Metaphor and Meaning*, New York: Oxford University Press, 1991, pp. 34–67.

[41] Another scholar who studied this archive is Kimmi Caplan. His articles were published in Hebrew: "The Development of Separation Circles among Haredi Zealots: The Case of Amram Blau," *Zion* 76(2) (2011), 179–218 (in Hebrew); *idem*, "'An Insolent, Dirty Convert Woman:' Amram Blau and Ruth Ben David Marriage Affair," *Iyunim Bitkumat Israel*, 20 (2010), 300–35 (in Hebrew).

[42] Refael Kadosh, *Extremist Religious Philosophy: The Radical Religious Doctrines of the Satmar Rebbe*. PhD Dissertation, The University of Cape Town, 2011 (in Hebrew); Norman Lamm, "The Ideology of the Neturei Karta: According to the Satmarer Version," *Tradition* 12(2) (1971), 38–53; Allan L. Nadler, "Piety and Politics: The Case of the Satmar Rebbe," *Judaism* 31(2) (1982), 135–52; Zvi Jonathan Kaplan, "Rabbi Teitelbaum, Zionism, and Hungarian Ultra-Orthodoxy," *Modern Judaism* 24(2) (2004), 165–78; and David Sorotzkin, "Building the Earthly and Destroying the Heavenly: The Satmar Rebbe and Radical Orthodox School of Thought." In: Aviezer Ravitzky (ed.), *The Land of Israel in 20th Century Jewish Thought*. Jerusalem: Ben Zvi Institute, 2004, pp. 133–67 (in Hebrew).

[43] After the completion of this research a doctoral dissertation on the biography of Rabbi Teitelbaum was published. Menachem Keren-Kratz, *R' Yoel Teitelbaum – The Satmar*

hagiographical literature, his collection of letters, and other scholarly works discussing Teitelbaum and his community in New York.[44] Following Teitelbaum's death in 1979 his followers split into several camps, each of which wrote a biography of the rabbi that suited its own positions and needs.[45] Comparing and contrasting these works yielded interesting insights into Teitelbaum's leadership and character. Collecting the clues and hidden messages from several sources led me to hypothesize that during and even after the Holocaust the rabbi articulated ideas that came close to those of Agudat Yisrael, including de facto acceptance of the Zionist movement.

The historical analysis of the rabbis' path includes extensive discussion of the way they chose to strengthen the Haredi community. In the case of Jerusalem, Rabbi Blau's authority was one of second fiddle, serving as an opposition to the leadership of the more moderate Agudat Yisrael movement. Blau constantly challenged their power with modesty campaigns, Sabbath demonstrations, and campaigns against modern education, which allowed him to demonstrate his zealotry and pushed the wider Haredi community to the extreme. As for Rabbi Teitelbaum, he used his power to build educational institutions that would block secular influence, developed a unique code of dress to emphasis his community's distinct identity, and later envisioned a segregated community – Kiryas Yoel – as a modern-day Haredi *shtetl* (the Yiddish term for the small Jewish towns of Eastern Europe in the days before the Holocaust).

I trace the ideology of Rabbi Teitelbaum through a discussion of the teachings of Rabbis Akiva Yosef Schlesinger (1838–1922),[46] Chaim

---

Rabbi (1887–1979): Biography, Tel Aviv: PhD dissertation, Tel Aviv University, 2013 (in Hebrew).

[44] On the Satmar community in New York, see: Israel Rubin, *Two Generations of Urban Island* (2nd edition), New York: Peter Lang, 1997; Jerome Mintz, *Hassidic People: A Place in the New World*. Cambridge: Harvard University Press, 1992; Solomon Poll, *The Hassidic Community of Williamsburg* (2nd edition). New Brunswick: Transaction Publishers, 2006.

[45] Dovid Meisels, *The Rebbe – The Extraordinary Life and Worldview of Rabbeinu Yoel Teitelbaum the Satmar Rebbe*. NJ: Israel Book Shop, 2011; Alexander Deitsch, *Butzina Kadisha*, 1–2. New York: Tiferes Publishing, 1998, 2000 (in Hebrew); Shlomo Yaacov Gelbman, *Moshian Shel Yisrael* 1–9. Kiryas Yoel: Ohel Torah Publishers, 1989–2008 (in Hebrew).

[46] Michael Silber, "The Emergence"; *idem*, "Alliance of Hebrews, 1863–1875: The Diaspora Roots of an Ultra-Orthodox Proto-Zionist Utopia in Palestine," *The Journal of Israeli History* 27(2) (2008), 119–47.

Elazar Shapira (the Munkacser Rebbe) (1871–1937),[47] and Yeshayah Asher Zelig Margaliot (1894–1968).[48] Like Teitelbaum, all these rabbis viewed the modern era as so degenerate that its only possible meaning could be the imminent arrival of the messiah. All these rabbis adopted a dualistic approach according to which the only proper Jewish way of life is radical ultra-Orthodoxy, while any deviation from this course represents the rise of Satanic powers, which are expected to grow prior to the End Times. My research led me to hypothesize that it is even possible that Rabbi Shapira saw himself as a candidate for the role of the righteous messiah.

This Haredi sub-culture in Israel and the United States made a supreme effort to block the advancement of women. I discuss at length the establishment of the dress code and its reinforcement by means of modesty campaigns and modesty patrols. Another aspect of gender roles is the debate over the secular education of women: on the one hand this is regarded as unwelcome; on the other, it proves essential for the financial survival of the movement.

Chapter 1 discusses the background to the rise of Neturei Karta, and in particular the circumstances that led to the assassination of Jacob-Israël de-Haan (1881–1924), the "foreign Minister" of the Old Yishuv (the well-established community of Jewish religious scholars living mainly in Jerusalem). De Haan, who was a Dutch writer and a journalist, joined the Old Yishuv and led it to a fierce struggle with the immerging Zionist Yishuv. His campaigns focused on the separation of his community from the authority of the Zionists, and he also tried to reach a peace treaty with the Hashemite dynasty, while undermining the Balfour Declaration. His diplomatic maneuvers led to his violent and premature death.

Chapter 2 examines the life and approach of Rabbi Amram Blau (1886–1974), founder of the radical ultra-Orthodox and anti-Zionist organization Neturei Karta. The chapter begins by presenting Blau's plan to establish an agricultural settlement for families from the Old Yishuv, to be situated on the outskirts of Jerusalem. The next section describes the establishment of Neturei Karta and its struggle to strengthen the Haredi enclave in Jerusalem, including the campaign for Sabbath observance and

---

[47] Allan Nadler, "The War on Modernity of R. Hayyim Elazar Shapira of Munkacz," *Modern Judaism* 14(3) (1994), 233–64; Ravitzky, *Messianism*, pp. 40–62. Levi Y. Kooper, *The Munkacs Rebbe Chaim Elazar Shapira the Hassidic Ruler – Biography and Method.* Doctoral Dissertation, Bar Ilan University, 2011 (in Hebrew).

[48] Yehuda Liebes, "HaEdah HaHaredit in Jerusalem and the Judea Desert Sect," *Jerusalem Research in Judaic Studies* 3 (1981), 135–52.

Haredi education. The research also identifies new components in Amram Blau's ongoing campaign against Zionism. In the field of Blau's personal life, the chapter offers some fresh insights into the path that took him to the leadership of HaEdah HaHaredit, and reveals documents that cast a new light on the scandal caused in his later life by his second marriage to the convert Ruth Ben David and their stormy relationship.

Chapter 3 continues the discussion of Blau's Neturei Karta, focusing on its modesty campaigns. The chapter explores the defensive stage of the modesty campaign, which was directed mainly at the Haredi enclave itself, and sought to strengthen it in its struggle against secular Jerusalem. This process included the establishment of the modesty patrols. The examination then progresses to the offensive campaign, including the struggle against mixed swimming pools and against a club operated by the Working Mothers' organization. The main purpose of this stage was to reinforce Neturei Karta's leadership position among the Haredi public in Jerusalem. It also explores the ethos of zealotry in the context of the torching of a sex shop in Tel Aviv.

Chapter 4 takes us to post First World War Czechoslovakia and a discussion of messianic tension in the biography of Rabbi Chaim Elazar Shapira (1871–1937), the Munkacser Rebbe, who was a prominent leader of radical ultra-Orthodoxy in his day. This chapter demonstrates intense tension that developed as a response to the First World War and continued until his death. His messianic activists included a trip to Jerusalem to crown the king messiah, which ended in a fiasco; a public dispute with the Gerrer Rebbe, Avraham Mordechai Alter, the most prominent Hasidic leader of the time, partly in order to disqualify the Gerrer as a messianic candidate and promote himself as an alternative candidate; and magical ceremonies that were intended to hasten the End.

Chapter 5 describes Yoel Teitelbaum's biography, focusing on three periods. The first part discusses his childhood and early career as a ruler-Rebbe in Hungary until the beginning of the Second World War. The second part describes his release from the Hungarian Ghetto in Klasenberg, his arrival in Switzerland on the Kastner Train, his brief stay in Mandatory Palestine, and his emigration to the United States. The third part presents the reconstruction of the Hasidic world in the United States by means of the religious enclave. It was this latter period that made Teitelbaum one of the greatest leaders of the post-Holocaust Orthodox world.

Chapter 6 presents the ideology of Hasidic radical ultra-Orthodoxy, focusing on the belief that the End Times are drawing near, a conclusion they reached due to the deterioration in the physical and the spiritual world of Orthodox Jewry. This ideology led them into a sharp dualism: They view themselves as the righteous ones, while all of their opponents – secular and moderate Orthodox alike – are seen as the reincarnation of Satanic powers.

Due to the importance of fundamentalist religious movements in contemporary affairs and their growing influence in the Jewish world, in particular, the final chapter is devoted to a comparison between ancient and modern Jewish religious radicals. I compared the pattern of religious zealotry as exemplified by three movements: radical ultra-Orthodoxy, messianic Religious Zionism and Second Temple zealots. I examine possible ideological similarities between the leaders of the Jewish Revolt of 66–70 BC and the modern movements. The chapter opens with a discussion of the term "zealotry" from both Biblical and rabbinical perspectives, before moving on to a comparison of the three movements according to several parameters: their attitudes toward violence, their position regarding eschatological expectations, and their relationship to Jewish nationalism.

The book ends with an epilogue discussing some contemporary topics among Neturei Karta and Satmar, and their future possible implications, such as the consequences of Haredi draft to the Israeli army, and the growth of reliance on welfare among Hasidic families in New York.

The de Haan assassination and the background to the formation of Neturei Karta

The late nineteenth century saw dramatic developments in the character of the Jewish community in Palestine with the commencement of Zionist immigration. The Old Yishuv in Jerusalem was a longstanding community of observant Sephardi and Ashkenazi Jews who adhered to the traditional perception of settlement in the Land of Israel as a religious and spiritual value of importance to the entire Jewish people. They believed that Jewish settlement in the Land of Israel must fulfill a religious and spiritual function – prayer and Torah study – and, accordingly, the Jewish Diaspora was urged to ensure the economic survival of this settlement. The Diaspora was therefore expected to meet economic and physical needs, while the Jewish community in the Land of Israel was to devote itself to maintaining the central values of traditional Jewish society: prayer and Torah study in the Holy Land. In principle, the Jews of Palestine saw themselves not as the recipients of charity but as the rightful recipients of remuneration as part of a barter system.[1] They argued that Jewish life in the Land of Israel was intended solely for the study of Torah, and accordingly they viewed themselves as a minority that must struggle and speak out against any dilution of this way of life.[2]

The commencement of British rule in Palestine (1918) did not lead to any significant changes in the relationship between the religious

---

[1] Menachem Friedman, *Society and Religion – Non-Zionist Orthodoxy in the Land of Israel, 1918–1936*. Jerusalem: Ben Zvi Institute, 5738 – 1978, pp. 1–2 (in Hebrew).

[2] Aviezer Ravitzky, *Messianism, Zionism, and Religious Radicalism*. Chicago and London: University of Chicago Press, 1993, pp. 40–78.

communities and central government. The Ottoman millet system, which granted administrative autonomy to the recognized religious communities, remained intact. However, the Balfour Declaration (1917) recognizing the right of the Jewish people to a "national home" led to the definition of the Zionist movement as the representative of the Jewish community in Palestine. In practical terms, this constituted a dramatic change, and Haredi Jews were forced to cope with the new political hegemony of the emerging Zionist community. During the Ottoman period, the Old Yishuv had exercised considerable governmental power over its communities through the institution of the Hakham Bashi (Sephardi chief rabbi). The transition to the British Mandate created a new balance of political power and led to friction between the Old and New (Zionist) Yishuv; the process of developing understandings and cooperation between the two sides took almost a decade. The turning point in the relations between the two sides began following the murder of Dr. Jacob-Israël de Haan in 1924. The disagreements provided the background to the establishment of Neturei Karta. Even prior to the political assassination of de Haan, however, the relations between the two sides were characterized by escalation and conflict in the legal and political arenas. This chapter will discuss de Haan's dramatic life and the events that led to his death.

Following the British conquest of Palestine in 1918, Zionist activists in Jerusalem established a single committee to represent all the Jews in the city. The separatist Haredi community refused to join the committee and established an alternative body known as the Ashkenazi City Committee under the authority of Rabbis Yosef Sonnenfeld (1849–1932) and Yitzhak Yeruham Diskin (1839–1925). The rabbis of the Old Yishuv objected to the national character of the main committee and feared that the new body would seize control of their assets, impose secular education, and collect taxes.

Rabbi Sonnenfeld was born in Slovakia, which at the time was part of the Austro-Hungarian Empire. He studied at Pressburg Yeshivah, the largest and most influential yeshivah in Central Europe in the nineteenth century, under the auspices of Shmuel Binyamin Sofer (the "Ktav Sofer"), the son of the Hatam Sofer. In 1873, he settled in Jerusalem with his wife and gained widespread recognition in the Old Yishuv as an erudite Torah scholar. He was one of the directors of the Hungarian Kollel, a position that was accompanied by considerable power in distributing charitable donations from abroad. Following the establishment of the branch of Agudat Yisrael in Jerusalem, Sonnenfeld became one of its most prominent leaders, thereby acquiring formal political support for his campaigns.[3]

The Zionists' demand that women be permitted to participate in the elections for the community and their refusal to obey the rabbinical authorities on the matter provided clear evidence of the rebellious nature of Zionism from the Haredi perspective. This heightened demands for absolute separatism, which could be interpreted in two ways: Firstly, as communal separatism, ensuring that observant and secular Jews would not live in the same community; and secondly, as total separation from the "evil ones" and their wicked ways.[4]

The Tenth Zionist Congress, held in 1911, decided to undertake educational and cultural activities in Palestine and the countries of the East in the spirit of Jewish nationalism. This decision led to a split in the Zionist movement. A large section of Orthodox Jews left the Mizrahi Movement that was part of the Zionist Organization and established Agudat Yisrael, a political movement founded in 1912 in order to unite all sections of the Orthodox community against the profound trend toward secularization in the Jewish world. The movement's main power-base was among traditional circles in Central and especially Eastern Europe. In Palestine, Agudat Yisrael was represented by circles who supported the principle of total separatism.[5]

The Hungarian model for the secession of the ultra-Orthodox community served to an extent as a blueprint for the population in Jerusalem identified with the Old Yishuv. Staking its claim to religious liberty, this community argued that it could not coexist in common institutions under the leadership of nationalist Jews. However this model was not appropriate in all stages of the struggle, and there is extensive evidence that Sonnenfeld was willing to cooperate with the Zionists under certain circumstances. Speaking at the San Remo Conference in 1922, for example, he advocated unrestricted immigration by Jews to Palestine as demanded by the Zionists. The memorandum he submitted to the conference sought to avoid phraseology that might be interpreted as an

---

[3] Yitzhak Hershkowitz, "Rabbi Chaim Yosef Sonnenfeld." In: Benjamin Brown and Nissim Leon (eds.), *Hagdolim: The People Who Shaped Haredi Judaism in Israel: A Collection of Essays in Honor of Professor Menachem Friedman*. Jerusalem: Van Leer (forthcoming) (in Hebrew).

[4] Menachem Friedman, *Haredi Society – Sources, Trends, and Processes*. Jerusalem: Jerusalem Institute for Israel Studies, 1991, p. 31 (in Hebrew).

[5] Yosef Fund, *Separation or Participation: Agudat Yisrael versus Zionism and the State of Israel*. Jerusalem: Magnes Press, 1999 (in Hebrew).

attack on Zionist goals.[6] This position changed after Dr. Jacob Israël de Haan arrived on the scene.

The story of de Haan's life and death is a fascinating episode that I will only be able to touch on briefly here. He was born into a traditional Jewish family in Smilde in the Netherlands; his father was a cantor and teacher. At an early age, de Haan left the religious lifestyle and joined various Communist groups. De Haan was a man of outstanding intellectual capabilities. He was considered one of the greatest Dutch poets of his time and also authored two novels that were the subject of considerable attention. He found time to gain a PhD in law and went on to teach law at Amsterdam University. He wrote an important report on the prisons of the Russian Empire, drawing global attention to the appalling conditions in these institutions. His books and poems openly raised themes reflecting his homosexual orientation, and in response the Social Democratic party began to distance itself from de Haan. He married a Christian woman, Johanna Van Maarseveen, who was nine years his senior and provided him with financial support. Even after assuming a Haredi way of life, he remained married to Van Maarseveen and maintained his contact with her. He was profoundly influenced by the anti-Semitism that was rife in upper-class social circles in the Netherlands. During the First World War, he responded to anti-Semitism by returning to Orthodox Judaism and joining the Mizrahi Religious-Zionist party. In 1919, he emigrated to Palestine, earning a living as a reporter for the Dutch newspaper *Algemeen Handelsblad* and working as a lecturer at the British Mandate School of Law and Economics in Palestine. He initially hoped to find his place in the Zionist leadership, but his services were declined. The Mizrahi movement also responded coolly to his advances and he failed to secure a place in the faculty of the Hebrew University. De Haan led a covert homosexual lifestyle in Palestine and testimony suggests that he had sexual relations with Arab youths.[7]

Shortly after migrating to Palestine, de Haan became profoundly disappointed, disillusioned by what he viewed as the bureaucratic and corrupt conduct of the Zionist leadership in Palestine. He was concerned

---

[6] Shlomo Nakdimon and Shaul Mayzlish, *De Haan: The First Political Assassination in the Land of Israel*. Tel Aviv: Modan, 1985, pp. 76–8 (in Hebrew).

[7] Nakdimon and Mayzlish's work offers the most comprehensive biography of de Haan, including discussion of his early life before he assumed a Haredi identity as well as an examination of his sexual orientation.

at the deteriorating relations between Jews and Arabs in Palestine and by attempts to exclude Arabs from the job market through the "Hebrew labor" campaign. As time passed, he became increasingly pessimistic regarding the prospects of Zionism.[8]

De Haan met Sonnenfeld during the course of his journalistic work and was enchanted by the rabbi. In March 1920, he decided to change his allegiance and became a member of the Ashkenazi City Committee. He then began to provide services as a counsel and "foreign minister" for the Old Yishuv. The activists of the Old Yishuv lacked the necessary skills to compete with the Zionists for the sympathies of the British rulers. De Haan, by contrast, was a recognized writer and sophisticated cosmopolitan who spoke numerous languages and enjoyed access to prominent figures around the world. De Haan encouraged the Old Yishuv to adopt a militant stance against Zionism. At one point, he even attempted to persuade the Hashemite dynasty to sign a political agreement undermining the Balfour Declaration. He met his end when a Zionist assassin fired three bullets directly at his heart.

In the legal arena de Haan sought to oppose the claim that the Jews constituted a single religious community according to the Ottoman model of the millet. Instead, he advocated the foundation of two autonomous communities – a national community and a Haredi community.[9]

One of the first struggles between the two factions concerned the establishment of the chief rabbinate. The British rulers demanded that a single rabbinate be established for Jews in Palestine, inheriting the Ottoman institution of the Hakham Bashi. The British recognized that a single Sephardi chief rabbi would be insufficient, and accordingly they agreed to the establishment of a parallel institution for Ashkenazim. The Zionist leadership chose Rabbis Avraham Yitzhak Kook and Yaacov Meir as the Ashkenazi and Sephardi chief rabbis, respectively. The chief

---

[8] Michael Berkovitz, "Rejecting Zion, Embracing the Orient: The Life and Death of Jacob Israel de Haan." In: Evan D. Kalmar and Derek Penslar (eds.), *Orientalism and the Jews*. Waltham: Brandeis University Press, 2005, pp. 109–24.

[9] The Haredi literature relating to de Haan presents a fuller version of his activities on behalf of the community. However, this literature ignores de Haan's personal life and provides a highly selective review of his actions. For further discussion of his legal and political campaigns, see: David Halevy, *Murder in Jerusalem: The Affair of the Murder of Prof. de Haan.* Bnai Brak: Tefutza, 1987 (in Hebrew); Zvi Meshi Zahav and Yehuda Meshi Zahav, *The Martyr Rabbi Yaacov Yisrael de Haan, May G-d Avenge His Blood: The First Zionist Murder in the Land of Israel.* Jerusalem: Institute of Haredi Judaism, Sivan 5746 – 1986 (in Hebrew).

rabbis' powers were confined solely to the enforcement of Jewish religious law and matters of personal status.[10]

The Old Yishuv in Jerusalem was profoundly disturbed by the establishment of the rabbinate and launched a direct attack on the institution, declaring a day of fasting and mourning. The Old Yishuv could not accept that their adversaries from the Zionist movement could control the area of religious services and launched a legal battle against the rabbinate's powers. De Haan played a leading role in this campaign, which sought to exclude from the rabbinate's authority the religious trusts representing the Old Yishuv, such as the kollelim and religious institutions, which were originally expected to come under the authority of the chief rabbinate. Thanks to de Haan's efforts, the British allowed the Old Yishuv to establish its own Office of Religious Trusts, independently of the chief rabbinate.[11] He also led a legal campaign to secure recognition for the right of the Haredi community to maintain its own system for the slaughtering of meat, separate from that of the chief rabbinate. The compromise reached required the Haredi slaughters to state expressly that they were not supervised by the rabbinate.[12]

Another legal front concerned exemption from payment of the "Matzah Tax" in Jerusalem. In 1921, the High Commissioner allowed the Jerusalem City Committee to collect a special tax on matzah for Passover in order to finance its activities. The Ashkenazi City Committee objected fiercely to the tax, arguing that it discriminated against its followers, who purchased large quantities of matzah for Passover, while the followers of the general City Committee were less strict about eating matzah. Over the course of the four-year struggle, the High Commissioner initially declined to recognize the existence of two separate Jewish communities. The Haredim refused to accept defeat and rejected various proposed compromises, and eventually the tax was abolished.[13]

According to the Haredi researcher David Halevy, de Haan's greatest achievement was preventing the adoption of the "Communities Constitution" in its original format. The format of the constitution adopted in January 1928 (after de Haan's assassination) reflected a compromise between the two sides. The Mandate authorities announced the establishment of a recognized Jewish religious community in Palestine and granted

---

[10] Friedman, *Society and Religion*, pp. 110–27, 367–88.
[11] Meshi Zahav and Meshi Zahav, *The Martyr*, p. 84.
[12] Nakdimon and Mayzlish, *De Haan*, pp. 107–10.
[13] Halevy, *Murder in Jerusalem*, pp. 84–92.

the Council of the Chief Rabbinate the status of a supreme court of appeals. The subsequent compromise clarified that membership of "Knesset Israel," the parliamentary institution of the Jewish residents of Palestine, was voluntary, and the authority of the chief rabbinate extended only to those Jewish subjects of the Mandate who chose to affiliate to the body. This compromise allowed a parallel organization in the framework of HaEdah HaHaredit ("the Haredi Community"), which was not officially recognized by the Mandate authorities. Although HaEdah HaHaredit did not receive parallel powers to those enjoyed by Knesset Israel, the right of secession constituted a considerable achievement for the non-Zionist Haredim. According to Halevy, 13,000 individuals exercised their right to secede from Knesset Israel, 10,000 of whom lived in Jerusalem.[14]

However, it was not de Haan's legal campaigns that would cost him his life. The breaking point came when he attempted to promote the so-called Arab option. The first signs of his initiative came during a visit to Palestine by Lord Northcliffe. Alfred Charles Harmsworth (1856–1922), Lord Northcliffe, was a British press tycoon who visited Palestine in 1922. Northcliffe was not a supporter of the Balfour Declaration and feared that the British government's support for Zionism would damage British interests in the Middle East. De Haan secured a meeting with the visitor, arriving in a delegation that also included Rabbi Reuven Shlomo Jungreis and Rabbi Moshe Leib Bernstein. The delegation sought to present the Haredi position on Palestine to Northcliffe. As the memorandum prepared ahead of the meeting shows, de Haan and his associates emphasized the refusal of the Haredi community to be subjected to the authority of the Zionist leadership. Their position was justified on the grounds of religious freedom. Among the general Jewish public, however, the meeting was perceived as an attempt to thwart the Balfour Declaration and to strengthen British public opinion against the establishment of a Jewish national home. After the visit, Northcliffe became a radical anti-Zionist, fiercely criticizing the Mandate and claiming that the Balfour Declaration had been a mistake. His position was widely attributed to his meeting with de Haan. Northcliffe subsequently employed de Haan as a reporter in Palestine for the Daily Express, a position he continued to occupy until his assassination.[15] Rabbi Sonnenfeld and de Haan published letters of clarification about their meeting with Northcliffe, rejecting the claim that

---

[14] *Ibid.*, p. 81.
[15] *Ibid.*, 100–10; Meshi Zahav and Meshi Zahav, *The Martyr*, pp. 108–31.

they spoke out against Zionist interests. De Haan wrote: "The delegation never conceived of speaking against the Zionist idea ... and also, of course, not against the Balfour Declaration, which is highly important to the Jewish people."[16] In his rebuttal, de Haan claimed that he had merely asked for changes to be made to the Balfour Declaration in order to secure the religious rights and freedoms of non-Zionist Jews, as well as non-Jews.[17] Sonnenfeld wrote: "My positive appraisal of the question of the realization of the Jewish settlement (Yishuv) in the Land of Israel has not changed in the slightest." Like de Haan, he emphasized that the Haredim were demanding "complete freedom for all the communities and religions so that [they] may keep the Torah and commandments."[18]

De Haan's audacious diplomacy reached new levels in 1923–1924, when he met several times with members of the Hashemite dynasty: Hussein Bin 'Ali, the ruler of Hejaz, his son Emir 'Abdullah, ruler of Transjordan, and King Feisal of Iraq. The Hashemite dynasty had come to rule extensive areas of the former Ottoman Empire thanks to its allegiance to Britain during the First World War. In June 1923 de Haan met with Emir 'Abdullah, who offered to sign a peace treaty with Agudat Yisrael that would allow Jews to live in peace under Arab rule, though without any special national rights. In 1924, de Haan again met with Kings 'Abdullah, Faisal, and Hussein. At this meeting, the Arab rulers repeated their proposal that Jews could enjoy equal rights in their kingdom, if their rule was extended over the western bank of the River Jordan. De Haan secured a written declaration from King 'Abdullah, which he proceeded to present to the Great Assembly of Agudat Yisrael in Vienna in the same year through the delegate Moshe Blau. Menachem Friedman claims that de Haan's proposal was in all probability rejected by Agudat Yisrael due to the sense of Jewish solidarity. Despite this, de Haan continued to pursue his contacts with Arab leaders.[19]

Following this meeting, de Haan arranged a summit conference attended by Rabbis Sonnenfeld, Jungreis, Chaim Ben Naeh (the rabbi of the Bucharian Jewish community), and de Haan himself with King Hussein of Hejaz. The conference was held on February 24, 1924 in Shuna, Jordan. The importance of the event to the Old Yishuv can be gauged from the fact that Rabbi Sonnenfeld revoked a vow he had taken never to leave the borders of the Land of Israel, appearing for this purpose before three Admorim who were visiting Palestine at the time – the Gerrer

---

[16] Nakdimon and Mayzlish, *De Haan*, p. 121.
[17] Meshi Zahav and Meshi Zahav, *The Martyr*, pp. 122–3.   [18] *Ibid.*, pp. 120–1.
[19] Friedman, *Society and Religion*, p. 239.

Rebbe, the Sokolov Rebbe, and the Gaon of Bendin.[20] The delegation declared that it was representing Agudat Yisrael, a body that comprised over one million registered members pursuing a life of Torah and commandments. Rabbi Sonnenfeld emphasized to the king that Agudat Yisrael was not accountable to the World Zionist Organization.[21]

Nationalist Jewish circles were appalled by the delegation's visit to Transjordan. The National Committee issued a declaration claiming that the delegation's objective had been to divide the Jewish voice and to suggest that all the Jews of the world did not share a common aspiration to build a national home in the Land of Israel. "This is a treacherous step that cannot be met with silence," the declaration added.[22]

De Haan planned to visit London in order to continue his diplomatic efforts to secure autonomy for the Haredi community by meeting with the British minister of justice. News of the planned visit was leaked to the press, and the day before de Haan was due to leave Palestine the decision was taken to assassinate him. Avraham Tahomi shot de Haan as he was leaving synagogue after evening prayers.[23] To this day it remains unclear who gave the order to send Tahomi on his mission. Haredi writers attribute the decision to the senior echelon of the Zionist movement – Ben Gurion and Weizmann. It is hard to imagine that a political assassination of this kind could have taken place without the approval of the commander of the Haganah in Jerusalem, Yitzhak Ben Zvi, who later became Israel's third president. It is certainly possible that Ben Zvi was acting under orders from even more senior quarters.

After his death, de Haan was crowned a martyr and became an iconic character in radical circles. Every year, Neturei Karta marks the anniversary of his death and publishes a poster in his honor written by Amram Blau.[24] However, it should be noted that the Haredi public as a whole has not joined in this adulation of de Haan, probably because of his homosexuality. Some members of the leadership of Agudat Yisrael sought to belittle his importance immediately after his death.[25]

---

[20] Meshi Zahav and Meshi Zahav, *The Martyr*, p. 161.
[21] Sonnenfeld's speech is quoted in full in Meshi Zahav and Meshi Zahav, *The Martyr*, pp. 164–5.
[22] *Ibid.*, pp. 179–80.
[23] Nakdimon and Mayzlish revealed Tahomi's identity as the assassin.
[24] http://onegshabbat.blogspot.com/2012/06/blog-post_19.html (accessed December 2, 2013). See also Blau's eulogies from 5721 to 5722 (1961–1962). In: Meshi Zahav and Meshi Zahav(eds.), *The Martyr*, pp. 300–3.
[25] Nakdimon and Mayzlish, *De Haan*, pp. 207–18.

Although Neturei Karta saw de Haan as a role model, neither de Haan himself nor Sonnenfeld should be seen as sworn anti-Zionists. Their struggle focused on communal isolationism but did not negate Zionism's right to establish an independent entity. De Haan's activities could be seen as the first example of an alliance between extreme Haredim and Arab nationalists. After his assassination, Rabbi Moshe Blau assumed the leadership of the Old Yishuv and Agudat Yisrael, adopting a more moderate policy that emphasized the common fate of Haredim and nationalist Jews. The Arab option was abandoned in favor of a pragmatic domestic Jewish policy. The next split would come in 1938 with the establishment of Neturei Karta, which adhered to a militant anti-Zionist approach.

Polish anti-Semitism and the closing of the United States to mass immigration from Eastern Europe led to a wave of immigration to Palestine by middle-class Jews during the period 1925–1929 (the Fourth Aliyah). This immigration included a large group of Hasidic Jews, particularly from the Ger dynasty, who sought to live a productive, economic life in Palestine, rather than one based solely on piety. In their country of origin, these immigrants had identified with Agudat Yisrael, but after arriving in Palestine they discovered that the movement was identified with an anti-Zionist position. The result was the gradual emergence of tension between the Old Yishuv and these new Haredi immigrants. The main point of contention was the realization that the position adopted by the members of the Old Yishuv was unrealistic in economic and social terms. These immigrants were absorbed by the growing Zionist community and integrated in the Jewish workforce. Moreover, they wished to provide their children with a certain level of secular education – a position that was fiercely opposed by the radicals. These tensions led to the first signs of division.[26]

The Arab riots of 1929, whose victims were mainly members of the Old Yishuv in Hebron and Safed, marked a turning point in the relations between Agudat Yisrael and the Zionist institutions. The tragic events, in which 133 Jews were murdered, underscored the common fate of the Jews in the conflict with violent Arab nationalism. Four years later, Hitler came to power in Germany. The rise of Nazism led to the recognition that Palestine was a key place of refuge, including for the leaders and supporters of Agudat Yisrael.

[26] Friedman, *Haredi Society*, pp. 33–7.

In the mid-1930s a delegation of Agudat Yisrael leaders from Poland visited Palestine and decided to remove the movement from radical ultra-Orthodox control and replace it with a joint leadership representing the veteran population in Jerusalem alongside immigrants from Poland and Germany. The changing character of Agudat Yisrael reflected a crisis in the principle of separatism. As a minority that was dependent on a non-Haredi majority in almost every facet of life, Haredi society could not adopt a separatist policy, yet it could also not afford to support the Zionist circles. Accordingly, it adopted a policy of essential cooperation, without which it could not survive, but which was not to be accepted on an a priori basis.[27] Some sections of the Haredi public mainly in Jerusalem refused to accept this policy; the opponents dubbed themselves the HaHayim association ("Association of Life"), a name that was later replaced by Neturei Karta.[28]

---

[27] Friedman, *Society and Religion*, pp. 351–8.
[28] Kimmy Caplan, "The Development of Separation Circles among Haredi Zealots: The Case of Amram Blau," *Zion* 76, 2 (2011), 179–218 (in Hebrew).

2

Rabbi Amram Blau, founder of the Neturei Karta movement

Amram Blau (1886–1974), founder of Neturei Karta, was a resolute religious leader who was not afraid to engage in quarrels and was willing to engage in frequent campaigns to protect the purity of the group he headed. His protests raised the issue of the struggle against the State of Israel and cooperation with its institutions on the agenda of the Haredi public in Israel and the Diaspora. Blau's demands for purity and integrity and his refusal to compromise made him a popular figure and an important role model for the Haredi community. Neturei Karta numbers just a few hundred followers yet exerts an influence far greater than its size would suggest.[1] This chapter examines the life and works of Amram Blau, focusing on key milestones in his life. It sheds light on documents that have only recently become available to researchers, and which were secured by Boston University Library by convoluted means. This material is supported by newspaper articles, archival documents, memorial books, and additional scholarship.

This chapter begins by presenting Blau's plan to establish an agricultural settlement for families from the Old Yishuv to be situated on the outskirts of Jerusalem. The next section describes the establishment of Neturei Karta and its struggle to strengthen the Haredi enclave in Jerusalem, including the struggle for the Sabbath and Haredi education. This chapter also identifies new components in Amram Blau's ongoing campaign against Zionism. In the field of Blau's personal life, the research offers some fresh insights into the path that brought him to the leadership

---

[1] Menachem Friedman, *Haredi Society – Sources, Trends, and Processes.* Jerusalem: Jerusalem Institute for Israel Studies, 1991, pp. 91–2 (in Hebrew).

31

of HaEdah HaHaredit, an umbrella organization that unites all of the anti-Zionist factions in Jerusalem, and reveals documents that cast a new light on the scandal caused in his later life by his second marriage to the convert Ruth Ben David. This chapter also examines some correspondence between the two that reveals their relationship and aspects of the rabbi's personal life.

AN AGRICULTURAL SETTLEMENT FOR YOUNG HAREDIM FROM JERUSALEM

In the 1920s and 1930s, a serious attempt was made by young Haredi men from Jerusalem to establish an agricultural settlement on the outskirts of the city. This episode, which is described as follows, raises questions regarding Haredi historiography, and particularly that of the Old Yishuv in Jerusalem. Is their loyalty to a way of life that requires the men to engage solely in Torah study, and their principled opposition to any form of secular life, truly the product of their adhesion to the ways and traditions of their ancestors, to which no changes must be made? The plan we shall discuss here suggests that this may not necessarily be the case. A further question: had this plan been successful, might Haredi history in Israel have moved in a different direction in terms of the community's opposition to secular work and employment? It is also interesting that this episode has been omitted from collective Haredi memory, and that no further attempts were made by the radicals to revive their plan, whether at Nabi Samwil or in any other location.

In 1921 a passionately worded broadsheet was circulated among the members of the Old Yishuv in Jerusalem. Its message was highly unusual, advocating the establishment of a commercial company to be called Keren Yeshu'ah (the Salvation Fund). The goal of the company was to establish an agricultural community for Torah scholars to be situated on the outskirts of the city. The residents would make a living from raising livestock and growing crops. The area chosen for the establishment of the settlement was close to the Arab village of Beit Iksa, by the road to the sacred tomb of the Prophet Samuel (Shmuel Hanavi in Hebrew and Nabi Samwil in Arabic).

The broadsheet explained that scattered plots with a total area of some two thousand dunams (approximately 500 acres) had been purchased decades ago by Jerusalem residents. However, the ownership of these plots could expire if the land was not settled.

The document also revealed that the Zionist movement had begun to show an interest in this land. Accordingly, in order to "save" this Jewish property, the Haredi settlement plan focused on this area. The broadsheet offered two key reasons for the need to establish the settlement: the desire to perform the religious commandments relating to the Land of Israel and the imperative to save Jewish property:

If we wish to raise the emblem of Torah sages in the Holy City [Jerusalem], which has become so poor in this world due to their appalling material condition, and if we wish to raise the emblem of the building and settlement of the Land as a firm and standing building to the honor and glory of our holy Torah; if we wish to save this vast Jewish property [...] whose immense value can no longer even be estimated, lest it be lost to strangers, G-d forbid. If you wish to revive in the Land those commandments that depend [thereon], that they may be pleasing to the Holy One, blessed be His name and memory, wherein the neglect of His commandments led to our terrible exile, then the Land will be able to observe the Sabbatical years, thereby surely rendering us deserving of full salvation and imminent redemption, then you must count yourselves among those fellows who help the Salvation Fund with your tithes, and by this privilege, in repentance and comfort, may we be speedily redeemed in our days, amen.[2]

The broadsheet advocated the establishment of an agricultural settlement in order to improve the material condition of the residents of the Old Yishuv, who as noted faced economic hardship. Such a settlement would also allow its inhabitants to observe the religious commandments relating to farming in the Land of Israel.

On 13 Tammuz 5681 (July 19, 1921), the Ramatayim Tzofim association was founded under the patronage of Akiva Yosef Schlesinger, shortly before his death (1922). Schlesinger was an unusual figure in the Haredi community. He immigrated to Palestine from Hungary and sought to establish an orthodox political entity that would function as a Toranic state (see Chapter 6).[3] He was active in purchasing land in Palestine to this end. A temporary committee was established for the association, including Schlesinger's son Shimon, Moshe Holtzman, and Amram Blau, who was also appointed secretary of the association. After the company was founded, its organizers managed to gather twenty people for the land purchase.

The purpose of the association was to found a chain of agricultural settlements intended for the inhabitants of the Old Yishuv in Palestine.

---

[2] Anonymous, untitled, undated, Blau Archive, Box 2, Property folder.
[3] Michael K. Silber, "Akiva Yosef Shlesinger – The First Zionist?" *Cathedra* 73 (1994), 78–105 (in Hebrew).

The first booklet published by the association clearly shows that the initiators of the plan saw their goal as being to compete with the Zionist movement over the settlement of the land, and to prove that Jewish agricultural settlements could be established while maintaining strict observance of the Torah and the commandments, unlike Zionist settlements such as the kibbutzim that followed secular and collectivist principles.

To all of our brethren who treasure the Holy Torah and observance of the commandments, and whose heart longs to build and settle our Holy Land and to observe its commandments, and yet whose heart also aches to see such building if it is not in the spirit of the Torah – to all these, we say: Come, dear brethren, and lend us your hand [...] and join the founding fund of Ramatayim Tzofim.[4]

This leaflet bears the signatures of approval of Rabbi Yitzhak Yeruham Diskin, the son of the late leader of the Old Yishuv, Moshe Yehuda Leib Diskin, and his successor as the head of the religious court, and Yosef Chaim Sonnenfeld. The leaflet was also signed by Rabbi Moshe Kliers, the head of the religious court in Tiberias. All these rabbis were respected leaders of the Old Yishuv.

Ramatayim Tzofim sought to bring together members, purchase land, and provide loans on advantageous terms for the construction of homes and acquisition of livestock and farming equipment. According to the constitution, the association was supposed to include three different types of members: Active members who purchased a plot in order to settle it; nonsettling members who wished to purchase a plot not for the purpose of settlement, but in order to perform the commandment of settling the land; and members of the founding fund, who were to contribute money to finance the members' loans.

The company decided that the plots of land would be allocated to the members by lottery. A committee of seven members was established to perform this task on a voluntary basis; the decisions were taken by a majority vote of its members. Although women were entitled to purchase land and to be association members,[5] they were not entitled to vote. In each colony, the construction of a synagogue, Talmud Torah for girls, and "Heder" for boys was envisaged, and these were to operate "without moving one inch from the path taken by our fathers and

---

[4] Anonymous, "A Clarion Call for Help," undated, Blau Archive, Box 2, Property folder.
[5] Binyamin Kluger said that out of 166 members, 20 were women. See: Binyamin Kluger, *The Neighborhoods Surrounding Jerusalem.* Jerusalem: self-published, 1979, p. 217 (in Hebrew).

their fathers." A Mikveh (ritual purification bath) for women and men was also planned in each colony.[6]

Considerable thought was given to the spiritual regulations that were to apply in the colony. The religious constitution reflected the position of the Old Yishuv on controversial issues of the time, beginning with a discussion of the question of labor during times of rest – Sabbath, the festivals, and the Sabbatical year. Naturally, the constitution stated that all these dates would be observed strictly and unquestioningly; neither would it be acceptable to employee non-Jews to circumvent the prohibition against labor on these days. A similar approach was taken to the question of offsetting tithes and observing the religious commandments relating to the land. On the broader question of religious lifestyle, the constitution stated that the synagogues would follow the Haredi style without introducing any changes. Every member was required to attend a quorum for the morning and evening prayers, together with his sons, and a compulsory Torah lesson lasting at least thirty minutes would be held every day after these prayers. Talmudei Torah would be established in the colony and the teachers responsible for educating the children would be vetted by the committee. As a general rule, youths under the age of eighteen would not be permitted to engage in crafts, in order to raise the children as Torah students.

The constitution also prohibited any changes in dress or in the requirement for men to grow bears and earlocks. Women were not to be permitted to go out in immodest dress: they were not to expose any flesh and were required to wear long sleeves and to cover their necks. Neither were they to go barefoot or to wear tigh-fitting clothing. Women were not to go out with their hair uncovered and could not wear a wig.

The study of foreign languages would be prohibited in the colony unless absolutely required by the law of the land. Moreover, the residents would be forbidden to speak Hebrew. The members of the association would not be permitted to visit the theater or cinema, as part of the effort to ensure that they devoted their lives solely to holiness "without tomfoolery."

"Outstanding" inspectors would be appointed to enforce these rules. No changes whatsoever were to be made to the constitution, even by way of a temporary provision, and even if a Torah sage permitted the change: "No relaxation shall be allowed." A member who violated the

---

[6] Anonymous, "A Clarion Call for Help."

constitution would be warned three times; if he persisted in his ways, his money would be returned and he would be banished from the colony.[7]

The economic logic behind the organization was relatively simple, perhaps unrealistically so. A share company was established to purchase the land, with the objective of issuing 3,000 shares, each costing 30 Palestine pounds. If all the shares were sold, the company would thus raise the sum of 90,000 pounds.

An initial sum of 11,250 pounds was to be invested in acquiring land, while the balance [78,250 pounds] could be lent to the purchasers. Loans in the sum of 200 pounds would be given to 400 members. Each member would repay 20 pounds a year, so that the association would receive total repayment of 8,000 pounds a year. At the end of the fifth, tenth, and fifteenth years, this would allow the association to purchase additional land for the sum of 2,500 pounds a year (a total of 7,500 pounds each time).

On the basis of this financial calculation, the association was officially founded in May 1926.[8] A report published by the association in 1927 stated that 345 dunams of land had already been acquired[9] in several areas close to Beit Iksa. The main areas of land were at Ras Uda (eighty-one dunams), purchased from the heirs of Abdulqadr Muhsin, and Ras al-Beit (fifty-eight dunams).[10] In order to ensure access to their land, the members of the association raised funds to build a road and requested permission from the governor of the Jerusalem District of the Mandatory government to operate a public transport line connecting Jaffa Road in Jerusalem to their land.[11]

In order to ensure the strict application of the religious constitution, the association chose to register the land in its name, thereby enhancing its powers of enforcement. However, this step created resentment among those who had invested their own money and who demanded that the land they had purchased should be registered in their own name. The Ashkenazi religious court instructed Amram Blau that the plots of land

---

[7] *Ibid.* See also, Anonymous, "Religious Constitution," undated, Blau Archive, Box 2, Property folder.

[8] See the letter from Attorney Benzion ben Aharon, dated May 2, 1926, Blau Archive, Box 2, Property folder.

[9] Four dunams equal approximately one acre.

[10] Anonymous, "Report," 22 Adar 5687 – 1927, Blau Archive, Box 2, Property folder.

[11] See letter from the Governor of Palestine, July 19, 1934, Blau Archive, Box 2, Property folder.

should be registered in the owners' names. One purchaser even contacted civil attorneys in order to register the land in his own name.[12]

The association employed fundraisers to try and find Diaspora Jews interested in purchasing land. A letter from Benzion Adler, one of the fundraisers, shows that the task proved harder than expected and Adler did not enjoy great success.[13]

Mismanagement and arrears in members' payments paralyzed the association, which began to accumulate a deficit. In January 1931 Amram Blau sent a letter to the members of the association begging them to meet their financial undertakings: "The forecasts have failed to materialize and the coffers remain empty." Blau chastised those members who had ceased to attend the general meeting, perhaps due to their disillusionment with the association, thereby preventing it from holding lawful meetings. He threatened to resign from the committee unless additional funds were found to cover taxes and levies.[14] Written ten years after the establishment of the association, the letter suggests that the initial enthusiasm had already waned and no actual preparations were being made to move on to the land.

In 1937, as the result of the association's inability to manage its accounts properly and to submit annual reports and statements as required by British Mandate law, the Registrar of Cooperative Associations in Jerusalem announced that an investigation would be undertaken into the association's accounts. Accountant M. Friedenberg was charged with undertaking the investigation, and his "interim report" stated that the association held 270 dunams of land in the Beit Iksa area intended for the purpose of settlement in a religious spirit. Some of the land was registered in the association's name while other plots were registered in the name of private individuals. In other cases, only contracts with the sellers had been finalized. Friedenberg reported that the association had some 140 members, each holding varying rights to areas of between one and ten dunams.

The investigator noted that no practical settlement activities had begun; neither had any plans been made for small farms or other forms of settlement on the land proving the ability to secure the association's goals in the land it had acquired. He defined the association's

---

[12] See letter from Attorney Moshe Grossman to Amram Blau, January 3, 1934, Blau Archive, Box 2, Property folder.

[13] Benzion Adler, untitled, undated, Blau Archive, Box 2, Property folder.

[14] Amram Blau, "Returned Letter," undated, Blau Archive, Box 2, Property folder.

bookkeeping as "in arrears and requiring correction," and revealed that the association had not provided any loans for its members. This last finding can be explained against the background of the miscalculations of the association's capital and the failure to estimate the true price of the land. The investigator also calculated that between 1933 and 1937 the association acquired a deficit of 842.038 pounds. Above all, however, the report reveals that his main concern was that the association could not realize the goals it had set itself: "The association should clarify whether it is possible to prepare a practical plan for housing or settling its members on the purchased land [...] and whether the association has the requisite means to realize such a plan."[15]

Amram Blau's response to the auditor's report revealed the main problems facing the association. Apart from mismanagement, the political situation in Palestine had begun to change beyond recognition, disrupting the settlement plans: "Steps have already been taken for settlement, but the 'Events' have delayed their actual execution."[16] Following the outbreak of the Arab Revolt in 1936, it was no longer practical for observant Jews to relocate to land within an Arab village. Since the association did not request protection from the institutions of the Yishuv, it was obvious even at this stage that it would be unable to establish its planned settlement.

In 1940, the Registrar of Associations of the Mandatory authorities ordered the liquidation of the association, which was duly dissolved in March 1948. This marked the end of the plan to establish an agricultural settlement for the members of the Old Yishuv in Jerusalem. The importance of the story of Ramatayim Tzofim lies in the indication it offers of the future public activities of Amram Blau: the protection and public inspection of modesty, maintaining traditional patterns of language use, campaigning against new educational content, and waging a broad-based struggle against modernism.

THE HAHAYIM ASSOCIATION AND NETUREI KARTA

Amram Blau's grandfather, also named Amram, immigrated to Palestine from Slovakia in 1868. He was a student of Shmuel Binyamin Sofer (known as the "Ktav Sofer") of Pressburg (1815–1871). The Ktav Sofer was the son of Moshe Sofer (the "Hatam Sofer,") a famous leader of

---

[15] M. Friedenberg, "Report," October 26, 1937, Blau Archive, Box 2, Property folder.
[16] Untitled, undated, Blau Archive, Box 2, Property folder.

Hungarian Jewry. According to his son's testimony, Amram Blau (the grandfather) decided to leave Hungary after facing persecution from reform-minded Jews who disapproved of his traditional style, and after he was unable to make a living as a community rabbi of Tranava.[17]

His son, Itzhak Shalom, married Shaine Ester and the couple had four sons. Amram Blau was born in Jerusalem in 1886; his eldest brother, Moshe, was born in 1880. As young men, Moshe and Amram became active in Agudat Yisrael and in the Ashkenazi City Committee. Moshe was the more prominent of the two brothers. Following the murder of Jacob-Israël de Haan in 1924, the path was cleared for Moshe to assume the leadership of Agudat Yisrael and the Ashkenazi Committee, and eventually he veered toward a policy of cooperation with the Zionists. The dispute within the Haredi community in Jerusalem regarding cooperation with the Zionists was reflected in a rift between the two brothers, Amram and Moshe.

At the end of July 1938 the institutions of the Yishuv organized a campaign to collect a poll tax to finance defense costs in the face of the Arab revolt. The guards trained publicly on the Sabbath and ate non-Kosher food, arousing the wrath of traditional Jews. Despite this, Agudat Yisrael decided not to express public opposition to the poll tax. This position accelerated the process of separation that led to the emergence of the HaHayim ("Life") association, named after Rabbi Chaim Sonnenfeld. Later the name was changed to Neturei Karta.[18]

The name Neturei Karta is taken from the Talmud (*Hagigah* 2:7) and means "guardians of the city" in Babylonian Aramaic. The opponents of the poll tax sought to convey their conviction that the armed guards stationed in Jerusalem were not the guardians of the city, but its destroyers. As the Talmudic passage argues, the true guardians of the city are its Torah sages and students. The new movement was led by Aharon Katzenelbogen and Amram Blau.[19]

The HaHayim association published a founding document detailing its principles. The following were some of the most significant aspects presented in the document:

A   *The essence of the Jewish people*: The manifesto opens with the argument that the foundation of the Jewish people is the Torah in

[17] Binyamin Kluger, *All of Rabbi Moshe Blau's Writings*, Jerusalem: Mashabim, 1983, pp. 20–4.
[18] I. Schochman, "From Inside the Walls," *Davar*, November 29, 1938, 5 (in Hebrew).
[19] Friedman, *Haredi Society*, pp. 88–9.

its entirety. Accordingly, the Nation of Israel cannot be as the other nations, which own national assets such as land, language, and race, but it can own solely the Torah. Thus the function of this nation is to place its trust in the Holy One and to impose the Torah on its way of life. All those who accept the yoke of the Torah are considered Jews. A person who is not of the "race of Israel" but accepts the yoke of the Torah and the commandments is bound to the Jewish people and becomes part thereof. Conversely, a Jew from the "race of Israel" who deliberately casts off the yoke of Torah, or who denies the authority of the Torah, and does not believe in the veracity of a single word of the Torah, is considered an apostate who has left Judaism, even if he has not converted to another religion. The Torah does not distinguish between an apostate and a heretic, both are subject to the same single law: "The Jewish people is obliged to separate itself from and to remove such persons."

It is interesting to note that the manifesto ignored the well-known saying that "an Israelite, though he has sinned, remains an Israelite" (*Babylonian Talmud, Sanhedrin* 44a). In Chapter 6 I will discuss the rejection of the lenient position toward sinners in the teachings of Rabbi Yeshayah Asher Zelig Margaliot, one of the spiritual leaders of the Jerusalem radicals, who claimed that all those who do not follow Neturei Karta's approach are considered "rabble."

B   *The bond between the Jewish people and its Land*: Just as God chose the People of Israel, so He chose the Land of Israel for His people, as the place where they were to keep the laws and commandments. The observance of the commandments in the Land of Israel carries special sanctity; indeed, many commandments can only be observed in this Land. Accordingly, in this era, the document argues, any Jew who is capable of doing so is commanded to settle in the Land of Israel. Rabbi Yoel Teitelbaum would later argue that the commandment to live in the Land of Israel did not apply in his generation; however, this was not the position of the manifesto (see Chapter 6 for further discussion of this aspect).

C   *The nature and manner of Jewish exile*: God exiled the Jewish people from its land due to their sins and scattered them among the nations. However, He promised that at a time of His choosing He would bring redemption through His rightful messiah, "and not through the autonomous redemption of mundane and human forces" – a phrase that alludes to secular Zionist action. Every Jew is commanded to anticipate redemption and to pray for the expedition of salvation. The manifesto quotes a comment by Maimonides that any person who does not anticipate the coming of messiah, or does not await his coming, denies not only the prophets who predicted the messiah but also the entire Torah and Moses. Thus the manifesto supports the principle of messianic passivity, a hallmark of Haredi thought and the underlying reason for its rejection of Zionism.

D   *The Old Yishuv*: The Jews who immigrated to the Land of Israel in order to observe the Torah and the commandments dependent on the Land settled in the holy cities (Jerusalem, Hebron, Safed and Tiberias) and their purpose was exclusively religious. Before the First World War they numbered several tens of thousands, all of whom observed the Torah and lived in peace with their Arab neighbors; their neighbors showed virtually no hatred or opposition to them. The HaHayim association represents this kind of Jew. The manifesto embodies a clear hostility toward any concept of Jewish life in the Land of Israel other than that of Torah study. It is important to note here that this approach could not have accommodated Blau's activities in Ramatayim Tzofim. We can therefore assume that the establishment of Neturei Karta was possible only after collapse of the agricultural experience.

E   *Zionist influence*: After the First World War, the British government declared the establishment of a national home for the Jewish people through negotiations with the World Zionist Organization. It did not recognize the Jewish people as the people of the Torah, and according to the authors of the manifesto, the Zionist Organization has no part in the Jewish people, since "its leaders are not akin to the nation of Israel in any matter." The Zionist movement decided at one of its congresses that the Jewish religion is a private matter for each individual and did not subject itself to the authority of Torah. Accordingly, "this organization has removed itself from *Klal Yisrael* (the totality of Israel)." Since the concept of the Zionist Organization is alien to the spirit of the Torah and the Jewish people, all the great Torah leaders opposed it from its inception. Due to the recognition of the movement by the British government, "this organization has seized the leadership and influence over the Jewish people during two decades [of activities] in the Land of

Israel." During this period, the manifesto says, the movement destroyed the religion and Torah of Israel and incited the Jews to leave God and His Torah. Their communities are devoid of any religious content and their education is completely irreligious. This leadership has caused the Jewish people to endure suffering and distress.

F   *The proposed Jewish state*: Regarding the proposal by the British government to establish a Jewish state,[20] the manifesto argued forcefully that the Torah opposes any such entity. The reasons for this are: 1) Release from exile must come through the rightful messiah – "the Jewish people cannot free itself from exile by its own forces;" 2) the state would be led by the members of the Zionist Organization, who are not fit to lead the Jewish people in accordance with the Torah; 3) the government handed to these people would endanger the Jewish religion, and even laws passed to protect religion could not remove this danger; 4) the exiled People of Israel must not arouse the hatred of its neighbors and the jealousy of the nations, thereby endangering Jewish lives.[21]

As can be seen the manifesto presents a radical stance, depicting Zionism as a movement of apostates. The manifesto emphasizes the principle of political passivity as a tool for expediting messianic redemption. Neturei Karta emerged as a counterreaction to the conciliatory trends that began to emerge among the Haredi leadership as Agudat Yisrael moved toward a retroactive acceptance of Zionism and cooperation with the movement in terms of social responsibility and governance. Neturei Karta rejected such partnership; its radical separatist approach refused to acknowledge the secular supporters of Zionism as proper Jews.

These hardline principles led to an ideological and political rift among the members of the Old Yishuv. The rift was effectively led by the two brothers, Amram and Moshe Blau. Although their disagreement involved principled and substantive issues, it is not impossible that it also reflected a personal conflict. This was an ideological row that split a family.

On the basis of the newly examined documents, I would like to suggest that alongside the principled disagreements, it is also possible to discern

---

[20] It is worth noting that the British government did not, in fact, advocate the establishment of a Jewish state, but rather of a "national home for the Jewish people." By the time the manifesto was written, however, it was already apparent that the idea of a state was crystallizing.

[21] Anonymous, "Society of Life," undated, Blau Archive, Box 3, Folder 9, Document 10.

an element of rivalry between the two brothers. I shall attempt to prove this hypothesis on the basis of the content of a strongly worded letter sent to Moshe Blau in January 1940 by his brother Amram. In the letter, Amram made a last-ditched attempt to convince his brother to abandon the approach taken by Agudat Yisrael, to repent his sins, and to "separate himself from the wicked." The letter also served as a "writ of divorce" between the two brothers. Amram warned his brother that if he failed to abandon the approach of Agudat Yisrael, he would have no choice but to distance himself from him. He claimed that the partnership with the Zionists would lead to a catastrophe and that there could be no compromise on this matter. The letter acknowledged that such a rift would be extremely painful on the personal level, but if Moshe failed to mend his ways this would be inevitable. The document suggests that, at the time, Amram did not believe that his brother had moved too far from him in ideological terms, and that he anticipated that he would indeed repent – in contrast to Agudat Yisrael, regarding whom he had already abandoned all hope.[22]

Further evidence of the personal rivalry between the two brothers can be found in their memoirs. Moshe Blau's memoirs, entitled "On Thy Walls, Jerusalem," does not even mention the fact that he had a younger brother (Amram); this fact was also omitted from a book edited by his children after his death. In this book, Moshe Blau's son, who was also called Amram, savagely attacked his father's adversaries, while maintaining a deafening silence regarding his uncle Amram.[23] Similarly, Amram Blau's own book of memoirs, published almost thirty years after his death, makes only the scantiest of references to the fact that he was the younger brother of the leader of Agudat Yisrael.[24]

The division led to a power struggle as both sides – HaEdah HaHaredit and Agudat Yisrael – competed for the right to represent the Haredi public in Jerusalem. The splinter faction no longer considered itself subject to the instructions of Agudat Yisrael; in other words, Amram no longer saw himself as subordinate to the leadership of his brother Moshe. However, he still considered himself loyal to the spiritual leadership of Rabbi Joseph Tzvi Dushinsky (1867–1948), the leader of both Agudat

---

[22] See: Blau Archive, Box 3, Folder No. 1, Document 18.

[23] Amram (ben Moshe) Blau, *Guardian of the Walls – Chapters in Memory of Moshe Blau.* Jerusalem: self-publication, 1976 (in Hebrew).

[24] Mordechai Mintzburg, *From the Diary of Rabbi Amram – Chapters from the Memoirs of the Rabbi and Tzadik Amram Barshi Blau, May the Memory of a Tzadik Be for a Blessing.* Jerusalem: self-publication, 5767 – 2007 (in Hebrew).

Yisrael and HaEdah HaHaredit. In August 1945, this faction received a legal seal of approval following the elections to the political leadership of HaEdah HaHaredit, which saw a fierce contest between Agudat Yisrael and Neturei Karta. Amram Blau competed against his brother for the position of leader on a platform demanding total separatism. Neturei Karta won the election due to a political maneuver: the movement ran in three different parties, thereby splitting the votes of Jerusalem Haredim.[25] After the elections, Neturei Karta assumed the leadership of HaEdah HaHaredit, which Amram Blau himself headed for many years. This political victory led to the final separation of Agudat Yisrael from HaEdah HaHaredit.[26] HaEdah HaHaredit emerged from the split as a small and weak movement, whereas the majority of Haredi Jews followed the more moderate leadership of Agudat Yisrael. It should be noted that Moshe Blau died suddenly soon after the schism. He contracted food poisoning while returning to Palestine by ship from a fundraising trip to Italy (June 7, 1946).

THE STRUGGLE FOR THE INTERNATIONALIZATION OF JERUSALEM

In 1947, the United Nations Special Committee of Palestine (UNSCOP) proposed the division of the mandate area into two states, Jewish and Arab. Jerusalem was to remain a separate international area (*corpus separatum*). The plan was adopted by a majority vote of the UN General Assembly on November 29, 1947. During the interim period between the approval of the plan, the expiry of the British Mandate on May 14, 1948, and the establishment of the State of Israel, a war erupted between Jews and Palestinians. After the British forces left, the Arab armies also joined the fighting. The outcome of the war led to the division of Jerusalem between the State of Israel and the Kingdom of Jordan.[27]

As the British Mandate in Palestine drew toward its close, Amram Blau became increasingly active in the political and international arena in an effort to protect the rights of his community. Although Blau's appeals for

---

[25] Unsigned, "Neturei Karta," *Hatzofeh*, August 7, 1945, 2; unsigned, "Jerusalem," *Hatzofeh*, July 25, 1945, 4; unsigned, "Radical Neturei Karta," *Hatzofeh*, July 26, 1945, 8 (all in Hebrew)

[26] Anonymous, "Record This for a Memory in Writing," *HaHomah* 24 (Ellul 5734 – 1974), 24–8 (in Hebrew); see also Friedman, *Haredi Society*, p. 94.

[27] Yoav Gelber, *Palestine 1948: War, Escape and the Emergence of the Palestinian Refugee Problem*. London: Sussex Academic Press, 2006.

intervention by international bodies ultimately had no practical effect, an examination of these activities is informative in terms of Blau's modus operandi and his willingness to act by any means possible in order to attack and embarrass Zionism in the international arena. His actions showed a willingness to adopt a forceful and uncompromising position and to pay a heavy price for his stance, to the point of being portrayed as a traitor.

Prior to the establishment of the State of Israel, Blau contacted four different bodies with the goal of preventing the future state from gaining sovereignty over the Haredi neighborhoods of Jerusalem. On November 19, 1947, just ten days before the vote on the partition plan, HaEdah HaHaredit sent a letter signed by Rabbi Dushinsky (as mentioned, he was also the chief rabbi of Agudat Yisrael) to the secretary-general of the United Nations, demanding that the city remain an international territory without sovereignty. According to Dushinsky, the Haredi community in the city had existed since before the establishment of the British Mandate and was the rightful heir of the longstanding Old Yishuv. He argued that this holy city should be secured by means of an international agreement, so that in any scenario all sides would respect its absolute neutrality. Accordingly the rabbi demanded that Jerusalem should not be included in the territory of any state and the residents of the city should not be subject to the citizenship of any state, and should enjoy solely citizenship of the holy city.[28] At the same time, Amram Blau and Aharon Katzenelbogen sent a further memorandum to the UN secretary-general in which they declared:

We shall not relinquish our right to demand your sponsorship and protection in the name of humanity, and we shall not abandon ourselves to a regime whose principles and methods desecrate all we hold sacred, and which is determined to undermine our religious life. Accordingly, we request that we be rescued from the Zionist regime by all means you consider worthy.[29]

This request was accompanied by further appeals to the Zionist Executive and Diaspora Jewry. In a letter to the Zionist leadership, Amram Blau demanded that HaEdah HaHaredit be recognized as an autonomous

---

[28] Anonymous, "Record This." It is worth noting that Dushinsky also met with the UN mediator Bernadotte on this matter see: Yuval Frankel, "Haredi and Religious Judaism in Jerusalem during the Siege," *HaTziyonut* 18 (1994), 247–89 (in Hebrew). See also: unsigned, "Radical Haredi Leaders Demand Equal Status to Their Community as the National Community," *HaMashkif*, July 16, 1947, 4 (in Hebrew).

[29] Anonymous, "Record This."

body, since the public it represented did not wish to share a common fate with Zionism. Blau claimed that the British government had recognized Haredi Jewry as a religious community and had allowed them to leave the National Committee and manage their religious affairs in accordance with their beliefs. Accordingly, they asked the Zionists to grant them the same autonomous status they had enjoyed under the British government.

In this context, the rabbi raised the issue of the "Three Oaths." A passage in the Babylonian Talmud (*Ketubot* 111a) is the source of this belief: "Why/What are these Three Oaths? One, that Israel should not storm the wall. Two, the Holy One adjured Israel not to rebel against the nations of the world. Three, the Holy One adjured the nations that they would not oppress Israel too much." Traditional rabbinical exegesis interpreted these oaths as a prohibition against collective migration to the Land of Israel prior to the End Times. Amram Blau argued that Zionism is a clear instance of rebellion against God. According to Aviezer Ravitzky, the Three Oaths are not a tactical device intended to protect the Jewish people and discourage rash action in Exile; rather, they form a substantive manifestation of Divine leadership and providence over the Jewish people. Zionism and the State of Israel were therefore viewed by the radicals as tantamount to a rebellion against God, and hence completely unacceptable.[30] Blau sought to identify reward and punishment in all human acts, interpreting the Holocaust as a grave penalty for the rebellion by Zionism against the Three Oaths. Those Zionists who sought to "expedite the End" by immigrating to Palestine and rebelling against the familiar world order were responsible for the terrible Divine penalty that emerged in the form of the Holocaust. In his letter to the Zionist leadership, Blau wrote:

We must oppose [the Zionists] for we do not wish to share their fate, and we have no interest in their state, particularly in light of our fear concerning our Sages of blessed memory, who warned us not to rebel against the nations, "if I do not permit," etc. We have seen with our own eyes how great and holy were the words of our Sages of blessed memory, for since [Zionism] began, Jewish blood has been spilled like water by the Bolsheviks and by Hitler, may his name and memory be erased [...], and the words of our Sages of blessed memory came true, for Jewish blood was abandoned with a cruelty unknown since humankind appeared on the earth, to the point of building factories to make soap from human corpses, G-d forbid[31] [...] and

---

[30] Ravitzky, *Messianism*, pp. 63–70.
[31] The rabbi alludes here to a rumor that has never been substantiated that the Nazis produced soap using fat taken from the bodies of Jews murdered in the concentration camps.

pity anyone who saw such things. So how can we not be afraid of this situation [...] we, Jews who believe in G-d and in the words of our Sages of blessed memory [...] We must take every opportunity to state that we do not belong to their cause.

Blau ended his letter by stating that HaEdah HaHaredit wished to commit itself in writing to accept the laws of the Torah, and did not wish to form part of the nascent state.[32]

Rabbi Dushinsky and Blau also cooperated with the efforts made by the Anglican bishop to halt the fighting between the different religious communities in the city. They met with the bishop several times and signed a petition he initiated.[33] During the siege of Jerusalem, Neturei Karta organized a demonstration in favor of a ceasefire. On April 4, 1948, Neturei Karta marched from the edge of the Meah She'arim neighborhood toward the British government center in the Russian Compound. The demonstrators carried cloth banners bearing the slogans "We favor peace – we demand a ceasefire." The rumor that Neturei Karta were marching with white flags and were ready to surrender soon reached circles close to the Haganah, who clashed with the demonstrators and even opened fire. No one was injured, but this was a highly significant incident – while soldiers were waging a desperate battle for Jewish Jerusalem, Neturei Karta were perceived as "stabbing them in the back."[34]

The activities urging the continuation of the British Mandate are corroborated in the Blau Archives in the form of an urgent letter sent by Amram Blau to the Haredi world leadership, urging them to apply international pressure on the Mandatory government to maintain its sovereignty in Palestine. In his letter, Blau explained that the Holy One had scattered the Jewish people around the world and, accordingly, the nations of the world were responsible for attending to their needs. The Jews should be loyal to the monarch of Britain and its dominion, and must ensure that the monarchy acts in their best interests. Even if there are Jews who seek to act against the interests of the kingdom (a reference to

---

[32] Amram Blau, "Request to the Zionist Government to Recognize HaEdah HaHaredit, Which Does Not Wish to Share a Common Fate with Them," undated, Blau Archive, Box 3, Folder 1.

[33] Anonymous, "Anglican Bishop Attempts to Make Peace," *Davar* February 22, 1948, 2 (in Hebrew).

[34] Unsigned, "The Demonstration of Haredi Jewry against the Zionist Leadership," *HaHomah* 43, Sivan 5708 – 1948, 4 (in Hebrew). Menachem Friedman, "Neturei Karta and the Sabbath Demonstrations in Jerusalem, 1948–1950." In: Avi Bareli (ed.), *Divided Jerusalem, 1948–1967: Sources, Summaries, Selected Incidents, and Ancillary Material*. Jerusalem: Ben Zvi Institute, 1994, pp. 230–31 (in Hebrew); Frankel, "Haredi."

the underground organizations that engaged in military action designed to encourage the end of the Mandate) the Jews are still bound by the oath not to rebel against the nations, for if they do so their blood will be abandoned "like the deer and roe of the fields."[35]

In a letter to his supporters Blau mentioned a further argument in favor of neutrality, which he described as a "natural cause." This reason reflected both tactical and strategic calculations. Blau predicted that the Yishuv would lose the battle against the Arab armies and, accordingly, it would be better to refrain from collaborating with the forces of the Yishuv. He noted the proposal to recruit women to the war effort,[36] claiming that this was intended to create a balance between the Israeli army forces and the Arab armies, with their "tremendous armed forces, with their modern weapons that exceed all the Zionist weapons, the skill of their soldiers, and their surprising number." Blau mocked the intention to launch a general recruitment drive, commenting that "they reckon that by including all the women, they will be able to withstand their enemies, who are one hundred times their number." Accordingly he advocated a stance of neutrality. A further reason he quoted for his certainty in the victory of the Arab forces was that "their enemies are not heretics to their faith and do not mock their rabbis and call on them to recruit their daughters." Blau's conclusion from his examination was that the ultra-Orthodox community should not enlist and should maintain its neutrality, so that after the Zionist defeat in the war it would not be identified with the losing side.[37]

Neturei Karta's desire to avoid being part of the State of Israel took a further turn in 1956. During the tempestuous Sabbath demonstrations (see later), Blau published a broadsheet urging the State of Israel to permit his supporters to cross to the Jordanian side of the city. Levi Avrahami, the commander of the Jerusalem police, presented this broadsheet to the commission of inquiry established to examine the Sabbath demonstrations. According to press reports, Avrahami stated that he had spoken to

---

[35] Amram Blau, "A Voice of Entreaty," Blau Archive, Box 3, Folder 1; Another appeal with similar arguments can be found in: Neturei Karta, "To Our Brothers in Exile," *HaHomah* 42, 29 Adar 5708 – 1948, 1 (in Hebrew).

[36] Neturei Karta sharply opposed the draft of women to the military, and the supreme court of HaEdah HaHaredit ruled that it is better to die and not allow women to join the military. See: Yosef Zvi Doshinsky, "Pesak Din," *HaHomah* (46), 21 (Av 5708 – 1948), 1 (in Hebrew).

[37] Amram Blau, "To Save Our Lives, Sons and Daughters," undated, Blau Archive, Box 1, Modesty file, Folder, Document 76.

Amram Blau, who claimed to have obtained the in-principle agreement of the Kingdom of Jordan to the passage of his supporters, and that the number of people involved was several dozen.[38] For his part, Avrahami supported the request and recommended the commission consider it seriously.[39]

In addition to Neturei Karta's fear of religious persecution following the establishment of the State of Israel, the new situation also raised a complex theological dilemma. As noted, the Three Oaths were interpreted as prohibiting any rebellion against the will of the nations. Neturei Karta had based its theological opposition to Zionism on these prohibitions, yet the State of Israel was established following a vote in the United Nations and with the support of the majority of the countries of the world. Accordingly, it could be interpreted as an approval by the will of the nations; indeed, Religious Zionist circles saw the vote in the United Nations as one of the harbingers of the messiah and the first signs of final redemption. The main response Neturei Karta evolved to this dilemma was to argue that the historical process in which the State was established was a divine test – an illusion that threatened the very survival of Torah Judaism.[40] Thus the vote by the United Nations actually represented the victory of Satan who had managed to gain the upper hand and enable the Zionist dream to come true. Thus, according to this view, God has allowed Satan to have victory in order to test the true believers. The Zionist success on the international stage should therefore be seen as a sign of the entrance into the age of the footsteps of messiah – the period preceding the coming of the messiah that is marked by grave sorrows and spiritual decline. The theological paradox is that the Jewish people continue to live under the yoke of exile, but this is imposed by Jewish hands.[41] An editorial in the newspaper *HaHomah* summarized this argument: "In our prayers we say 'because of our sins we were exiled from our

---

[38] Menashe Darash argues that in 1957 Blau sent a letter to the king of Trans-Jordan with a request to resettle his community in the Jewish Quarter of the Old City. See: Menashe Darash, *Neturei Karta of Meah She'arim*. Jerusalem: Atnahta Publishing House, 2010, p. 71 (in Hebrew). These negotiations started prior to the establishment of the state. See: M. Vitlin, "Also Neturei Karta's Rabbi is Willing to Move to the Patronage of Abdullah," *Heruth*, August 15, 1949, 1 (in Hebrew).

[39] Anonymous, "Avrahami Suggests Passage of 'Neturei Karta' or Their Dispersal in Israel," *Davar*, February 21, 1956, 2 (in Hebrew).

[40] Unsigned, "For Those Who Believe in God," *HaHomah* 27, 11 Shevat 5708 – 1948, 1 (in Hebrew).

[41] Unsigned, "Where are We Coming?" *HaHomah* 26 (2nd edition), 20 Kislev 5708 – 1948, 1 (in Hebrew).

Land.' Can anyone find a false opinion claiming that because of our sins we will be redeemed?" The editorial thus concludes that the State of Israel cannot possibly embody redemption or even the beginnings of redemption. It is rather a manifestation of false messianism, and the community of the faithful should rally to oppose it. The editorial demanded the establishment of a "wall of fire" between the believers and the infidels and argued that only strict observance of the laws of modesty and the ways of the past could secure the ultimate and genuine redemption of the just messiah.[42] The subsequent outbreak of the War of Independence in 1948 was seen by Neturei Karta as proof that Israel's establishment was indeed against the will of the nations.

THE SABBATH DEMONSTRATIONS

After the establishment of the State of Israel, Neturei Karta continued its campaigns against the actions of the authorities in Jerusalem when these contradicted its conservative interpretation of Orthodox law and custom. The campaigns waged on the city's streets focused on issues relating the observance of the Sabbath laws. The demonstrations began with small groups, but the police response, including beatings and arrests, led wider circles to join in the protests. At the time of Israel's establishment, the Haredi public suffered from low self-esteem due to the sense that Haredi society had following the Holocaust and the trend to secularization. The Sabbath demonstrations, as well as the demonstrations on the issue of modesty, (which I shall discuss in the next chapter), strengthened Haredi morale and led to a sense of resurgence against the background of the antireligious atmosphere in Israel at the time, under the hegemonic leadership of the Socialist Mapai party.

Tensions between the Haredi and secular populations in Jerusalem concerning activities on the Sabbath had begun during the British Mandate period. The Union of Hebrew Workers (Histadrut) offered walking tours in Jerusalem on the Sabbath and soccer matches were also held. Moreover, fresh food and milk passed along Meah She'arim St., the center of Haredi life, on its way to Tnuva, the Histadrut-owned company for the marketing of agricultural produce.[43]

---

[42] Unsigned, "The Insolent Smear Me With Lies, but With My Whole Heart I Keep Your Precepts," *ibid*, 1 (in Hebrew).

[43] Freidman, *Neturei Karta*, pp. 225–6.

After the end of the War of Independence, the border in Jerusalem ran close to the neighborhood of Meah She'arim. Indeed, the Mandelbaum Gate crossing point was close to Batei Ungarin, home to one of the most extreme groups. The Mandelbaum Gate operated seven days a week, while Meah She'arim St. itself provided the quickest and most direct route between the gate and Schneller Camp, the base used by the IDF brigade in the area. Army vehicles driving along on the road were a routine sight on the Sabbath in this period, and this reality sparked Neturei Karta into action.

During the Passover festival in 1949, an Israeli officer serving as an observer in the United Nations check point was attacked while he was on his way to Mandelbaum Gate. A few days later, an army vehicle broke down in the area. After the driver stopped and attempted to repair the vehicle, he was attacked. In response, he opened fire on the demonstrators.[44]

However, the incident that brought out the demonstrators in their masses was the opening of the Edison Cinema, situated close to a Haredi neighborhood, on the Sabbath. The Haredi public organized demonstrations against the desecration of the Sabbath and the police responded by attacking the protestors with batons. Many Haredim were arrested and transported (on the Sabbath) to the police headquarters in the nearby Russian Compound. The demonstrations established the subject of the desecration of the Sabbath as a key priority for the Haredi public and Neturei Karta became the vanguard of the campaign on this issue.

After an agreement was reached with the army ending the passage of military vehicles along Meah She'arim St. on the Sabbath, the focus of the demonstrations moved to "Sabbath Square" – the intersection of Geula St. and Strauss St. in downtown Jerusalem. In this period, this area was not yet part of the Haredi heartland. As mentioned earlier, Tnuva used these roads to transport fresh milk from the dairies, including on Sabbath – particularly during the summer, in order to prevent the milk going sour in the heat.

As the vehicles passed along, they were subjected to verbal attacks from Haredim shouting "Shabbes!" (the Yiddish pronunciation of Shabbat – Sabbath). Sometimes stones were hurled at the passing cars. A cycle of escalation ensued. Sometimes the drivers would stop and confront the demonstrators, only to find themselves surrounded quickly by an angry Haredi crowd. In response, young kibbutzniks would come on the

---

[44] *Ibid.*, p. 234.

Sabbath to defend the roads, confronting the Haredim and sparking violent incidents between the two sides. Police intervention served only to exacerbate the clashes. The Sabbath demonstrations continued for years on the roads bordering on Meah She'arim, and eventually ended in a Haredi victory, leading to the dwindling use of these roads on the Sabbath.[45]

One particular incident acquired mythical status in the history of Neturei Karta. During one of the Sabbath demonstrations, Amram Blau hung onto the rear end of a truck passing along the road. The driver continued his journey for some distance before stopping to confront Blau. Blau was arrested by the police, though he was later released. He was summonsed to a trial but refused to sign the summons, and was therefore arrested again and accused of an unlawful gathering, riotous behavior, and causing damage. Amram Blau refused to participate in the trial, declaring that he did not recognize the authority of the court. He refused to answer the judge's questions, arguing that Jerusalem was an international area in accordance with the decision of the United Nations, and accordingly he was a resident of Jerusalem and not of the State of Israel. The judge decided not to sentence Blau on that day, since his son was due to be married the same evening, but Blau refused to post bail. He was sentenced to three months in jail and required to wear prison clothes. In recognition of the arrest and the personal price Blau had paid, the spiritual leader of the Haredi public, the "Hazon Ish" Rabbi Avraham-Yeshayah Karelitz, visited him in the detention center in a show of solidarity.[46]

In 1956 the government decided to establish a commission of inquiry to examine the Sabbath demonstrations in Jerusalem. The commission was formed following the death of one of the demonstrators, Pinchas Segalov. Neturei Karta blamed his death on police violence, though an autopsy showed that Segalov died after an artery burst in his head due to pressure from the mass of demonstrators. Although many of the leaders of the religious public in Israel participated in the funeral, including those identified with Religious-Zionist Mizrahi and Agudat Yisrael, Amram Blau gave the main eulogy.[47] The commission of inquiry was unable to reach agreed conclusions and each of its members presented a separate

---

[45] *Ibid.*, pp. 238–40.

[46] The visit took place on August 23, 1953. Anonymous, "Record This," 27.

[47] Anonymous, "A Victim of the Sabbath Demonstrations Buried," *Davar*, September 3, 1956, 4 (in Hebrew).

report. However, the majority view was that, as far as possible, vehicles should avoid traveling through Haredi neighborhoods in Jerusalem on the Sabbath. A minority position advocated the prohibition of all traffic on certain roads, with the exception of emergencies.[48] This recommendation was eventually implemented, de facto, and to this day roads in Haredi neighborhoods are closed on Sabbath and the festivals.

According to Ehud Sprinzak, the Sabbath demonstrations enhanced the prestige of Neturei Karta among the Haredi public, which saw the movement as the main force protesting the desecration of the Sabbath and securing victories at a heavy personal price. Since the demonstrations were generally restrained and nonviolent, and Neturei Karta avoided involvement in political affairs, the different governments preferred to avoid excessive clashes with the movement. Over time, the self-confidence of Neturei Karta grew, as did their realization that in a democratic system they could protest against the state without facing undue penalization.[49]

OLD AND NEW EDUCATION

One of the struggles between Neturei Karta and Agudat Yisrael related to educational reforms. A hallmark of modernism is change in educational methods, with an emphasis on secular scientific education. Amram Blau saw the campaign against such changes as one of his key objectives. Moreover, since his approach negated any form of cooperation or receipt of support from the Zionist state, the effort to distinguish his movement from the educational stream of Agudat Yisrael became an important component of his campaign.

Toward the end of the British mandate period, the Haredi Education Committee in the Land of Israel was established under the supervision of Rabbi Dushinsky, with the support of Rabbi Yitzhak Zeev Soloveichik (1886–1959). The goal of the committee was "to strengthen old education," and it promised to identify and oppose any change in educational methods and any addition of new fields of study.

According to the committee's constitution, its activities would include building educational centers, Talmudei Torah, "in the traditional Jewish spirit, without any change whatsoever, and without any alien admixture

---

[48] Anonymous, "Three Separate Reports Published by the Commission to Investigate the Sabbath Demonstrations in Jerusalem," *Davar*, June 6, 1957, 4 (in Hebrew).

[49] Ehud Sprinzak, *Brother against Brother: Violence and Extremism in Israeli Politics from Altalena to the Rabin Assassination*. New York: Free Press, 1999, pp. 87–112.

or external wisdoms such as have been prohibited by our holy rabbis." Regarding girls' education, the constitution stated that girls should be educated to modesty and God-fearing behavior without any religious studies. The teaching of foreign languages to girls was absolutely prohibited, including the teaching of Hebrew. It should be noted that the spoken language used by this community in their schools was Yiddish.

The committee launched vicious attacks against the Beis Yaacov educational network, which became the main component in the education system of Agudat Yisrael. The Beis Yaakov schools provided a vocational education for girls enabling them to integrate in the job market, particularly as teachers. This educational reform enabled Haredi households to enjoy financial stability. The women gained a useful vocation and went out to support the family, thus allowing the men to continue to study Torah. The educational revolution in gender relations in Haredi society occurred in the early 1950s.[50]

The Beis Yaakov educational network had operated under the patronage of Agudat Yisrael since 1919, and in the 1930s the network began to operate in Palestine. The network adopted a more progressive approach to girls' education, including foreign language studies (English) and teaching in Hebrew.[51]

Amram Blau launched a fierce attack against this educational approach, and particularly against the use of Hebrew as the language of teaching. He claimed that Zionist nationalism was based on two pillars – language and land. Hebrew was the Zionist weapon for strengthening nationhood. "This is the Hebrew the infidels used to deceive the Jews and to poison the children of Israel with false views, infidelity, and heresy." He ordered the Haredi public not to send its daughters to these schools until this aspect was remedied.[52]

After the establishment of the State of Israel, the education stream of Agudat Yisrael and Po'alei Agudat Yisrael[53] was recognized as a fourth

---

[50] Agnieszka Oleszak, "The Beit Ya'akov School in Krakow as an Encounter between East and West," *Polin* 23 (2010), 277–90; Caroline Scharfer, "Sarah Schenirer, Founder of the Beit Ya'akov Movement: Her Vision and Her Legacy," *Polin* 23 (2010) 269–75.

[51] Judith Tudor Baumel and Jacob J. Schacter, "The Ninety-Three Bais Yaakov Girls of Cracow: History or Typology?" In: Jacob J. Schacter (ed.), *Reverence, Righteousness, and Rahmanut: Essays in Memory of Rabbi Dr. Leo Jung.* Northvale, NJ: Jason Aronson, 1992, pp. 93–130.

[52] Amram Blau, "To Quench the Thirst," undated, Blau Archive, Box 1, Education folder, Document 62.

[53] Po'alei Agudat Yisrael, active from 1948 to 1981, was a Haredi labor party. The movement had 14 affiliated settlements and was a member of the Histadrut, the Zionist

educational stream (known as the "independent" stream, alongside the three existing Jewish educational streams – state, state-religious, and the workers' stream). The education system enjoyed full autonomy, with the exception of minimal educational requirements in the fields of language, science, and history. State recognition and funding enabled the network to flourish in financial terms and ensured that the teachers enjoyed regular and orderly employment.[54]

Neturei Karta found it difficult to compete with the financial support enjoyed by the educational network of Agudat Yisrael. Nevertheless, the effort to withstand this pressure and the struggle to prevent schools and individuals from joining the fourth stream became one of the struggles wages by Amram Blau. In 1949, in an effort to stem the flow, the rabbis of HaEdah HaHaredit convened and issued a *Da'at Torah* (statement of "Torah opinion") prohibiting affiliation to the fourth stream. They claimed that any contact with the Zionist education system "was akin to the abandonment of Torah study and its delivery to those who stalk our holy Torah to uproot, demolish, and destroy it." They threatened that any gabbai or director of a Talmud Torah who broke this barrier "would be damned and a fence-breaker, may a snake bite him." The rabbis also prohibited educators to work in these institutions and forbade parents to send their children to them.[55] Amram Blau contacted schools that were considering joining the network and implored them not to do so, while promising to ensure their financial security.[56]

Over the years Neturei Karta attempted to revive the boycott of the independent education stream, particularly following the waves of mass immigration, which brought to Israel large numbers of Jews from Arab

---

labor organization. At its peak the movement had three seats in the Knesset. During the Fourth Knesset (1959–1961), MK Binyamin Mintz from Po'alei Agudat Yisrael served as postal minister.

[54] Zvi Zameret, *Education during the First Decade*. Tel Aviv: Open University Press, 2003 (in Hebrew).

[55] Untitled, 13 Kislev 5709 – 1948, Blau Archive, Box 1, Education folder, Document 56. Similar bans published in Neturei Karta's newspaper: Unsigned, "On the Outrage Regarding the Education Danger," *HaHomah* 58, 21 Kislev 5709 – 1949, 1; Zelig Reuven Bengis, "Great Warning," *HaHomah* 59, Tevet 5709 – 1949, 2 (in Hebrew).

[56] For example, Blau contacted the Committee of the Bukharians and asked them not to agree to the offer by Moshe Porush for them to join the Independent education system. Blau promised that if the committee split as a result of the decision, he would ensure that an alternative institution opened in another building. See Amram Blau, "The Distinguished Rabbis of the Committee of the Bukharians, may they live days that are pleasant and long," 11 Kislev 5709 – 1948, Blau Archive, Box 1, Education folder, unnumbered document.

countries with traditional religious backgrounds who provided a significant pool for recruitment to the Agudat Yisrael network.[57] In broad terms, however, these efforts failed to secure their objective. Neturei Karta was unable to compete with the economic prosperity the State of Israel could offer the Independent stream and those who worked in it. This may explain why this particular campaign never became the central plank in the work of Amram Blau, and served merely as another stick in his efforts to attack Agudat Yisrael.

One of the main innovations in the field of education in HaEdah HaHaredit was the establishment of an education system for girls. The researcher Raphael Shneler has shown that the education system for boys was deeply conservative, continuing almost unchanged from the practices of the nineteenth century and focusing exclusively on religious studies. By contrast, the very concept of an education system for girls was a radical innovation that emerged only in the 1930s. Shneler explains that since this time boys' education has continued to be static and traditional, while the girls' education system has seen ongoing change. His research shows that women in HaEdah HaHaredit sought to strengthen their status and demanded a broader education – both Jewish and general, particularly against the background of their efforts to integrate in the job market. The girls' education system was established in response to this pressure, and particularly due to the presence of the Beis Yaacov girls' education system of Agudat Yisrael, which constituted a source of competition. Indeed, Shneler found that over time the curriculum of the new girls' education system became increasingly similar to that of Agudat Yisrael.[58]

This instance suggests that the ban on women's education by the leadership of HaEdah HaHaredit came to be seen as an edict that could not be accepted by the public, particularly since Agudat Yisrael permitted such education. The involvement of women in the workplace became crucial to the survival of Haredi society. Pragmatic solutions that modified the ways of the past and brought modernization to HaEdah HaHaredit were adopted after the efforts to withstand such changes proved ineffective.

---

[57] See: "Decisions Taken at a Meeting of the Torah Sages and Yeshivot in the Holy City of Jerusalem, may it speedily be rebuilt," 5 Tammuz 5714 – 1954, Blau Archive, Box 1, Education folder, unnumbered document.

[58] Raphael Shneler, *The Educational System of the Jewish Radical Haredim in Jerusalem as their Main Contributor to Continuity and Change.* PhD Dissertation, Bar Ilan University, 1977 (in Hebrew).

THE CAMPAIGN AGAINST PARTICIPATION IN THE ELECTIONS

The main issue separating Neturei Karta from the remainder of the Haredi public was their demand for the community to remain separate and to refrain from participating in the Zionist enterprise and the State of Israel. In this context, a particularly sensitive issue was that of participation in elections and representation in the political and governmental echelons. The system of proportional representation used in elections to the Knesset enabled the Haredi public to exercise considerable power and influence in the corridors of government, thus reinforcing their ability to maintain their lifestyle and to strengthen their educational institutions, thanks in no small part of state funding.[59] However, participation in Israeli politics implied the de facto recognition of the State of Israel; since Neturei Karta opposed such recognition, it refused to participate in the political process.

In the booklet, *The Judge in Your Days*, Blau explained the principles shaping the opposition of Neturei Karta to Haredi involvement in Israeli politics, and they can be summarized as follows:

The first principle is the need for separation. Blau argued that participation in the elections meant joining together with a public that had turned its back on the Torah and rebelled against God. Accordingly, those who participate in the elections do not merely join with the evil for utilitarian goals, but become part of evil themselves: "Each voter is included in this public and this leadership, whatever happens, he is a limb or a part in the wild beast that is devouring the soul of Israel, this infidel beast that rebels against the Kingdom of Heaven."[60]

Accordingly, Blau continued, participation in the political system implied the acceptance and recognition of a leadership based entirely on rejection of the Torah. Moreover, since there can be no Israel without Torah, the use of the epithet "State of Israel" is an act of forgery and deception. Only those who observe the Torah can use the name "Israel." Participation in the elections and the recognition of infidels as the leaders of the people means paying respect and honor to criminals – "placing an

---

[59] Samuel Heilman and Menachem Friedman, "Religious Fundamentalism and Religious Jews: The Case of the Haredim." In: Martin E. Marty and Scott Appleby (eds.), *Fundamentalism Observed*. Chicago: University of Chicago Press, 1991, pp. 197–264.

[60] Amram Blau, *The Judge in Your Days*. Jerusalem: Horev, undated [probably published in Tishrei 5720 – October 1959], p. 5 (in Hebrew); found in: Blau Archive, Box 3, Folder 1, Document 23.

idol in the Temple."[61] Rapprochement and cooperation between observant and infidel Jews opens the door to "their toxic influence." Accepting budgets and jobs and drawing near to the pleasures of power allow them to exert their influence, thereby endangering the entire public.

A further rationale raised by Blau was the prohibition against the participation of women in the elections. He stated that the Halakhah rules that a woman is not permitted to judge. Accordingly, allowing women to take part in government is tantamount to degrading the Torah.

Blau claims that Israeli sovereignty entails a declaration of Israel as a "fighting people" – that is, fighting against the nations, while according to the oaths rendered to the Jewish people by God, it must not rebel against the nations of the world. Accordingly, faithful Jews must separate themselves from those who rebel against the nations, since they are liable to cause a terrible disaster. Participation in elections entails partnership in the rebellion against the nations.[62]

Another principle is that participation in elections prevents separatism. The faithful Jew who sees the results of Zionism – that Blau claims was the reason for the Holocaust and the murder of six million Jews, as well as tens of thousands more in Israeli wars – must protest and rail against this act of infidelity. To sit at the same table as the infidel and rebel leadership, and to receive budgets and help from them, prevents such protest. Moreover, even if the Haredim were to protest and then once again sit at the same table, "and again share the funds and dance with their every move, the protests, even if they actually occurred, would have no value."[63]

Blau attacked the widespread argument in Haredi circles that participation in the elections was a matter of "rescue." The argument was that if the Haredim refused to participate in elections and to take part in the leadership of the state, this would represent an even greater threat to the world of Torah, since it would be left without defense. Blau's counterargument was that separatism is an act of defiance that had an inherent force of its own that far exceeds that of the principle of "rescue." Moreover, the Haredi parties had negligible power, and the money provided by the Zionists is no more than "bribery." Moreover, the infidels take no heed of their opinions, and in most cases the Haredim do not even bother to express their opinion. The result is that rather than influencing the situation, they are influenced by it. "Any honest mind recognizes that the outcome is that they are swallowed in their belly, G-d forbid."[64]

---

[61] *Ibid.*, p. 8. [62] *Ibid.*, p. 13. [63] *Ibid.*, pp. 17–18. [64] *Ibid.*, p. 26.

This approach explains Blau's fierce attack against the Council of Torah Sages of Agudat Yisrael. He argued that there had never been such an institution within the religious Jewish world, and that the council had been formed to combat Zionism. Since Agudat Yisrael had now chosen to join forces with the Zionists, however, what purpose could such a body have? Moreover, Blau argued that the council did not include the true Torah sages, such as the "Hazon Ish" Rabbi Avraham Yeshaya Karelitz and Yitzhak Zeev Soloveitchik (the "Brisker Rebbe.") Instead, the council was full of appointees who supported the approach of the political activists. Accordingly, Blau concluded, the Council of Torah Sages had no authority, since it legitimized heresy, and real authority should rest solely with the Beit Din Tzedek, the supreme court of HaEdah HaHaredit.[65]

Blau viewed the concept of Jewish nationhood as a false idea. An independent state established by mundane action contradicts the belief in messianic redemption and in the power of God. Involvement in Zionist action leads to chaos and the blurring of boundaries, something that Blau feared would lead to the mass and public desecration of God's name. Accordingly, he declared that he had no part in the leadership of the state and no interest in its affairs. The Haredim should not participate in the elections, and the state does not represent them.[66]

Blau's principled position did not change over the years since he founded Neturei Karta and through to the time when he presented his ideological approach in writing. The constant theme is the identification of Zionism as heresy and the abandonment of the path of Judaism, and the consequent emphasis on extreme separatism and protest.

THE MARRIAGE OF AMRAM BLAU TO RUTH DEN DAVID

In the latter part of his life, after his first wife died, Amram Blau became embroiled in a major scandal due to his desire to marry the convert Ruth Ben David. The story of Madeleine Ferraille, who later became Ruth Ben David, is a fascinating episode in its own right. Few Haredi women have attracted such sustained public interest in Israel. Her personal story is one of dramatic changes. She grew up in a Catholic family in France, was converted by a liberal rabbi in Paris, and later (in 1952) immigrated to

---

[65] *Ibid.*, p. 32.
[66] Amram Blau, *Clarifying Matters*. Jerusalem: Horev, 5720 – 1959 (in Hebrew); found in: Blau Archives, Box 3, Folder 1, Document 23.

Israel and joined Kvutzat Yavne, where she raised her only son, Uriel, and underwent an Orthodox conversion. The religious kibbutz did not provide her with sufficient religious stimulation, and her journey took her on to Meah She'arim.

In 1960, her life took a dramatic turn when she was recruited to kidnap the boy Yossele Schumacher and smuggle him out of Israel. The family of the boy, who was seven at the time, had immigrated to Israel from the Soviet Union and the boy was being educated on a temporary basis by his grandfather, Nachman Schtraks, in Meah She'arim until his parents settled and found an apartment and work. After a few months, his parents purchased a home in Holon and registered the child at a state-religious school. Schtraks opposed the education intended for his grandson, and decided to remove him from his parents' custody. Various elements in the Haredi community hid Yossele in different locations, including Safed and Moshav Komemiyut that was affiliated with Poalei Agudat Yisrael, and then decided to smuggle him out of Israel. They contacted the French convert, who agreed to help smuggle Yossele out of the state. The boy was hidden for three years in Haredi communities in Switzerland, France, and the United States, with the material and logistical assistance of the Haredi businessman Yerahmiel Domb, a resident of London known for his support of Neturei Karta. The affair provoked a storm of protest in Israeli public opinion.[67]

The leadership of Agudat Yisrael initially supported the kidnapping but changed its position following the furious public reaction; MK Shlomo Laurentz even attempted unsuccessfully to locate the boy and reunited him with his parents. Prime Minister David Ben Gurion ordered the secret services to locate the boy, although the affair had nothing to do with national security. Uriel, the son of Ruth Ben David, was summonsed for questioning and revealed his mother's involvement in the affair. Following his testimony Ruth Ben David was located by the Mossad in France and kidnapped for questioning. After a plea bargain was signed, she revealed the location of Yossele in return for a promise that she would not be imprisoned.[68]

After converting to Judaism, Ruth Ben David had remained unmarried for many years; having divorced her Christian husband, she was unable to

---

[67] For example, see: K. Shabbtai, "At the Gates of Mass Hysteria," *Davar*, May 25, 1962, 2 (in Hebrew).

[68] See Ruth Blau, *Guardians of the City*. Jerusalem: Eidanim, 1979 (in Hebrew). Cf.: Isser Harel, *The Yossele Campaign*. Tel Aviv: Yediot Acharonot, 1982 (in Hebrew).

find a partner. After the exposure of the Yossele affair she became a cultural hero among the Haredi population. In 1963, Amram Blau's wife Hinde, who had borne him nine children, passed away. A quick-thinking matchmaker suggested to Blau that he might marry the convert, who was twenty years his junior, and so it transpired. On September 7, 1964, the traditional *Wort* matchmaking and engagement agreement was signed by the couple. The agreement required Ruth Ben David to adapt her dress to the modesty codes of the Haredi community, including black stockings, and to cover her head with a black scarf. The agreement did not set a date for the wedding.[69]

When word of the engagement became public, the Neturei Karta community erupted in shock. Could "Rabbi Amram" really be intending to marry a convert? Young radicals, including three of Amram Blau's own sons, turned to the supreme court of HaEdah HaHaredit and asked the court to prohibit the marriage, which it did. The court ordered Blau to avoid the proposed match.[70] To add insult to injury, the head of the court, Rabbi Pinchas Epstein, had himself wished to marry Ruth and was furious after he was rejected.[71] The court gave the following grounds for its ruling:

1. Blau was sterile and accordingly the marriage entailed an element of "deception," since the bride would not be able to have children.
2. There was an enormous age gap of over twenty years between the couple.
3. The rabbi was a leading Torah sage whereas the bride was a convert – this constitutes a desecration of God's name, since a convert was popularly regarded as someone who is not sufficiently decent or modest. This would result in rumors and make a mockery of Neturei Karta.[72] According to the press, the zealots published broadsheets depicting Ben David as an educated and well-traveled woman, and hence someone unsuitable to serve as the bride of a leading rabbi.[73]

[69] Blau Archive, "*Wort*," Blau Archive, Box 3, Ruth Ben David folder. See also: Blau, *Guardians of the City*, p. 172.

[70] B. Yehoshua, "Reb Amram Refuses to Break his Engagement to the Convert," *Ma'ariv*, July 14, 1965, 18 (in Hebrew).

[71] Darash, *Neturei*, pp. 72–3.

[72] Amram Blau, *The Claim of Amram Blau against the Court of HaEdah HaHaredit in Jerusalem*. Jerusalem: self-published, 5725 – 1964/5 (in Hebrew); found in: Blau Archive, Box 3, Ruth Ben David folder.

[73] The ruling was copied to Amram Blau's response to the court mentioned in Blau, *The Claim*. See also Yehoshua, "Reb Amram," 18.

Blau decided to disobey the court and marry the convert, although the row delayed the wedding for over a year. In order to explain why he had chosen to disobey the *Beit Din Tzedek* of HaEdah HaHaredit, Blau composed a pamphlet, printed in just ten copies in order to prevent its widespread distribution. He also sent a letter adding further arguments to those presented in the pamphlet.

On the basis of both these sources we may divide Blau's response into two types of arguments: spiritual and Halakhic on the one hand, and mundane and practical on the other. It seems that the court's main concern was the issue of public gossip, since Blau devoted most of his response to this aspect. He argued that the desecration of God's name should be determined by the essence of an action and not by the way it is perceived by the public. Accordingly, he sought to inquire whether marriage to a convert constitutes a prohibition, and hence "desecrates God's name." Since he argued that there is no Halakhic impediment to marriage to a convert, it follows that no attention should be paid to public gossip.

Blau continued by mentioning various figures whom tradition reports were married to converts: Joshua married Rahab, Boaz took Ruth, and King David also married a convert (whose name is unknown). Rabbi Akiva took the wife of Tornoseropos as his wife.[74] Indeed, Elazar, the son of Aaron the Priest, married one of the daughters of Pottiel, despite the gossip among the tribes directed at his son Pinchas.[75] According to the traditional principle that each generation is less worthy than its predecessor, Blau argued that if the early generations were greater in Torah, the concern of desecration of God's name in their marrying converts must have been even greater. Despite this, these marriages went ahead and were not cancelled due to public gossip.

Moreover, Blau argues that it is God's wish that Jews should love the convert, who for all purposes is to be considered equal to a Jew by birth – "the alien living with you must be treated as one of your native-born" – and must not be separated from the general public. Accordingly, it is gossip about converts that desecrates God's name. Those who oppose the convert's wish to marry him are opposing God's will. Meeting the will of a convert, through the desire to honor and complete God's will, is actually even greater than such an action in the case of a Jew by birth, since there exists the additional commandment to "love the stranger."[76] Those who consider the convert less worthy violate explicit commandments from the

---

[74] Blau, *The Claim.*   [75] *Ibid.*, p. 5.   [76] *Ibid.*, pp. 8–10.

Torah, and Blau comments "certainly no consideration is to be paid to those with such opinions and to such gossip."[77]

Regarding the question of "deceiving the convert," Blau chose a different interpretation to that of the court. He argues that "deceiving the convert" means that she must not be considered flawed or less worthy. He emphasizes that Jews by birth have no superiority over converts.[78]

Blau therefore asked whether consideration should be given to those with a "foolish and delinquent" opinion who regard the convert as less worthy and gossip about a man who is great in Torah. He asked whether a distinction should be made between converts and those born Jewish on the basis of the foolishness of those who transgress against Torah. "Is this thinkable?!" he asked, with an overtone of challenge.[79]

Blau noted that had he chosen a "born Jew" as his wife the court would not have intervened in the match. This creates a situation in which there is one law for born Jews and one for converts – in contradiction of the provision in the Torah that "There shall be one standard for you; it shall be for the stranger as well as the native, for I am the Lord your God" (Leviticus 24:22).

Blau also found support from scriptures in response to the claim regarding the age gap between himself and Ben David. According to the Biblical story and the traditional exegesis of the Book of Ruth, Boaz married Ruth when he was eighty years old and she was just forty.[80] Blau claimed that the Book of Ruth reflects the approach of the Torah to the commandment to love strangers, showing that the decision to take a convert as a wife is a great sanctification of God's name.[81]

After concluding his spiritual and Halakhic arguments, Blau presented other claims. Firstly, he had already made an undertaking to the convert, and he could not now withdraw his vow. Moreover, he was afraid of "the terrible prohibitions regarding the nullification of marriage."[82]

Secondly, the court's ruling would effectively render Ben David an *agunah*,[83] since she would be unable to marry. This had provoked public fury against the court and against Judaism as a whole; "who knows what

---

[77] *Ibid.*, p. 10.   [78] *Ibid.*, p. 10.   [79] *Ibid.*, p. 11.   [80] *Ibid.*, p. 14.

[81] *Ibid.*, pp. 16–17.

[82] Amram Blau, "To the Great Rabbis the Members of the Beit Din Tzedek, May They Live a Long Life, Amen," 17 Menachem–Av 5725 (August 15, 1965), Blau Archives, Box 3, Ruth Ben David folder.

[83] A woman whose husband has abandoned her or disappeared, so that she cannot obtain a religious divorce and remarry.

results this will have," Blau warned, alluding to the widespread public reaction to the affair, including coverage in the international media.[84]

Thirdly, Blau was determined to marry the convert come what may. Accordingly, the decision of the court risked dividing the Haredi camp and creating a public schism, devastating "the surviving remnant of Judaism."[85] After his marriage, he indeed caused a split in HaEdah HaHaredit after he established his own branch of Neturei Karta.[86]

As for the question of fertility, Blau's answer is unclear and elusive. However, his position casts doubts on the honesty of his Halakhic argument concerning the requirement to love and refrain from deceiving converts. Blau begins his pamphlet with the ruling from the Halakhic compilation Shulhan Arukh stating that the Torah requires that he marry a woman who will bear him children. As explained earlier, the court argued that since Blau was sterile he had no need to marry, and indeed this would be tantamount to deception. Blau hinted obliquely that since his intended bride was a convert, this problem was resolved: "Though my heart hesitates [about the marriage], it is interesting that my body (as two of the members of the *Beit Din Tzedek* have known for some years) frees me of these hesitations."[87] He later repeats this argument: "If a Jew like myself had the opportunity of such a marriage and the intended wife were a Jew by birth, this would certainly be a desirable match for him, but since I have hesitations, as I have mentioned, there is actually an advantage in this match, as distinct from a match with a Jew by birth."[88] In my opinion, Blau's comments imply that since he is sterile, his marriage to a convert solves the problem created by the fact that the marriage will not produce any children. In other words, his argument was based on the concept that a convert has a lesser status than a Jew by birth. This leads me to conclude that Blau's Halakhic arguments were merely a cloak for his desire to marry the young and attractive woman, since these later arguments contradict his earlier claim that converts are in no way inferior to Jews by birth. After Blau's death, Ruth Blau attempted to refute the rumors of her late husband's sterility. In her autobiography she claimed that some five years after they married, when she was approximately fifty

---

[84] James Ferons, "Israeli Sect Head to Wed a Convert; Orthodox Chief, 72, Leaves Holy City for Divorcee, 45," *New York Times*, August 2, 1965, 11. See also: Anonymous, "Mazal Tov! Rabbi Amram Has Married His Convert," *Yediot Acharonot*, September 5, 1965, 21 (in Hebrew).

[85] Blau, *To the Great Rabbis.*

[86] Unsigned, "HaEdah HaHaredit is splitting," *Davar*, August 19, 1965, 14.

[87] Blau, *The Claim*, p. 1.   [88] *Ibid.*, p. 6.

years old, she indeed became pregnant. However she fasted on Yom Kippur, against her physician's orders, and the fetus was lost.[89] It is highly unlikely that this story has any foundation.

Following the scandal created by this affair, the Satmar Rabbi, Yoel Teitelbaum, attempted to solve the problem by offering Ruth Ben David financial compensation in return for the cancellation of the marriage; however, she declined the offer.[90] The Satmar Rabbi did not order Blau to cancel the match, providing him with the excuse he needed to pursue his plan. Blau's insistence on marrying Ben David, in contradiction of the instruction of the court of HaEdah HaHaredit, forced him to leave Jerusalem and move to Bnei Brak.[91] The wedding took place in September 1965 and the price Blau paid was his excommunication from the community in which he had spent his entire life, and whose struggles he had led over a period of dramatic changes. Two years later, however, Blau managed to placate his community and was able to return to his home in Jerusalem. Kimmy Caplan claims that Blau's return was conditioned upon giving up his leadership role in Neturei Karta.[92] The affair described here emphasizes Blau's character as an independent man willing to take unpopular decisions and to challenge his own religious authorities.

The writer Menashe Darash revealed several personal letters between Ruth and Amram that suggest that the two had a stormy relationship that included both passionate love and bitter arguments.[93] While Ruth was visiting France in order to sell her apartment, she wrote to her husband:

My beloved, may you live a long life – Amen – pray for me and for us, also on the Sabbath my beloved by the Torah, pray for me for I long to be by your side in Jerusalem as speedily as possibly. I am very sad without you my beloved and I ask that in your prayers you beseech the Holy One, blessed be He, to soften the hearts of the persons regarding my apartment that they may come to speak with me soon and we can complete this matter quickly and successfully.

Ruth uses the Biblical Hebrew word *"dod"* (beloved) to address her husband, creating echoes of the Song of Songs, where the beloved is depicted as perfect and flawless. In Jewish tradition the character of the beloved came to be interpreted as an allegory for God, while the wife was likened to the Jewish people. The wife's love for her beloved in the Song of Songs is depicted as a tempestuous one replete with erotic language.

---

[89] Blau, *Guardians*, pp. 198–99.   [90] Yehoshua, "Reb Amram," p. 18.
[91] Ibid., See also: Blau, *To the Great Rabbis*.
[92] Kimmy Caplan, "An Insolent, Dirty Convert Woman."
[93] Darash, *Neturei*, pp. 85–9.

Ruth's choice of this term and the tone of her letter reflect her profound affection for Amram.

In the same letter, however, the first signs can already be seen of the issues that would later cloud the couple's relationship. The most significant problem was the rejection of the marriage by the Haredi community, and in particular the fact that the opponents included Amram's children from his first marriage. Ruth continues: "I hope you will not bring me into disgrace and will not bring such people into our home. As I have told you, they should not be in our home as long as they fail to repent." We cannot be certain regarding the identity of these persons whom Ruth does not wish to enter their home. It is reasonable to hypothesize that they were supporters of Neturei Karta who had opposed the marriage from the outset, so that she does not wish them to enter the martial home until they apologize.

Another letter quoted by Darash reveals that Ruth left her husband two years after their marriage. Another voyage to France was for the purpose of medical treatment due to stomach problems, and she also wished to undergo treatment for infertility. However, she also used the trip as an excuse not to return to her husband; his reply asking her to change her mind suggests that the reason she left was his sterility, which he refers to obliquely as a defect in his body. The correspondence shows that Ruth was aware of the arguments her husband had presented to the Beit Din Tzedek in order to justify his marriage to a convert, who was considered a second-class wife. Her departure from Jerusalem, and apparently a conversation with a woman referred to as "Mrs. Ratterbart," reopened the wound and Ruth decided to leave Amram. He attempted to dissuade her from this course of action:

[Regarding] the defect you have found in my body, and I do not wish to state the name of the defect, for things happen and the letter might fall into strange hands, and this is not good – it is not fitting that strangers should know to what the matter refers. I already told you while you were still in Jerusalem that this is not a defect that has emerged only at this juncture. While I was a married student I already suffered from this defect. With this disadvantage I have found myself in diverse company – at gatherings, meetings, and demonstrations, at weddings and circumcisions, among rabbis and Admorim, with yeshivah students, merchants, and relatives – and other than you, no-one has ever commented to me on this defect, neither associates nor strangers, neither friends nor enemies. I do not claim that this defect or disadvantage is not present in me, or that you are incorrect, but while I did not particularly sense this defect, you came to me on that Sabbath and told me in such a drastic manner that you cannot stand me because of my defect and that for this reason you would remain in France. Yet you know that even then I promised you that I would correct this defect. Thus you left me when you departed – in peace and tranquility, yet now you are suddenly reopening the wound in such a provocative manner.

I know of no other matters in which I have embittered your life to the point that you state that you no longer wish to be an "embittered rag." What the women there told you [...] did not go as you thought, but that is not my fault. You write – do I not think that I am the center of everything? Since when do I think that I am the center? I do not know how I have prevented you from being content. It seems to me that lately there was no special matter between us other than that which I mentioned at the beginning of my letter. [...]

You are already not so angry with me, and surely you will change your decision, for I miss you very much. Be healthy and strong, happy wherever you go and turn. Rest and be satisfied and joyful, and may we soon together welcome our just Messiah. Greetings from your longing husband, Amram Blau. (85–6)

As is clear from the letter, Ruth was aware of her husband's infertility problem and he had promised to attend to the matter. Her accusation that he was self-centered may be connected to his failure to deal with this issue, which he emphasizes is not his fault. The impression is that Blau believed that his wife's desire to become pregnant was unrealistic; as noted, he had promised the Beit Din Tzedek that he would not have children with Ruth.

Ruth was not placated and evidently continued to accuse Amram of various offenses and improprieties toward her. She demanded that he mend his ways and punished him by remaining in France during the High Holydays, leaving her without him. Amram sent a further letter proclaiming his love for her, quoting from Proverbs 10:12: "After all, Scripture says 'Love covers all wrongs'" (86). He promised to repent his ways but added: "Why do you now try to hurt me in your letter? In correspondence with a husband far away, one should try as far as possible to write in a friendly manner and not (Heaven forfend) to be hurtful" (87).

Amram's pleadings failed to soften his wife's rage. She refused to return, declaring that she did not wish to do so in a state of mental anguish. She claimed that Amram had disrespected her status and their marriage: "Now I understand what will happen on the eve of this Yom Kippur. You will be with your children like a widow who has lost his precious wife – like a husband without a wife. You will tell them, or you will allow them to understand, that you are still their mother's husband, while I am nothing." She went on to complain that Amram did not refer to her as "my darling:" "In the last letter you sent to me with Uri [Amram's eldest son], you did not write 'my darling Ruth' so that Uri would not think that I am your wife" (88).

Blau replied:

My darling Ruth, I received your beloved letter. You cannot imagine how much joy you bring to my soul when you tell me that you are a little calmer now, even if only a little. You make me the happiest of men. You bring me a new soul.

You are angry at me because I wrote "dear" rather than "my darling" and you build a whole construction on this basis. I tell you, I really did not mean anything. And you could argue that the adjective "dear" is greater than "my darling," since dear means dear to the whole world, while my darling means you are dear only to me. (88–9)

The exchange of letters reveals something of the relationship between Amram and Ruth. Although they had already been married for two years at this point, it is clear that their relationship was still clouded by the cool response to the marriage among Amram's supporters. Amram was forced to maneuver between his wife on the one hand and his followers on the other. This balancing process infuriated Ruth to the point that she considered leaving her husband and threatened not to return after she traveled to France. Amram's infertility was a further source of concern. Although it is clear from the letters that Ruth had been aware of this problem, she nevertheless decided (at the age of 47) to travel to France in order to seek treatment at a gynecological clinic, and she informed him that she had once again begun to get her period. Accordingly, she was furious at him for failing to address his own problem. Clearly Ruth was determined to have children with him, perhaps in part in order to put an end to the gossiping in Haredi circles.[94] Since Amram had emphasized that he did not wish to have children with Ruth during his proposal, he was disappointed by the aggressive tone of her letters. It is possible that her demand that he "repent" refers to the suggestion that he deceived her. As will be recalled, the claim of deception was one of the grounds quoted by the Beit Din Tzedek for opposing the marriage.

Amram expressed displeasure at the fact that Ruth signed her letter: "Sad Ruth who no longer believes that there is even a little joy in the world for her" (89). He attempted to console her: "The truth is you should be happier than usual, for the Blessed Lord has helped you and you are now a Jew; everything else is nothing" (89). Amram's replies to Ruth imply that he indeed loved and missed her and was doing his best to console her. These letters illuminate a less familiar side of his personality:

---

[94] In her own book Ruth emphasizes her desire to have children: Ruth Blau, *Guardians*, p. 198.

he was not only a bellicose and stubborn man, but also a gentle romantic. The letters explain why he insisted on marrying her even at the cost of disobeying the Beit Din Tzedek: He was in love with her, and evidently she loved him. However, she was mortally wounded by the insults, gossiping, and the giggling of children behind her back as she walked through the streets of Meah She'arim.[95]

Amram Blau passed away in 1974, aged in his late eighties. Thousands of mourners participated in his funeral procession. Ruth was in Australia when her husband died and his sons quickly buried their father alongside his first wife Hinde. Ruth was unable to attend the funeral and was left helpless and angry as her beloved husband was buried alongside another woman.[96]

After Blau's death, Ruth decided not to transfer his personal archive to his sons and to keep the material in their home. Toward the end of her life, she handed the private archive to Yoel Rappel, with whom she had been acquainted since spending part of her life in Kvutzat Yavne. Rappel's father, David Rappel, had prepared her for her Orthodox conversion to Judaism. Blau's archive was transferred to the Elie Wiesel Center at Boston University due to the personal relationship between Professor Elie Wiesel and Yoel Rappel. The decision followed an undertaking by the university authorities to invest in preserving and maintaining the archive. Institutions of higher education in Israel were either been unwilling to make such a commitment or demanded conditions Rappel found unacceptable.

NETUREI KARTA AFTER THE DEATH OF AMRAM BLAU

Aharon Katzenelbogen (1894–1979), Amram's partner in the leadership of Neturei Karta, was a relatively unknown figure not prone to belligerent activism. His power stemmed mainly from his religious knowledge, but he refused to participate in the movement's demonstrations. Katzenelbogen died a few years after Blau.

Blau's marriage to Ruth had led to the first split in the movement as Amram's followers seceded from HaEdah HaHaredit. The death of the two leaders led to a further split among their sons, each of whom claimed to be the legitimate heir to the leadership of the movement. Neturei Karta effectively disintegrated as a result of these feuds, with each faction

---

[95] *Ibid.*   [96] Darash, *Neturei*, p. 90.

comprising no more than a small band of supporters. Amram's son Uri assumed the leadership position in 1974 but subsequently led his followers back to the fold of HaEdah HaHaredit, which his father had left after refusing to obey its edicts. Chaim Katzenelbogen established a rival organization called "Neturei Karta of Torah and Awe" that seized control of Neturei Karta's assets, including the newspaper HaHomah, expelling Uri Blau from the movement. This movement continues to function outside the framework of HaEdah HaHaredit.[97]

Another figure who came to prominence from the 1970s was Moshe Hirsch (1930–2010), who came to be known as "the foreign minister of Neturei Karta." Hirsch was appointed to the position in 1974 following the death of Amram Blau in order to put an end to the rivalries that were splitting the movement at the time.[98] Hirsch attempted to revive the idea of the "Arab option" as raised by the Jerusalem zealots and publicly expressed support for the Palestinian Liberation Organization (PLO). He declared his desire to affiliate to a Palestinian national entity, and in 1994 he was appointed Minister for Jewish Affairs in the government of Yasser Arafat, chairman of the Palestinian Authority.[99] Hirsch was a marginal figure from the most extreme faction who lacked influence and was not supported by HaEdah HaHaredit. In 1990 he survived an assassination attempt by an unknown assailant. His activities focused mainly on the movement's public relations and on attempts to promote the "Arab option."[100]

Another provocative figure who gained prominence in these circles was Yehuda Meshi Zahav (born 1952). Meshi Zahav was one of the organizers of mass demonstrations in Jerusalem, some of which were particularly fierce, and gained the military-style epithet of "operations officer of HaEdah HaHaredit." As a young man he sprayed graffiti on the gravestone of Benjamin Zeev Herzl, the Zionist visionary. In 1996 he established an organization called Identification of Disaster Victims (known by its Hebrew acronym Zaka), which attends to the bodies of victims and ensures that they are brought for Jewish burial. The organization was established following a wave of Palestinian suicide bombings after the signing of the Oslo Accords and during the Second Intifada. In

---

[97] Darash, *Neturei*, pp. 100–101.

[98] Unsigned, "Children of Amram Blau Elected as Leaders of Neturei Karta," *Ma'ariv*, July 17, 1974, 4 (in Hebrew).

[99] Unsigned, "Rabbi Hirsch Gave Arafat an Amulet to Prevent Harm," *Davar*, July 7, 1994, 4 (in Hebrew).

[100] Darash, *Neturei*, pp. 96–9.

2003 Meshi Zahav was invited to light a beacon at the annual Independence Day ceremony marking the foundation of the State of Israel. His participation in this event inevitably entailed his departure from the ranks of the anti-Zionist HaEdah HaHaredit. "Then I still thought that if I dress in rags and put ashes on my head and walk through the streets of Meah She'arim on Independence Day declaring that I do not recognize the State of Israel, I am thereby sanctifying God's name. Today I know that the opposite is the case – this is actually a desecration of God's name."[101]

CONCLUSION

Over the course of his life, Amram Blau became one of the most famous figures in the Haredi community of Jerusalem. Although he led a relatively small faction numbering no more than a few hundred families, he enjoyed considerable influence. The moderate Haredi leadership was forced to consider his reactions to their decisions and Neturei Karta's position was clearly and publicly heard.

The Haredi community has produced only a few heroic characters who have led its struggles and can serve as role models for its younger generations. Amram Blau's militant personality made him a perfect candidate for this role. His willingness to engage in stubborn campaigns at a heavy personal price, including frequent imprisonment, humiliation, and beatings heightened his appeal (even his sterility was explained as the consequence of a severe beating by policemen at one of the demonstrations he attended). The end result was that Blau enjoyed a unique status in the Haredi community.

Blau was an individualist and a leader. He constantly sought to position himself at the vanguard of his community. However, he was no Don Quixote tilting at windmills: he always sought to persuade others to join him. The Blau archives provide countless examples of gatherings and meetings Blau organized in an effort to convince his fellow Jerusalemites to join his campaigns. He never launched a campaign without ensuring that he had supporters, and even his decision to marry Ruth Ben David went ahead only after he was convinced that he had support for his move (even though his support came from outside the religious court of his own community). His archives include numerous letters of support and encouragement following his decision to marry the convert.

---

[101] *Ibid.*, p. 108.

Blau was not a spiritual leader, nor did he lead a yeshivah. He sought to reinforce his leadership by appealing directly to Haredi public opinion. He did so through broadsheets urging an extremist approach and opposing any compromise, and through deliberate provocations such as demonstrations bordering on violence against symbols of the state, or through the fierce language he used to attack his opponents within the Haredi community. Blau even organized demonstrations against such opponents, such as the demonstrations outside the Beis Yaacov schools, while viciously attacking Haredi politicians, and even holding public cursing ceremonies against them. His power and influence came mainly from the fiery rhetoric he employed in thousands of articles, as well as from his militant actions. The broad support for Blau and his approach eventually won him support among the rabbis and leaders of the Haredi community, who were left with little choice but to grant post factum approval for his actions. He also led the community into major public campaigns, such as the Sabbath and modesty wars, dragging the Haredi leadership along once the momentum had been established.

Blau's resolute opposition to Zionism and his uncompromising campaign against de facto Haredi cooperation with Zionism made him a benchmark for the Haredi public, and others were obliged to fall into line with his positions. Blau was perceived as a "zealot" – an uncompromising man who acted according to his personal conscience and embodied perfection. The broader public admired him for this, but found it difficult to follow his path due to the tendency to weakness and compromise. The Haredi public supported his campaigns, even when his protests were directed against what he considered the overly compromising positions of Agudat Yisrael. Blau thus exemplifies the moral strength of the zealot within the fundamentalist community: the zealot is viewed not as a fifth column or as someone who seeks to destroy the community from within but as a role model, and accordingly the public accepts his presence among them.

Blau advocated a strongly separatist approach that negates any contact with the secular world. His fierce opposition to Zionism, including attempts to embarrass and harm the movement on the international stage, were a product of his theological worldview, which saw Jewish political activism as a desecration of the faith that would bring down God's wrath on the Jewish people. His rejection of any contacts with secularism marks him as a stubborn and uncompromising fundamentalist leader who advocated withdrawal combined with protest. Alongside his total rejection of Zionism, his approach was also marked by opposition to any changes in the traditional content of studies; an increasingly strict stance on questions of dress; and a constant campaign against the desecration of the Sabbath in Jerusalem.

The abandonment of the idea of Haredi agricultural settlement came hand in hand with the disengagement from Agudat Yisrael. The latter, and especially its worker's movement Poalei Agudat Yisrael, adopted the settlement ideology, with the assistance of Zionist protection. Blau could not countenance such political ideas and felt obliged to oppose them.

Blau's position on violence and civil disobedience also won him considerable prestige among the Haredi public. He encouraged the public to participate in frequent demonstrations, which had the benefit of bringing a little "action" into the monotonous routine of young Torah students. However, the demonstrations never descended into unbridled violence, and, as a result, the State of Israel was able to continue to grant him freedom of demonstration, and he was not sentenced to long periods of imprisonment or exiled from Jerusalem.

Blau was a complex and contradictory figure. He opposed secular life in the Land of Israel yet participated in an attempt to establish an agricultural settlement. He advocated political passivity but intervened in political affairs, particularly during the period leading up to the declaration of Israel's independence, in an attempt to protect his community.

Neturei Karta continues to embody this tension to the present day. Is its demand for the dismantling of the State of Israel (albeit "by peaceful means") not a manifestation of political activism? Current reality, in which the existence of the State of Israel is an accomplished fact, demands activism even on the part of those who are utterly opposed to this approach.

3

The modesty campaigns of Rabbi Amram Blau and the Neturei Karta movement, 1938–1974

This chapter discusses the influence of Neturei Karta on the status of women in Haredi society in Jerusalem. The modesty campaigns initiated by Rabbi Amram Blau sought to gain power and control not just over women but also over the entire Haredi enclave. I will review the campaigns from their initiators' perspectives and consider their overt and covert agendas.

On the level of principle, as we have seen, Haredi society rejects the innovations of the modern world and demands that its members live in a manner similar to that of the Jewish shtetl of Eastern Europe.[1] One of the most prominent innovations of the modern era is the change in the status of women and in relations between the sexes, and accordingly this social development has become one of the main challenges faced by Haredi communities.[2] In this chapter I will examine modesty campaigns led by Neturei Karta circles from 1938 through 1974.

GENDER CONTROL IN RELIGIOUS FUNDAMENTALISM

Gender control is one of the hallmarks of modern fundamentalism. Many religious traditions view the observance of religious commandments in the family and the education of children to the religious lifestyle as key

---

[1] Menachem Friedman, "Jewish Zealots: Conservative versus Innovative." In: Laurence J. Silberstein (ed.), *Jewish Fundamentalism in Contemporary Perspective – Religion, Ideology, and the Crisis of Modernity.* New York: NYU Press, 1993, pp. 148–63.

[2] Samuel Heilman and Menachem Friedman, "Religious Fundamentalism and Religious Jews: The Case of the Haredim." In: Martin E. Marty and Scott Appleby (eds.), *Fundamentalism Observed.* Chicago: University of Chicago Press, 1991, pp. 197–264.

components of religious behavior. Accordingly, changes in the family unit will also impact on religion. Fundamentalist movements have seen one of their central functions as the struggle against any threat to the traditional family unit. In order to avoid such threats these movements have not hesitated to restrict the leeway open to women and children. These positions thus constitute a reaction to openness and modernization and to the concept of the advancement of the status of women in society.[3]

From the end of the nineteenth century the feminist movement began to question the traditional roles of women and hitherto-accepted definitions of femininity.[4] The American fundamentalist movement was founded in an age of anxiety surrounding gender relations. For American Protestants the traditional family came to emblemize the ideal social order, and Christian fundamentalism placed a return to these values at the center of its religious objectives.[5]

Islamic fundamentalist movements emphasize male superiority and reaffirm the moral authority of men, as supported by the Koran, to oversee their wives and children. Fundamentalists claim that gender superiority forms the kernel of Islamic religious doctrine. Thus, for example, the first constitutional step taken by Ayatollah Khomeini after consolidating the Iranian Revolution in 1979 was to nullify laws granting rights to women, and particularly a law introduced in 1967 permitting women to divorce and to receive alimony.[6]

The control of norms of dress is another key characteristic of Islamic fundamentalism. This control is intended to prevent the sexual excitement of men. Radical movements have sometimes used coercion to impose these rules. Thus Khomeini imposed the penalty of caning on immodestly dressed women after the revolution.[7] The fundamentalist movements pay

---

[3] Charles W. Peek, George D. Lowe, and L. Susan Williams, "Gender and God's Word: Another Look at Religious Fundamentalism and Sexism," *Social Forces* 69(4) (1991), 1205–21.

[4] Margaret L. Bendorth, *Fundamentalism and Gender 1875 to Present*. New Haven: Yale University Press, 1993, pp. 31–53.

[5] Helen Hardacre, "The Impact of Fundamentalisms on Woman, the Family, and Interpersonal Relations." In: Martin Marty and Scott Appleby (eds.), *Fundamentalism and Society: Reclaiming the Sciences, the Family, and Education*. Chicago: University of Chicago Press, 1993, p. 132.

[6] Shahla Haeri, "Obedience versus Autonomy: Women and Fundamentalism in Iran and Pakistan." In: Martin Marty and Scott Appleby (eds.), *Fundamentalisms and Society: Reclaiming the Sciences, the Family, and Education*. Chicago: University of Chicago Press, 1993, pp. 181–213.

[7] Hardacre, "The Impact of Fundamentalisms," pp. 139–40.

particular attention to issues of feminine sexuality, which is perceived as dangerous, polluting, and capable of ensnaring men, leading them to lose their self-respect and destroying the family. These movements saw the campaign for modesty as a key component of their struggle against modernism.[8] In the Islamic world, the veil became the emblem of a struggle. While secular Islamic nationalism encouraged the modernization of women, including more revealing clothes, one of the symbols of the return to religion has been the adoption of modest clothes by women, including use of the veil.[9]

The Orthodox Halakhah (Jewish religious law) does not grant equal status to men and women. Women are not permitted to hold the status of legislators or judges and are excluded from the law-making process.[10] Although women enjoy inheritance and property rights in several instances, they are denied the right to study Torah – the central ethos of Jewish culture. Throughout Jewish history women have lived in a world controlled and defined by men.[11]

Orthodox Jewish society was organized on a voluntary basis and included a particularly strict approach to processes of social supervision in order to prevent the loss of the younger generation. In Israel, this community adopted a particularly strict approach to modesty from its inception.[12]

MODESTY CAMPAIGNS IN THE HAREDI ENCLAVE

Haredi society followed a traditional modesty code practiced by the Old Yishuv.[13] Once Neturei Karta made modesty one of its major activities,

[8] Andrea B. Rugh, "Reshaping Personal Relations in Egypt." In: Martin Marty and Scott Appleby (eds.), *Fundamentalism and Society: Reclaiming the Sciences, the Family, and Education.* Chicago: University of Chicago Press, 1993, pp. 151–80.

[9] Hala Sukrallah, "The Impact of the Islamic Movement in Egypt." In: Darlene M. Juschka (ed.), *Feminism and the Study of Religion: A Reader.* London: Continuum, 2001, pp. 180–97.

[10] Leonard D. Gordon, "Toward a Gender–Inclusive Account of Halakhah." In: Tamar Rundavsky (ed.), *Gender and Judaism – The Transformation of Tradition.* New York and London: NYU Press, 1995, pp. 3–12.

[11] Jay M. Harris, "Fundamentalism: Objections from a Modern Jewish Historian." In: John S. Hawley (ed.), *Fundamentalism and Gender.* New York: Oxford University Press, 1994, pp. 137–73. See also Tamar Ross, "Orthodoxy, Halakhah and the Challenge of Feminism." In: Yosef Salmon, Aviezer Ravitzky, and Adam Praziger (eds.), *Jewish Orthodoxy: New Aspects.* Jerusalem: Ben Zvi Institute, 2006, pp. 255–96 (in Hebrew).

[12] Heilman and Friedman, "Religious Fundamentalism."

[13] Margalit Shilo, *Princess or Prisoner? Jewish Women in Jerusalem, 1840–1914.* Waltham MA: Brandeis University Press, 2005, pp. 69–107.

gender supervision became a prominent hallmark of this movement. A distinction can be seen between two key phases in Neturei Karta's modesty campaigns. In the first stage, mostly in the 1930s and 1940s, the campaign was waged within the Haredi neighborhoods in an effort to combat lax public attitudes toward women's clothing. This campaign was characterized by insulation, the closing of chinks in the armor of the community itself, and the separation of the Haredi community from the general public. Thus this stage was essentially an internal process within the Haredi community. Blau's role in the modesty campaign reflected initiative and leadership and the strict rules he imposed concerning women's dress are still followed to this day. Blau established the modesty patrols, which operated as an internal police, to enforce these rules. The patrols operated under an instruction from the *Beit Din Tzedek* [the Court of Justice] of HaEdah HaHaredit and gained a reputation for their willingness to use forceful means to impose their authority.[14]

From the late 1940s, and particularly in the 1950s and 1960s, the modesty campaign was expanded beyond the confines of the Haredi neighborhoods. The main goal now was to prevent mixed cultural and sports activities in the secular part of Jerusalem. This approach represented a break with the traditional approach of Neturei Karta as a body devoted to defending the borders of its community. This campaign might seem illogical, since the opposed activities took place outside the Haredi neighborhoods and involved individuals whom Neturei Karta did not even consider to be proper Jews. I would suggest that this phase was intended mainly to reinforce Neturei Karta's leadership position among the Haredi public in Jerusalem at the expense of Agudat Yisrael, a movement that was a partner of the Zionist state. Moreover, the modesty offensive by Neturei Karta took place alongside another major campaign by the movement – the campaign over the Sabbath. In this case, too, its activists went out from Meah She'arim to protest against the opening of the Edison Cinema on the Sabbath.[15]

The modesty campaign of Neturei Karta under Blau's leadership is consistent with the efforts of fundamentalist movements in general to restrict the status of women. The campaign began as a response to increasing laxity and openness; it strengthened male authority within the family unit, since the man was defined as responsible for the modest

---

[14] Ehud Sprinzak, *Brother against Brother: Violence and Extremism in Israeli Politics from Altalena to the Rabin Assassination*. New York: Free Press, 1999, pp. 87–112.

[15] Friedman, *Neturei Karta*.

appearance of the women in the household; it imposed severe restrictions on the external appearance of women in order to prevent externalized manifestations of sexuality; it established a strict system of enforcement in the form of the modesty patrols; and it imposed restrictions on women's education. As discussed in the previous chapter, Neturei Karta fiercely attached the education system of Agudat Yisrael, which permitted certain innovations regarding women's education.

THE MODESTY CAMPAIGN: THE DEFENSIVE STAGE

The earliest evidence of the existence of modesty patrols can be found in an anonymous letter from 1938 preserved in the Blau archive. The letter reveals that once a week people would pass through the markets and distribute propaganda on the subject of modesty.[16] A notice from that period written by Blau complained that women were deliberately walking through the Haredi neighborhoods in immodest dress and that there was no one who could oppose this.[17] A few years later the term "modesty patrols" appeared for the first time in a letter written by Blau, in which he demanded that guards be placed on the streets of Meah She'arim on Mondays and Wednesdays from 10:30 to 11:30 a.m.[18]

An important milestone in the elaboration of the function of the modesty patrols came in 1945, when the *Beit Din Tzedek* of HaEdah HaHaredit issued a warning to the residents of the Haredi neighborhoods to pay strict attention to the dress of their daughters and wives:

With heavy, sad, and broken heart we turn to you, our dear ones, with a merciful request and plea. Our hearts have been broken with shame to hear and see how far we have deteriorated and how, in many homes of those who keep the Torah, the impure plague of immodesty, Heaven protect, has spread in indecent clothes, short dresses, failure to ensure long sleeves, and so forth. This hellish custom corrupts from tip to toe and removes the Divine Presence from Israel, G-d forbid, and the spiritual woes bring in their wake physical woes, Heaven protect. All this has come upon us because of our negligence and silence, which have led to the widening of the opening in such an awful manner, Heaven protect. Thus we have come to ask each father and household to dedicate themselves to removing this appalling ugliness from your homes and to restore your former dignity. Let each man take the harness of supervision in his hand and supervise the daughters of the house, to ensure they are dressed in modest garments (and particularly to supervise the sewing of dresses). We are also obliged to supervise neighbors and

---

[16] Unsigned, untitled, Box 1, File 10, Doc. 43 (hereinafter "the Modesty File").
[17] Modesty File, Doc. 16.   [18] Modesty File, Doc. 49.

relatives, to warn and to protest, so that we may not bear responsibility. [...] This
is particularly so since once this opening has occurred, it is no easy matter to
uproot it, and we must adopt strident means, to awaken from the general slumber
and silence, and to awaken ourselves and others [...]. To explain the depth of
ugliness of this matter, and the gravity of the prohibition in accordance with our
holy Torah be a holy educator, and there can be no punishment unless a warning
is given, lest we be forced, G-d forbid, to take unpleasant steps against the
violators. Happy he who listens, takes heed, and warns others; his reward shall
flow as a river and he shall dwell securely and safely, in blessing and calm, with a
fair livelihood and all good in spirit and soul.[19]

The leaflet carried a warning to the residents of Meah She'arim to pay
attention to modest dress, including the threat of sanctions. The call was
for the husbands to be responsible for their wives and daughters' behavior. The declaration echoes Maimonides' ruling that it is the male's
responsibility to supervise women and children in their household.[20] In
order to enforce the rules of modesty it was first necessary to determine
what constituted desirable dress. To this end, Blau formulated a dress
code including a series of stringent conditions:

1. The dress of a Jewish woman must be long, reaching at least to
    below the knees in such a manner that even if she is seated her
    knees will not be visible.
2. The dress must be wide and not excessively tight on the body.
3. The sleeves of the shirt must be long and reach almost to the hand.
4. The dress must not be made from transparent or red cloth.
5. Slippers must not be transparent or flesh-colored.
6. The obligation of modesty applies to girls from the age of three.
7. A married woman must cover her hair with a head kerchief, and
    shall also wear a veil on leaving the house.[21] In May 1964, a
    prohibition was added to the modesty code forbidding the wearing
    of the "*peruk*"-type wig, with hair that appears natural – "which
    desecrates G-d's name, so that many cannot distinguish between
    immodest hair and a wig, causing many improprieties."[22]

---

[19] Rabbi [Zelig R.] Bengis, Rabbi Pinchas Epstein, and Rabbi David Jungreis, "Notice and
      Warning," 20 Sivan 5705 (June 1, 1945), unnumbered, Modesty File.
[20] Shilo, *Princess or Prisoner?* p. 85.
[21] Amram Blau, "Instructions on Modesty to the Jewish Woman," undated, Modesty File,
      Doc. 28.
[22] Selection of Articles of the *Patrol of Our Walls* from the Members of Neturei Karta,
      17 Sivan 5724 – 1964, 156 (in Hebrew).

Blau explained that the reason why Jewish women must cover their bodies modestly is in order not to lead men to improper sexual thoughts. He argued that a Jewish woman who dresses immodestly causes the public to fail and is considered a "pursuer" (*rodef*); as such, according to the Halakhah, she is liable to the death penalty imposed by God.[23] Moreover, immodest dress constitutes a "turning of the back on the Holy One, blessed be He"; "a public desecration of G-d's name"; and a phenomenon that will lead "to the removal of the Divine Presence from above the Jewish people."[24] Thus Neturei Karta's regulations were aimed first and foremost at ensuring men's moral conduct, guarding them against any possible temptations. The easiest way to do so was by restricting women's behavior. Women's code of dress was established in order to prevent any chance that men's desire might be aroused.

Since Haredi society views itself as the guardian of righteous traditions dedicated to the worship of God, modesty became as one of its outmost values. According to their perspective, a woman wearing immodest clothing was committing not only a personal offence but also a public one. Since the Divine punishment for immodesty will be imposed on everyone, it is a communal duty to fight it.[25]

In July 1950 the subject of the modesty rules gained further prominence after Blau convened a special gathering of Jerusalem rabbis to discuss the problem. During the meeting a clear and binding code was drafted for setting and enforcing standards of modesty. The code served as the foundation for a protracted modesty campaign that was not confined solely to the Haredi community but extended to other parts of the city without any Haredi presence. It also consolidated Blau's position as a leader in the Haredi community: He determined that the community would be mobilized on this issue; he pressured rabbis, who needed only to support his work on this matter of principle; and he even dared to engage in an offensive relating to the character of Jerusalem as a whole,

---

[23] *Din rodef* (the law of the pursuer) is based on the precept that "If a man comes to kill you rise early and kill him first." This law applies whenever a person's life is endangered and the "pursuer" may be killed in order to remove the danger. This law of self-defense applies whether or not a Sanhedrin is in existence. The obligation and right to save life applies at any time and to any person who recognizes that his life, or that of others, is endangered. For further discussion, see Eliav Shuchtman, "Jewish Government Cannot Be a 'Pursuer'," *Tehumin* 19 (5759 – 1999), 40–8 (in Hebrew).

[24] Amram Blau, "Instructions on Modesty to the Jewish Woman," undated, Modesty File, unnumbered.

[25] Shilo, *Princess or Prisoner?* p. 70.

rather than confining himself to maintaining modesty within his own neighborhood of Meah She'arim.

The summary of this meeting is a fascinating document. Decisions were taken on a range of subjects:

A. *Avoiding the immodest*: The community was urged to supervise women and girls in order to ensure that they dress and act modestly to the highest possible standards; to distance women from their friends who do not observe these rules and who visit theaters and cinemas – behavior considered indecent for religious women; to distance women from any place where there are immodestly dressed women; and to bring together women who dress modestly in order to strengthen them in their modesty.

B. *Reproach*: On the High Holy Days, after the reading from the Torah, a special blessing was to be recited for women who dress modestly; reproach must be used to create social pressure – each man must be urged to scold his brothers, neighbors, and relatives; in the case of the "offenders" themselves, the reproach should be indirect, through a parent or relative or person able to exercise influence.

C. *Protest and support*: The community must protest and take a scornful and humiliating attitude toward "these wild hussies (*prutzot mitpartzot*) who darken the world through their arrogant and ugly dress." Conversely, ways must be found to strengthen the "might and force" of those who dress modestly.

D. *Public protest*: The community should take to the streets and proclaim, "We do not wish hussies and wild and naked women, Heaven protect, on our streets." Notices should be posted bearing slogans against immodest dress; educational material should be published to alert the public and recruit it to public protest.

E. *Implementation*: A committee dedicated to improving modesty standards should be established in each neighborhood; women should be recruited to the committees to encourage and connect modest women and to distance the immodest; educational means should be used in the women's galleries of the synagogues.

F. *Worthy proposals*: The *gabbai* (the rabbi's assistant) should make "pleasant" comments to those whose daughters and wives fail to conform to the modesty rules; all invitations to celebrations should emphasize that women must come in modest dress and that the immodestly dressed are not invited.

In order to enforce the modesty code gabbais were asked to announce the code in the synagogue and to organize elections for modesty committees. The gabbais also raised funds for this purpose. A group of twenty to thirty young men went from one synagogue to the next in the city and helped organize the local committees. In the short term it was agreed that propaganda and notices should be used to recruit public support. In order to mobilize the community around the campaign a mass petition was launched and the campaigners decided to organize "noisy protest marches of 'brigades of demonstrators' to parade through the streets of the Haredi neighborhoods from time to time shouting slogans against immodesty." The ultimate purpose of the campaign was to prepare the foundation for demonstrations on this issue.[26]

The establishment of the modesty committees in the early 1950s was the first time that women were recruited to participate in a public campaign. Women have only rarely participated in the campaigns of Neturei Karta (another case is that of Ruth Ben-David, as discussed in the previous chapter). Women's participation was intended to create social pressure and to present a united community stance on the issue.

It is unclear at what stage the modesty patrols began to use violence in order to secure their goals. During the British Mandate it seems probable that Neturei Karta activists preferred to turn to the police in order to solve modesty issues that it could not resolve without recourse to violence. An example of this appears in an incident described in Blau's archives in 1938. After learning that a home in Meah She'arim was being used as a brothel where prostitutes met with their clients at night, Blau asked the police to close the place before the matter "leads to public outrage."[27] By contrast, in a testimony from 1966, some thirty years later, concerning an incident in which merchants from Meah She'arim asked Blau to "purify their neighborhood" of Mandel Green, they claimed that the soda salesman was a secret missionary who placed crosses on the walls of his shop and publicly desecrated the Sabbath. By this time the modesty patrols had come to resemble an internal police force that did not confine its attention solely to modesty issues.[28]

---

[26] Modesty File, Doc. 29, Summary of Meeting, 5 Menachem–Av 5710 – 1950.

[27] Amram Blau, "To the Commander of the Jerusalem Police," 10 Adar 5698 – 1938, Box 1, File 6, unnumbered. On the general topic of prostitution in Jerusalem at these times see: Haim Avni, *Clients, Prostitutes and White Slavers in Argentina and in Israel.* Tel Aviv: Miskal, 2009, pp. 162–70.

[28] File 6, unnumbered.

As the leader of the modesty patrols Blau was able to achieve an authority that placed him on the same level as the spiritual leadership of the Haredi community. Whereas the rabbis gained their authority from their rabbinical knowledge, Blau gained his power from his activities in the field of inspection and enforcement.

The defensive stage focused strongly on a separatist approach that negates any imitation of the secular way of life. This campaign emphasized that the supervision of clothing of Jewish women is a collective duty, and women's dress, ostensibly their private affair, came to be considered a communal symbol. Therefore women's modest garbs were to be considered for the entire nation's sake, while immodest cloths were viewed as a desecration of God's name that might bring God's punishment. The archive yields little information on the subject of men's dress. The modesty campaign focused on women's clothing and made no mention of men's clothing. A few references to men's garb can be found, however. In a leaflet entitled "Ours – Not Ours," Blau emphasized the external differences between Haredi yeshivah students and those from the Mizrahi stream of Religious Zionism:

Ours have long earlocks; those who are not ours have clipped earlocks and short hair in hoodlum style; ours wear head coverings in awe of their Maker; those who are not ours wear blue and white head coverings or with the emblem of the State of Israel, may the name of the evil rot.[29]

This leaflet emphasizes the Haredi opposition to any change in clothing, including that of men. In another case Blau was asked whether it was permissible for a man to continue to wear the same clothes as his ancestors, even if these differed from the clothing customs of Jerusalem. Blau replied that if the clothes reflect the customs of the man's ancestors and are not a form of "dandification or progress," this does not constitute immodesty. He noted that Rabbi Yitzhak Zev Soloveichik did not alter his dress after arriving in Jerusalem, yet his presence glorified the city.[30]

Not all members of HaEdah HaHaredit agreed with Blau on this matter. In 1924 the Slabodka Yeshivah emigrated from Russia to Hebron in order to avoid the draft of its members to the Russian army. In 1929 the yeshivah moved to Jerusalem after the Arab riots and the massacre in Hebron, when 69 Jews were murdered by an Arab mob. The students of this institution did not adhere to the Old Yishuv's dress

---

[29] Amram Blau, "Ours – Not Ours," undated, Modesty File, Doc. 78.
[30] Amram Blau, untitled, undated, Modesty File, Doc. 93.

code: they wore modern suits, grew forelocks, shaved their beards, and wore black hats.[31] Rabbi Yeshayah Asher Zelig Margaliot (whom I discuss at length in Chapter 6) sharply criticized their appearance and penned an entire book devoted to an attack on this new fashion in yeshivah circles. He argued that the traditional appearance, with long earlocks and an unshaven beard, embodies a proper image of God and is therefore immutable. He regarded the shaving of beards by the Slabodka Yeshivah students as the product of incitement by the *Sitra Ahra* (Satan) who blinded their eyes to their own transgression. He also claimed that the growing of the forelocks by these students could be perceived as an attempt to look like women, which is a grave sin.[32]

The modesty campaign was one of Blau's main spheres of activity, allowing him to demonstrate authority and leadership. The patrols he established became the practical instrument for imposing strict codes of dress on the Haredi population in Jerusalem.

As Margalit Shilo clearly demonstrates, Haredi women were a weak force in the old Yishuv community, and modesty prohibitions were strictly enforced upon them.[33] Therefore they were vulnerable targets for Blau and his modesty patrols. Since the Haredim view themselves as embodying a unique spiritual nature, they were willing to accept more restrictions and regulations.

THE OFFENSIVE STAGE

In 1946 a mixed swimming pool was opened in Ramat Gan. The opening of the first pool in the Zionist Yishuv aroused the wrath of the zealots in Meah She'arim and Blau launched a public campaign on the issue.[34] It might seem strange that Blau would launch a campaign concerning a pool situated far from Jerusalem, established by those whom he already regarded as heretics and rebels. The reason for his outrage was his concern that the opening of this swimming pool might set a precedent

[31] Shlomo Tikochinski, "The Transfer of Lithuanian Yeshivot to the Land of Israel: The Story of the Hebron and Ponivez Yeshivot." In: Immanuel Etkes (ed.), *Yeshivot and Batei Midrash.* Jerusalem: Zalman Shazar Center Press, 2006, pp. 273–314 (in Hebrew).

[32] Yeshayah Asher Zelig Margaliot, *Amudei Arazim.* Jerusalem: Maarav Print, 5692 – 1931, p. 2 (in Hebrew).

[33] Shilo, *Princes or Prisoner?* pp. 70–5.

[34] On the development of swimming pools as leisure resorts and a place of integration of sexes and races, see Jeff Wilste, *Contested Waters: A Social History of Swimming Pools in America.* Chapel Hill, NC: UNC Press, 2007.

for further mixed pools – a concern that proved accurate. As Blau feared, just a few years later a mixed swimming pool was also opened in Jerusalem.

Neturei Karta activists engaged in various actions in an effort to prevent the opening of the pool in Ramat Gan.[35] They secured 4,000 signatures on a petition opposing the opening of the pool (this number represents almost all the adult members of the Haredi community in Jerusalem at the time.)[36] The petition, submitted to the High Commissioner, demanded the cancellation of the opening of the swimming pool in order to protect young people from depravity and defend the honor of the Land of Israel.[37] According to Blau's perspective, immodesty detracted from the Land of Israel's sanctity. The High Commissioner denied their request.[38]

Neturei Karta activists also undertook other actions in an effort to close the swimming pool. They submitted a request to the Ramat Gan council and organized meetings and protests in Jerusalem and Ramat Gan with the assistance of the council of Bnai Brak, a Haredi city adjacent to Ramat Gan. Contacts were also made with factories in Ramat Gan, asking for their support in closing the pool and threatening a consumer boycott of their products.[39] Although the campaign against the pool was unsuccessful it illustrated Neturei Karta's organizational strength and its ability to mobilize protests.

Some ten years later Blau's fears materialized: preparations began to open a mixed swimming pool in the German Colony neighborhood of Jerusalem. He was concerned about the possible temptation and attempted to act preemptively. In January 1958, after news of the plan emerged, Jerusalem rabbis held an emergency meeting. They decided to hold various protest actions: in addition to demonstrations, a boycott of municipal taxes was organized, as well as boycotts of all those involved in the construction of the pool.[40] Neturei Karta published its boycott in

[35] Unsigned, "Protest March against Galei-Gil," *HaHomah* 23, 28 Iyar 5707 – 1946, p. 4; unsigned, "Jerusalem," *Davar*, September 17, 1946, 4 (in Hebrew).

[36] According to a census conducted in 1947, the Haredi community in Jerusalem included 4,445 men and women above the age of 18. See Yuval Frankel, "Haredi," 247–89, and particularly 256.

[37] Unsigned, "His Excellency the High Commissioner," undated, Modesty File, Doc. 7.

[38] *Ibid.*

[39] Unsigned, "Preparing for the Meeting against Galei-Gil," undated, Modesty File, Doc. 112.

[40] Resolutions of the Public Protest Meeting, Modesty File, Doc. 90.

several languages – English, German, Arabic, and Spanish – in an effort to apply economic pressure on the owner of the pool, Chaim Schiff, who was also the owner of the President Hotel in the city, by encouraging consumers to avoid the tourism services he marketed.

Neturei Karta even employed sorcery, imposing curses on Schiff and Jerusalem Mayor Gershon Agron:

They shall light a wax candle with the name of the evil one, the above-mentioned individual, and if there is no wax then another candle, and they shall all recite Psalm 109 and direct their intentions to the above-mentioned head of evil, and after finishing the psalm they shall overturn and cast off the extinguished candle and say that just as this candle has been extinguished, so shall the candle of the above-mentioned individual be extinguished, Amen Selah, etc.[41]

The candle is preserved in the archive, inside a folded piece of paper bearing the names of Schiff and Agron. According to anthropologist Mary Douglas, sorcery is a source of authority. Those holding the powers to bless or curse are considered uncontrolled and dangerous, and their mystical powers give them social control.[42] This is yet another example of Blau's hunger for power.

Neturei Karta was eventually forced to admit that its campaign had failed. The pool opened and operated without incident, although Schiff was ultimately obliged to sell the pool to Kibbutz Shoresh after the Chief Rabbinate removed the Kashrut certificate from all his businesses.[43] This incident illustrates the moral force of the Jerusalem zealots and their ability to influence the Chief Rabbinate, a state-sponsored organ, which acted against Schiff according to the approach dictated by Neturei Karta.

Neturei Karta was more successful in a further campaign against mixed swimming. In 1961, a plan was initiated to open a beach in Tiberias. A private buyer reached an agreement with the Tiberias municipality to remove a sewage pipe that had channeled waste into the Kinneret for many years, thus enabling the establishment of a beach on the site. Religious dignitaries in Tiberias, not all of whom were identified with Neturei Karta, asked Blau to launch a public campaign against the plan on the grounds that the road to the Tiberias cemetery passed through the planned bathing beach, as did the road to the grave of Rabbi Meir Ba'al

---

[41] Modesty File, Doc. 105.

[42] Mary Douglas, *Purity and Danger: An Analysis of Concepts of Pollution and Taboo.* New York and Washington: Psychology Press, 1966, p. 99.

[43] Unsigned, "Ministry of Finance is willing to Loan 100 Pounds to Agudah for Purchasing the Pool," *Heruth,* May 29, 1958, 8 (in Hebrew).

Ha-Nes.[44] In addition to the usual demonstrations, Blau also contacted a wealthy philanthropist, Yaakov Pinchas Gewirt, whose donation of 90,000 Israeli pounds enabled the purchase of the beach from the promoter and closed, removing the threat.[45]

The strategy of resolving tension between religious and secular Jews by purchasing the property in dispute was employed in the case of the "Club Affair" in Jerusalem. In 1954–1955, a fierce debate erupted between the secular and religious communities in Jerusalem. Neturei Karta organized turbulent demonstrations against a club operated by the Working Mothers' organization. The club, situated on the edge of the Meah She'arim neighborhood, held joint after-school classes for boys and girls.[46] Neturei Karta claimed that mixed dancing also took place there. Approximately 170 people were arrested at the demonstrations, held on a daily basis over almost a year, and arrested for periods of up twenty-eight days. Blau himself was detained for twenty-one days for participating in an unlawful gathering. He rejected a proposed compromise by which a wall would be constructed to separate the club from Meah She'arim.

In his vitriolic attacks against the club, Blau argued that:

All the sum of humanity might find its place in the holy city of Jerusalem; any scoundrel, and dirty or filthy one, any base and despicable adulterer, all the people of the lowest circles will come to spread their filthy abominations in the holy city of Jerusalem. To deface and pollute Jerusalem and to foul and poison the air with all manner of wantonness and depravity.[47]

He was determined to remove what he described as the pollution that was contaminating the holy city. The protracted protests became a struggle for the character and nature of the city. The secular public also initiated protests against religious coercion. The Mapai party, for example, urged its members to go to Meah She'arim to support the club and ensure it remained open.[48]

Against the background of this war of principles, it is interesting to consider the real motives behind the affair as revealed in the Blau archive.

[44] Unsigned, "Fervent Ceremonies against the Beach were Given in Synagogues in Tiberias," *Heruth*, January 27, 1962, 4 (in Hebrew).

[45] Amram Blau, "To Our Distinguished Friend, etc. etc., R. Yaakov Pinchas Gevirt, May He Live Days That Are Pleasant and Long," 9 Adar 5722 – 1962, Modesty File, unnumbered.

[46] Unsigned, "The Discussion on the 'Club Affair' was Transferred to the Interior Committee," *Hatzofeh* December 15, 1954, 1 (in Hebrew); Unsigned, "Sabbath Demonstrations Continued the Entire Sabbath," *Heruth*, November 27, 1954, 4 (in Hebrew).

[47] Amram Blau, "Remember, Lord, What We Had," Modesty File, unnumbered.

[48] Unsigned, "The Club in Dispute in Jerusalem – Institution under State Supervision," *Davar*, November 25, 1954, 8 (in Hebrew).

It emerges that a large girls' school was situated alongside the club. The school was attended by some 700 girls and was suffered from severe over-crowding. Due to the proximity to the club and the unacceptable standards of modesty from the Haredi perspective, the educators refused to allow the girls to use the school courtyard. Neturei Karta was asked to demonstrate in order to close the club and enable the use of the building by the school. Blau's letter to the Satmar Rebbe in New York, Yoel Teitelbaum, describing the campaign reveals that the owner of the property was asking 7000 Israeli pounds for its sale. After more than a year of demonstrations, the owner agreed to sell the property for 2,000 Israeli pounds. Blau contacted influential rabbis in the United States, such as the leaders of the Satmar and Stropkov Hasidic courts, in an effort to raise the required sum. The property was eventually purchased by Yechiel Benedict, a philanthropist.[49] Thus the demonstrations served purposes not necessarily confined to lofty concerns of modesty and purity. Practical considerations such as shortage of space in Meah She'arim also underpinned the protests as the Haredi community sought to expand its presence beyond the confines of the enclave.

From as early as the 1940s, consumer boycotts were widely used in order to "correct" businesses that acted in a manner contrary to the desires of Neturei Karta. The Haredi public learnt to use this tool, and due to its monolithic character it has been able to use, it continues to employ it effectively to the present day.

The appeal to Diaspora philanthropists illustrates another recurring pattern in Neturei Karta's actions. The movement itself and several of its followers and functionaries were sponsored by the Jewish Diaspora, as was the old Yishuv. Conflict resolution techniques thus included the purchase of properties at points of friction in order to resolve the campaign successfully. This pattern was seen in the case of the beach in Tiberias and the "Club Affair" in Jerusalem.

THE LIMITS OF ZEALOTRY: THE BURNING OF THE EROS SEX SHOP IN TEL AVIV

In 1972, a shop called Eros opened in Tel Aviv selling pornography and sex-related items. Unsurprisingly the development aroused the wrath of

---

[49] Amram Blau, "To the Glory of Our Heads, Our Teacher Rabbi Yoel Teitelbaum, May He Live Days That Are Pleasant and Long," undated, Modesty File, Doc. 70. See also Amram Blau, "To Our Distinguished Friend, Our Teacher Rabbi Yechiel Benedict, May He Live Days That Are Pleasant and Long," 8 Sivan 5716 – 1956, *ibid.*, Doc. 67.

the Haredi zealots. Two young Haredim who torched the shop were prosecuted and sentenced to eighteen and twelve months in jail.[50]

The arson attack became the subject of lively debate within Haredi circles. On the one hand, the religious public certainly considered a campaign against pornography a legitimate goal. On the other hand, the action taken by the two young men went beyond the normal confines of protests, such as demonstrations and propaganda. The arson attack constituted an offense against the laws of the state, endangered the well-being of individuals, and was a clear instance of individuals taking the law into their own hands. Rabbis and religious circles raised all these arguments as they distanced themselves from the attack.

By contrast, Blau justified the arsonists' approach and claimed that it was consistent with the Halakhah. He explained his position by reference to the Biblical story of Pinchas, the son of Elazar the priest, which will be discussed in detail in Chapter 7. The Biblical story supports spontaneous acts of violence in order to sanctify God's name.

Taking this precedent as his point of departure, Blau emphasized that he did not condone violence or underground actions. However, it could not be claimed that the two men acted in a manner that was contrary to the Halakhah. He acknowledged that the Torah does not permit individuals to do "that which is right in their own eyes," but added that a clear and detailed Halakhic solution can always be found to such problems. Blau asked why Pinchas had not obeyed Moses' instruction, choosing instead to act on his own. Answering his own question, he declared frankly: "Because when there is desecration of God's name, one does not pay respect to the rabbi." Thus in such an extreme state of debauchery and abomination there is no need to wait for instructions from the rabbis; action must be taken even without an explicit order.

Blau then embarked on a discussion of the principle of "accepting the yoke of Torah and the commandments." He argued that the giving of the Torah on Mt. Sinai and the acceptance of the Torah by the Jewish people made them "partners in an unlimited business" – that is, a binding partnership. Accordingly, each partner must prevent and protest any action liable to destroy the business. Every Jew is responsible for every other Jew, and accordingly what one Jew destroys will affect everyone. Blau claims that the Biblical story of Pinchas gives individual the right to take the law into his own hands, since Pinchas did not wait for official

---

[50] Unsigned, "Two Yeshivah Students were Convicted of Torching Eros," *Ma'ariv*, August 5, 1972, 5 (in Hebrew).

permission to act in violence. Accordingly, this is the Halakhic approach. It is interesting to note that in this interpretation, Blau does not distinguish himself from the seculars, and sees them all as being parts of the same organ, unlike his previous statements.

Blau further emphasizes that the Jewish people is not a democracy, since it accepted the Torah, which is not democratic. He characterizes democracy as "each one doing what is right in his own eyes," whereas the Torah determines the proper course for the Jewish people. There can be no deviation from this course and penalties are prescribed for any violation. The Jewish people accepted the Torah as a collective and all are committed to it, he argued. Accordingly, anyone who acts in the name of the Torah is not to be considered wicked or criminal. The two men did not torch the shop out of wickedness or out of a desire to commit a crime such as a bank robbery. They acted on the basis of their religious sentiment of respect for the Torah, and the public supported their action. Accordingly, their faithful devotion to the Torah clears them of any offense.[51]

Blau's defense argument echoes the French judicial category of *crime passionnel* committed under the influence of sudden or extreme passion. Killing an adulterer or adulteress upon the sudden discovery of adultery is characterized as a crime committed in the heat of passion, and as such entailed a reduced penalty or even acquittal.[52]

Blau's response reflects the dialectics of Neturei Karta zealotry. He himself would not send men to commit such an act, since he advocates a passive and nonviolent struggle. After the act has been committed, however, it can only be justified, and those who committed it must be defended against their many opponents within the Haredi public. Although the intention was that the modesty campaigns would take the form of nonviolent protest, the danger is always present that a protester who considers himself a zealot may engage in serious physical violence. This approach carries the potential for a descent into violence, although most cases did not reach this extreme.[53]

---

[51] Modesty File, Doc. 60.

[52] Ruth Harris, "Hysteria and Feminine Crimes of Passion in the Fin–de–Siècle," *History Workshop* 25 (1988), 31–63; Robert Ferrari, "The 'Crime Passionnel' in French Courts," *California Law Review* 6.5 (1918), 331–41.

[53] During the Gay Pride march in Jerusalem in 2005, one of the participants was stabbed by a young Haredi, Yishai Shlissel, who was later sentenced to twelve years in prison and fined NIS 280,000. This incident is further proof of the potential for zealous protest to descend into violence.

CONCLUSION

This chapter has examined the subject of the modesty campaigns led by Rabbi Amram Blau as the leader of the Neturei Karta movement, with the support of the Court of Justice of HaEdah HaHaredit.

In many cases the modesty campaigns were used to bolster Neturei Karta's leadership position among the Haredi public in Jerusalem at the expense of Agudat Yisrael, a movement that was a partner of the Zionist state. It is worth noting that during the modesty campaign Neturei Karta published fierce and strongly worded statements against Agudat Yisrael for operating in the Knesset and the Municipality of Jerusalem.[54]

With the benefit of hindsight, the defensive modesty campaign can be judged a great success. The rules imposed on women's clothing in the 1940s are still enforced today, with minor variations. Conversely the offensive modesty campaign may be judged a failure. Neturei Karta was unable to prevent the secular development of Jerusalem. Even from 2003 through 2008, when Jerusalem had a Haredi mayor, Uri Lupoliansky, this did not prevent the opening of places of entertainment on the Sabbath, let alone mixed swimming or dancing. Eventually, Neturei Karta virtually abandoned its offensive modesty campaign. However, the demonstrations raised the self-esteem of the Haredi public and created an aura of heroism around the campaigners for modesty.

The rise of religious fundamentalist movements can be explained as a reaction to secularity; their actions are intended to regain political powers after years of feeling attacked by secular society and state.[55] One of the main characteristics of this response is creating an enclave, a safe haven where the particular lifestyle can be maintained without outside interference. Joining the enclave is voluntary; therefore religious adherence is strictly enforced.[56]

---

[54] Neturei Karta even imposed a *pulsa di–nura* curse on Meir Yitzhak Levin, the political leader of Agudat Yisrael, who agreed to serve as the Minister of Welfare in the first government of Israel (1948 – 1952). The *pulsa di–nura* (literally, in Aramaic, "lashes of fire") is a curse calling for a person to meet with an unnatural death. See: Amram Blau, "A Warning Advice to a Hostile Enemy of Israel," Blau Archive, Box 3, File 1, No. 6.

[55] For an historical account of fundamentalism as a global phenomenon see Karen Armstrong, *The Battle for God*. New York: Ballantine Books, 2001.

[56] Almond, Appleby, and Sivan, *Strong Religion*, pp. 23–89.

In a controversial article published in 1983, "Extremism as a Religious Norm," the Israeli political scientist Charles Liebman argued that extremism embodies the adage "the more the better." This is true, firstly, in the expansion of religious law to include the public as well as the private realm, and in the imposition of ever-greater restrictions and hardship on implementing the law. The second dimension in which this adage is applied is that of isolationism, while the third is the rejection of cultural norms that are indigenous to the religious traditions. Liebman argued that the rise of extremism in the Jewish world is due to the breakdown of the Jewish community and the breaking of the institutions that were able to restrain the radicals. In addition, the search for a harsher interpretation of the law consistent with the desire to assure one's self and others that one is indeed living accordance with what is commanded to do.[57]

Adding to Liebman's argument, Gil S. Epstein and Ira N. Gang developed a mathematical model that explains the rise of extremism in a fundamentalist movement. They claim that the laws and regulations in a fundamentalist movement are becoming harder to follow, and followers may find themselves unsure of exactly what rules they are supposed to observe. It is the followers' ignorance and their desire to do what is right according to their religion that drives the increasing level of observance, which they assume increases the probability of meeting religious law. The severest position results in the greatest certainty that God's will is being performed.

Religious leaders apply fundamentalism by using religion to control behavior, thereby securing benefits from their followers or adherents. The leaders are assumed to possess more knowledge regarding the laws and rules that should be obeyed than their followers. Leadership rivalry leads to a race to the top in observance level, not to the bottom. The desire to hold on to members radicalizes clergy.[58]

These theories can inform our understanding of the success of Blau's modesty campaigns. The establishment of the Haredi enclave in Jerusalem was intended to block secular influence. Blau and his movement competed for power, thereby adopting increasingly extreme modesty demands. The expansion of the modesty rules was possible due to the community's

---

[57] Charles Liebman, "Extremism as a Religious Norm," *Journal of the Scientific Study of Religion* 22(1) (1983), 75–86.
[58] Gil S. Epstein and Ira N. Gang, "Understanding the Development of Fundamentalism," *Public Choice* 132(3/4) (2007), 257–71.

inherent insecurity and its assumption that "the more the better." Women constituted a weak link in the structure of this society, as had always been the case historically. Neturei Karta adopted an extreme position regarding modesty rules and other authorities were unable to challenge these without weakening their own leadership position. In such conditions, there was no incentive for Blau and Neturei Karta to halt or moderate the modesty campaigns.

4

Messianic activism in the work and thought of Rabbi Chaim Elazar Shapira (the Munkacser Rebbe) in the interwar period

The life and theology of Rabbi Chaim Elazar Shapira (1871–1937), the Munkacser Rebbe, were characterized by a profound messianic tension. Beginning in the period following the First World War and for the remainder of his life, this tension was manifested in eschatological calculations; sermons of a supernatural nature intended to expedite the End Times; a visit to the Land of Israel during which Shapira hoped to crown the King Messiah (and which ended in failure and disgrace); and a fierce and public dispute with the Gerrer Rebbe, Avraham Mordechai Alter, which I believe can also be attributed to tension regarding the personal identification of the messiah.

Chaim Elazar Shapira was born in Galicia on December 17, 1871, after his parents had attempted unsuccessfully to have children for many years. His family moved to Munkacs after his grandfather, Shlomo Shapira (1831–1893), was appointed the city's chief rabbi. At the turn of the twentieth century Chaim Elazar was appointed chief justice of the rabbinical court, and after the death of his father, Zvi Hirsch (1850–1913), he also assumed the role of spiritual leader of the Hasidic court. Shapira, a prolific author who published dozens of books, had a tough and argumentative character. Shapira died on May 12, 1937, aged sixty-six years.[1]

Although modern research has devoted little attention to the Munkacser Rebbe, there is no disagreement regarding his importance.[2] Shapira

---

[1] See Levi Cooper, *The Munkaczer Rebbe Chaim Elazar Shapira the Hassidic Ruler – Biography and Theology*. Ramat Gan: PhD Dissertation, Bar Ilan University, 2011, pp. 64–76.

[2] Allan Nadler, "The War on Modernity of R. Hayyim Elazar Shapira of Munkacz," *Modern Judaism* 14(3) (1994), 233–64; Aviezer Ravitzky, *Messianism, Zionism, and Religious Radicalism*. Chicago and London: University of Chicago Press, 1993, pp. 40–62.

was the leader of a significant Hasidic court in Hungary[3] and represented an extreme wing of Hasidic Jewry that rejected any modern innovations, and particularly modern Jewish politics. Shapira was one of the fiercest Orthodox opponents of Zionism, together with the sixth Rebbe of the Lubavitch dynasty, Yosef-Yitzhak Schneerson. He also devoted great efforts to preventing the introduction of changes to the traditional educational curriculum, and accordingly was a fierce opponent of Agudat Yisrael.

The Munkacser Rebbe died before the outbreak of the Second World War and almost all his followers were annihilated by the Nazis. As a result, few testimonies remain to his life and works. To date, three studies have been published about Shapira. Allan Nadler accurately described Shapira's antimodern beliefs and noted his messianic tendencies, though he did not discuss this aspect in depth. Aviezer Ravitzky offered an appraisal of Shapira's fierce opposition to the settlement of the Land of Israel and the development of the Land by means of secular professions. Levi Cooper published a doctoral thesis examining Shapira's role as a spiritual leader and Halakhic arbiter. In this chapter I will seek to offer additional insight into the thought of radical Hasidic circles during the interwar period, focusing on the messianic tensions that developed in the Munkacs Hasidic court.

MESSIANISM IN THE HASIDIC MOVEMENT AND MESSIANIC EXPECTATIONS IN ORTHODOX JEWRY DURING THE INTERWAR PERIOD – THEORETICAL BACKGROUND

Researchers of Hasidism are divided regarding the manner in which we should understand messianism in Hasidic thought and practice. The major outbreak of messianism that followed the spread of the Sabbatean movement ended in disillusionment. Hasidism, which was founded in the eighteenth century, approximately one century after the decline of Sabbateanism, did not share the collective messianic tension of the earlier movement. However, from the 1990s, strong messianic fervor developed

---

[3] According to the Yad Vashem website, the Jewish population of Munkacs was approximately 10,000, and included several Hasidic movements, Mitnagdim, Zionists, Neologs, and other streams. Shapira led the largest of the Hasidic sectors, though Satmar and Belzer Hasidim were also present in the city. See:
www.yadvashem.org/yv/en/exhibitions/communities/munkacs/between_two_wars.asp (accessed May 9, 2012).

in the Habad movement, challenging previous assumptions regarding Hasidic messianic passivity.

Martin Buber and Shimon Dubnow both argued that Hasidism no longer included an element of acute messianism.[4] However, the dominant strand of research into the Hasidic movement, as identified in particular with the renowned scholar Gershom Scholem, adopted a more dialectical view of Jewish history. Scholem suggested that Hasidism had "neutralized" the apocalyptical and collective fervor of messianic thought as manifested in the Sabbatean movement.[5] These approaches cannot provide a convincing explanation for the eruption of messianism in the Habad Hasidic court or among Hasidic zealots, as described later. Moshe Idel offered a more nuanced analysis, emphasizing that Hasidism is a diverse and longstanding movement. Accordingly, rather than a single, excusive trend, efforts should focus on identifying diverse responses. According to Idel, the central theme of the first two generations of Hasidism was the spiritualization of the messianic age, with an emphasis on the possibility of individual and mystically oriented redemption, rather than a collective perception. In later generations, the movement tended more to the collective, apocalyptic, and acute end of the messianic spectrum. Idel attributes this change to Rabbi Yitzhak Eizik Yehuda Yehiel Safrin, the founder of the Komarno Hasidic dynasty.[6] It is worth noting that Chaim Elazar Shapira was married to Safrin's great-granddaughter, and her father played an important role in Shapira's visit to Jerusalem, as I shall discuss later. Another approach, represented by Mor Altshuler, argues that the messianic impulse formed the driving force of Hasidism in the movement's early stages, among the disciples of Rabbi Yechiel Michal, the Maggid of Zlotchov, but was sidelined after his death due to the failure of the messianic plan and the rapid growth of Hasidism from an esoteric sect to a mass movement. Altshuler suggests that this sidelining was not final, however, and that the inherent messianic impulse is liable to reemerge in particular circumstances.[7]

Research into messianism in the Ger Hasidic dynasty presents a complicated picture. Yoram Jacobson argues that exile and redemption are

---

[4] Quoted in: Moshe Idel (ed.), *Messianic Mystics*. New Haven and London: Yale University Press, 1998, p. 212.

[5] Gershom Scholem, *The Messianic Idea in Judaism*. New York: Schocken Books, 1972, pp. 176–202.

[6] Idel, *Messianic Mystics*, pp. 212–47.

[7] Mor Altshuler, *The Messianic Secret of Hasidism*. Haifa: Haifa University Press, 2002 (in Hebrew).

vital themes in that dynasty. In his writings, Rabbi Itzhak Meir Alter ("the Rim," 1799–1866) developed a two-stage approach arguing that collective redemption can be achieved through personal spiritual ascent. This ascent does not entail the "neutralization" of the messianic idea, and the eschatological vision remains the essential goal of the spiritual quest. In the first stage the believer should overcome "nature" through faith and devotion, whereas the second stage is marked by self-denial and the revelation of truth. Thus the commitment to faith is the tool for hastening the End, allowing the believer to move from one stage to the next.[8] According to Jacobson, the book *Sefat Ha'emet* ("The Language of Truth") written by the Rim's grandson, Rabbi Yehuda Lieb Alter (1847–1905) was replete with messianic tension. However the Lurianic theosophy that lies at the center of this piece was transformed onto the spiritual and personal level; from this private level, it then also influenced the national and cosmic levels. Accordingly, this essay combines personal experience with collective salvation.[9]

According to Zvi Mark, messianic tension developed in the Ger Hasidic court and was personified in the character of the Rim. Mark presents evidence showing that the Rim saw himself as a potential messiah, and accordingly felt obliged to fight the evil Armilus (an anti-messianic figure), whom he identified with the Russian Tsar Alexander II (1818–1881). The Rim thus supported the Polish peasant revolt against the Tsar that began in 1830. After a long period in which he believed he could lead the entire Jewish people and expedite the End, the Rim suffered a crisis in his own self-perception. Nevertheless, he believed that his successor Yehuda Lieb Alter would inherit his messianic role.[10]

Rabbi Nachman of Breslov is another key messianic figure in Hasidic history. The exposure of the hidden Secret Scroll of the Hasidic court of Breslov allowed deeper observation into the portrait of the messiah, as this was revealed in the rabbi's talks. Zvi Mark argues that the messiah's image, according to the scroll, is a faithful copy of the image of the Tzadik, which in itself is based on the characteristics of Rabbi Nachman of Breslov himself. After his son's death, Rabbi Nachman also reached the

---

[8] Yoram Jacobson, "Truth and Faith in Ger Hassidic Dynasty." In: Joseph Dan and Joseph Hakar (eds.), *Studies in Kabbalah, Jewish Philosophy and Ethics and Contemplation Literature*. Jerusalem: Magnes Press, 5746 – 1985, pp. 593–616 (in Hebrew).

[9] Yoram Jacobson, "Exile and Redemption in the Ger Hassidic Dynasty," *Da'at* 2/3 (5738–5739, 1978), 175–216 (in Hebrew).

[10] Zvi Mark, "Messianic Hopes in Ger Hassidic Dynasty," *Tarbitz* 87(2) (5768 – 2007), 295–324 (in Hebrew).

conclusion that the chance for redemption had been missed and that another opportunity would only emerge after a period of one hundred years.[11]

The outburst of messianism in Munkacser Hasidism should be understood against the background of the particular circumstances pertaining at the time as well as the prevailing views in Orthodox Judaism around the turn of the twentieth century. The roots of messianic tension lay in influences from the surroundings of Hasidism and in the dramatic changes in the condition of the Jews during this period.

Some of the explanations offered by Orthodox leaders for the enormous changes in the condition of the Jews drew on analogies with the messianic age. They argued that modern reality should be interpreted as the realization of prophecies relating to the period preceding the coming of messiah. We may divide the exponents of this position into two categories – optimists and pessimists.[12] The optimistic approach is identified mainly with Religious Zionist thinkers, and in particular with the philosophy of Rabbi Avraham Yitzhak Kook, who explained that the rise of Jewish nationalism represents the "first pangs of redemption," that is – the beginning of the messianic process. According to this approach, which is based on natural messianism as described in Maimonides' writings, mundane actions by the nonreligious Zionist pioneers reflect the first stages of redemption, which may be realized in full through the actions of mortals.[13] Neo-Orthodox leaders of Agudat Yisrael such as Yitzhak Breuer also shared this approach, which facilitated cooperation between the movement and Zionism.[14] An opposing trend depicted modern times in dismal and pessimistic terms as the "pangs of messiah" – a period of distress and spiritual decline. Their approach was based on passages from the Babylonian Talmud describing the period of the *ikvata de-meshiha* (the footsteps of messiah) as one marked by severe material and spiritual hardship.[15] Those

---

[11] Zvi Mark, *The Hidden Scroll – the Secret Messianic Vision of Rabbi Nachman of Breslov*, Ramat Gan: Bar Ilan University Press, 5766 – 2006 (in Hebrew).

[12] Gershon Bacon, "Birth Pangs of the Messiah: The Reflections of Two Polish Rabbis on Their Era." In: Jonathan Frankel (ed.), *Studies in Contemporary Jewry 7: Jews and Messianism in the Modern Era: Metaphor and Meaning*. New York: Oxford University Press, 1991, pp. 86–99.

[13] Dov Schwartz, *Religious Zionism: History and Ideology*. Boston: Academic Press, 2009; idem, *Faith at a Crossroads – A Theological Profile of Religious Zionism*. Leiden, Boston and Koln: Brill, 2002.

[14] Yosef Fund, *Separation or Integration: Agudat Yisrael confronts Zionism and the State of Israel*. Jerusalem: Magnes Press, 1999, pp. 19–63 (in Hebrew).

[15] For example, see Babylonian Talmud, Sanhedrin 97a.

who adopted this position include the Lithuanian Rabbi Yisrael Hacohen of Radin, who ordered his students to study the laws relating to the priests in the Temple in anticipation of imminent redemption, and his disciple Rabbi Elhanan Bonim Wasserman, who composed the influential book *Ikvata de-Meshiha*, in which he interpreted the collapse of religious life as a sign of the approaching End Times.[16] During the interwar period, the Habad Hasidic movement also developed an acute messianic tension that would intensify still further after the war.[17] The Munkacser Hasidim adhered to the latter pessimistic school of thought and indeed took this position to its logical and extreme conclusion.

CHAIM ELAZAR SHAPIRA – BIOGRAPHY AND AFFINITY TO MYSTICISM AND MESSIANISM

Chaim Elazar Shapira was the great-great-grandson of Rabbi Zvi Elimelech Shapira (1783–1841), who served as the leader of the Dinov Hasidim. Zvi Elimelech later became one of the leaders of the radical stream in Hungarian Jewry, advocating a complete separation from any nontraditional way of life, and also engaged in the demonization of non-Orthodox Jews, referring to them by the obscure Biblical term "mixed multitude."[18]

Chaim Elazar Shapira eventually inherited the leadership of the Hasidic court from his father. He suffered from serious illnesses as a child, but subsequently recovered, and in accordance with Jewish tradition the name "Chaim" (Life) was added to his given name. He worked as a ritual circumciser for his living and married Haya Rabinowitz, but divorced her ten years later after the couple failed to produce any children. In 1903 he was appointed head of the religious court of the Munkacs community. Two years later, he married Rachel Peril, the

---

[16] Gershon Greenberg, "Foundations for Orthodox Jewish Theological Response to the Holocaust: 1936–1939." In: Alice Eckardt (ed.), *Burning Memory: Times of Testing and Reckoning*. Oxford: Pergamon Press 1993, pp. 71–94.

[17] Shalom Ratzbi, "Anti-Zionism and Messianic Tension in the Thought of Rabbi Shalom Dover," *HaTzyonut* 20 (5756 – 1996), 77–101 (in Hebrew); Menachem Friedman, "Messiah and Messianism in Habad–Lubavitch Hasidism." In: David Ariel-Joël [et al.] (eds.), *War of Gog and Magog: Messianism and Apocalypse in Judaism – Past and Present*. Tel Aviv: Yediot Acharonot Publishers, 2001, pp. 161–73 (in Hebrew).

[18] David Sorotzkin, *The Supra-Temporal Community in the Era of Change: The Emergency of Perceptions of Time and Collective as the Basis for Defining the Development of Jewish Orthodoxy in Modern Times*. PhD Dissertation, The Hebrew University of Jerusalem, 2007, pp. 193–203 (in Hebrew).

daughter of Rabbi Moshe Safrin of Komarno.[19] The couple had one daughter, Haya Frumme Rivka. Shapira was a consistent supporter of the Old Yishuv, and particularly of the Rehovot ha-Nahar Yeshivah, which had a Kabbalistic orientation.[20] He also established a neighborhood in Jerusalem called the "Munkacs Houses." The wedding of his only daughter was a major event in the Hasidic world, attended by thousands of visitors.[21] Shapira authored numerous works, including a seven-volume collection of rabbinical response entitled *Minhat Elazar*.

Many details regarding the biography of Rabbi Elazar Shapira are provided in the hagiographic essay *A History of Our Rabbi*, authored by the Hasid David Kahane. This essay was published in 1938, one year after the rabbi's death. According to Levi Cooper the book was written by the rabbi's close followers; although it was written in a hagiographic style, "one should not reject its value."[22]

According to Kahane, the First World War caused considerable psychological shock to the rabbi. The enormous scale of the death and destruction led him to identify the conflict with the war of Gog and Magog that precedes the coming of messiah. For Shapira, the war proved that his era was indeed one of the "pangs of messiah." Kahane wrote: "As a prophet and critic before the Lord, he warned and shouted that the date of redemption was approaching, and we must repent fully before God's great day arrives."[23] During the war, the battles reached the outskirts of the city, but it escaped unscathed. Shapira's followers attributed the good fortune of the city to a miracle thanks to their rabbi's piety.[24]

External confirmation can be found for Kahana's statement. During the war, Shapira published a book titled *Mashmia Yeshua* ("Announce Salvation,") in which he claimed that the war created the possibility to

---

[19] Moshe Idel notes that "the first rabbi of Komarno possessed and extremely heightened sense of messianic self awareness and simultaneously had strong mystical experience." Idel, *Messianic Mystics*, p. 239.

[20] Yonatan Meir, *Rehovot ha–Nahar: Kabbalah and Esotericism in Jerusalem (1896–1948)*. Jerusalem: Ben Zvi Institute, 2011, pp. 48–50, 89–90 (in Hebrew).

[21] An interesting depiction of the wedding, and of Jewish life in Munkacz in general, can be seen in the attached link. The footage reflects a diverse community in which Hasidim, Zionists, conservatives and modernists lived together. The Kleizmer band that played at the wedding is particularly interesting, as all its members were shaven and had a modern appearance:
www.youtube.com/watch?v=rp1OeIfoDowandhl=iw (accessed August 19, 2014).

[22] Cooper, *Rebbe*, p. 119.

[23] David Kahane, *A History of Our Rabbi*. Brooklyn, NY: Emet – Or Torah Munkacs, 5758 – 1998, p. 67.

[24] *Ibid.*, p. 45.

hasten the End. According to his narrative the messiah must come from a situation of distress and misery. In order to seize the opportunity for salvation, one should not pray for rescue and prosperity but for God's redemption. He emphasized that Jews must pray for collective redemption rather than personal salvation, which does not address the underlying problem. Indeed, when Israel prays for personal instead of collective salvation, God's anger grows so intense that people's prayers are left unheard. Since humans cannot overcome their personal grief, there is a need for a Tzadik, a righteous man who can assume the burden of redeeming the entire world from exile.[25] In this book Shapira addressed for the first time the connection between distress and redemption, and delineated the role of a Tzadik as a vessel through which it is possible to bring collective redemption. This perception would later become a prominent component of his messianic expectations.

The rabbi was involved in magic and mysticism[26] ("his head reaches into the Heavens,") and he devoted himself to the goal of preparing for the messianic era. As part of this approach he fought consistently and fiercely against any sign of change in the Jewish way of life.[27]

The Rebbe's followers believed that his mystical powers included the ability to bless and curse. Shapira was particularly inclined to numerology and to mystical combinations of letters, and his blessings included remedies for infertility (though evidently he was unable to use these to his personal benefit). Kahane devotes particular attention to his ability to impose curses. Shapira used his sermons during the High Holy Days for magical purposes. In his Rosh Hashanah sermon in 1917, for example, Shapira cursed the Tsar of Russia, "and in the same year, the dominion of the mighty king of Russia, may the name of the evil rot, was cut short." This depiction of the events is not without its irony, since the regime that followed the Tsar – the Communists – proved even more hostile to traditional Judaism. A year later, the rabbi cursed the "princes of the nations," and his disciples watched in awe as many kings and dukes lost their thrones in the aftermath of the world war.

Shapira's faithful biographer is honest enough to record that the rabbi also cursed the British Empire due to its support for the goals of Zionism

---

[25] Chaim Elazar Shapira, *Mashmia Yeshua*. New York: Emet – Or Torah Munkacz, 5751 – 1990 (originally published in 1919) (in Hebrew).

[26] Idel defines "mysticism" as "intimate connection, sometimes described as a direct contact with God, strong though often indefinable, which is designated in some extreme cases as 'mystical union,'" Idel, *Messianic Mystics*, p. 1.

[27] David Kahane, *A History of Our Rabbi*, p. 68.

and its adoption of the Balfour Declaration, which he referred by means of a play on words as Ba'al Pe'or, the name of a Canaanite god. The Bible mentions Ba'al Pe'or as an example of the connection to alien culture that leads to the abandonment of sexual prohibitions and to intermarriage. According to Itzhak Kraus, this approach should not be dismissed as mere semantics. It reflects his demonological view, which sees the success of Zionism as a proof of the rise of the evil powers that tempt Jews with false redemption.[28]

Kahane explains that the failure of the curse on Britain was due to the fact that the public did not support his supplication, and accordingly it was not accepted by God.[29] This comment implies that even Shapira's own followers did not share his fierce opposition to Zionism. Shapira attacked Zionist emigration to the Land of Israel, and his biographer declares that his warnings – or perhaps curses – proved accurate when, in 1929, "the savage Arabs suddenly assaulted them [the Jews], killing more than a few Jewish souls [...] And now all admitted: our Rabbi of Munkacs was correct, and we are shamed."[30] This comment refers to the 1929 riots, when 133 Jews, mainly from the Old Yishuv, were murdered by Palestinian nationalists.

Shapira's biographer notes that a further manifestation of his magical powers involved the halting of a typhoid epidemic that struck Munkacs in 1933. The rabbi blamed the Zionists for the epidemic, since they "are poisoning Jewish boys and girls with the venom of complete apostasy from the Torah of Moses." Accordingly, the rabbi strived to uproot "the house of idol worship," and thanks to repentance the epidemic ended.[31] Allan Nadler astutely observes that in this instance the rabbi's followers adopted the anti-Semitic narrative that Jews are responsible for spreading diseases.[32] It should be noted that ultra-Orthodox Judaism developed a consistent pattern of accusing Zionism for every ill that befell the Jews. The most virulent example was Yoel Teitelbaum, who accused Zionism of responsibility for the Holocaust.[33]

As part of his strong campaign against change, Shapira launched a bitter attack on the Gerrer Rebbe, Avraham Mordechai Alter, who at the time was one of the strongest Hasidic leader in the Jewish world, with a

---

[28] Itzhak Kraus, "The Theological Responses to the Balfour Declaration," *Bar Ilan* 28–9 (5761 – 2000), 81–104 (in Hebrew).

[29] David Kahane, *A History of Our Rabbi*, p. 69.   [30] *Ibid.*, pp. 105–6.

[31] *Ibid.*, p. 103.   [32] Nadler, "War on Modernity," 238.

[33] Ravitzky, *Messianism*, p. 63–70.

following of some 100,000 Hasidim. Shapira's wrath was aroused after Alter reached an agreement with Agudat Yisrael. In response, he supported a competing organization, "the Office of the Faithful on the Orthodox Foundation," which sought to curtail the influence of Agudat Yisrael among the Jews in Hungary and the surrounding countries.[34]

According to Kahane, Shapira felt depressed and humiliated in his later years as the coming of messiah continued to be delayed. His followers published a book describing Shapira's spiritual endeavors to cause the arrival of messiah during the last year of his life.[35] Shapira died of an incurable disease on May 12, 1937 at the age of sixty-six years.

SHAPIRA VISITS JERUSALEM TO CROWN THE MESSIAH

The main testimony regarding the rabbi's visit to Jerusalem in 1930 comes from the essay "Jerusalem Travels" by Moshe Goldstein, an associate of the rabbi who accompanied him on his journey.[36] The book, which was published during Shapira's lifetime and enjoyed his support, has been distributed widely and translated into several languages. Another highly important testimony was provided by Rabbi Yeshayah Asher Zelig Margaliot, who adds significant comments regarding the purpose of the visit.[37] The following discussion is based on both these sources.

In 1925, Shapira's court received a letter from the Munkacs Kollel in Jerusalem presenting an unusual request. An elderly man by the name of Shlomo Eliezer Alfandri, known by the epithet "the Holy Grandfather," had asked to move to the Munkacs Houses neighborhood, open a Beit Midrash (house of study) and donate his extensive library.

In his youth, the Holy Grandfather had served as a spiritual inspector in Istanbul. He subsequently served for several years as the chief rabbi of Damascus and later assumed the position of chief rabbi of Safed. In his old age he lived in Jerusalem among the residents of the Old Yishuv.[38] Among the local zealots the Holy Grandfather was considered the

---

[34] Kahane, *A History of Our Rabbi*, pp. 83–6.

[35] Yitzhak Adler, *The Order of the Last Year*. New York: Emet – Or Torah Munkacz, 5758–1997 (in Hebrew).

[36] Moshe Goldstein, *Jerusalem Travels*. New York: Emet – Or Torah Munkacz, Marheshvan 5764 – 2004 (in Hebrew).

[37] Shimon Margaliot, *Azamer bi-Shvahin: The Life of the Hasidic Kabbalistic Rabbi Yeshayah Asher Zelig Margaliot, May a Sage's Memory Be a Blessing*. Jerusalem: self-publication 5763 – 2003, p. 70 (in Hebrew).

[38] Moshe Goldstein, "Article of A Life of Fire," *Jerusalem Travels*, pp. 201–37.

greatest mystic in Jerusalem. His personal assistant was Rabbi Yeshayah Asher Zelig Margaliot, a close associate of the Munkacser Rebbe and the moving force behind the request in the letter.

The letter from Jerusalem piqued Shapira's curiosity. After investigations lasting several years and including the forwarding of references (some of which are quoted in the book), he decided to travel to Jerusalem in person in order to meet the Holy Grandfather. His impending visit to Jerusalem filled Shapira with enormous expectations. Goldstein's account of Shapira's joy ahead of his visit paraphrases several verses from the Song of Songs describing loving relations between a man and a woman, which have traditionally been interpreted as an allegory for the relations between God and the Jewish people. The Song of Songs also includes an oath and a warning not to awaken love "until it so desires" (2:7, 3:5, 8:4). The Jewish Sages drew from these verses a prohibition against any action deliberately intended to expedite messianic redemption.[39]

Goldstein describes Shapira as "becoming bound from afar by bonds of love for the Holy Grandfather." The description of this love continues: "And the longing grew so strong in our Rabbi and awoke the love until it so desires, to skip on the mountains and dance on the hills, saying: I shall travel and see it."[40] These passages reflect a tremendous passion, which Goldstein describes in pseudoerotic language to disobey the prohibition against messianic action, to awaken love, and to expedite the End. The rabbi is aware that he is prohibited from acting in this manner yet he decides to attempt to do so. The audacity this entailed is all the greater given Shapira's inherently conservative nature.

Shapira interpreted Alfandri's request as a call to joint mystical action with messianic goals. It should be noted that all the associates of the rabbi involved in his visit to Jerusalem were mystics motivated by acute messianic tension. Margaliot was one of the pioneers of the anti-Zionist campaign in Jerusalem, a struggle he depicted in messianic terms. Another important figure involved in the visit was Rabbi Chaim Shaul Dweik, the head of Rehovot ha-Nahar Yeshivah,[41] which was involved in deliberate attempts to expedite the End Times, including magical prayers offered during a *Tikkun Hatzot* (a midnight Kabbalistic service).[42]

Steve Weitzman argued that messianic characters throughout Jewish history have shown a dialectical pattern whereby their public presentation

---

[39] Ravitzky, *Messianism*, pp. 211–34.   [40] Goldstein, *Jerusalem Travels*, p. 22.

[41] For extensive details about this institution, see Yonatan Meir, *Rehovot ha-Nahar*.

[42] Idel, *Messianic Mystics*, pp. 308–20.

of the messianic message is preceded by a process combining external-
ization and exposure, depending on the circumstances. Weitzman likens
this process to that of "coming out of the closet," where the individual has
self-awareness as a homosexual but reaches the point of publicly external-
izing this characteristic after a protracted period in an intermediate or
"gray" reality.[43] A similar pattern can be seen in the relations between
Shapira and Alfandri. After Shapira agreed to the request and expressed
his willingness to leave Hungary immediately in order to meet with
Alfandri, the two men began to correspond with a view to executing the
visit. The correspondence takes the form of "wooing" on the part of
Shapira, who was enthusiastic to meet Alfandri as soon as possible, while
the latter was more hesitant and reluctant to commit himself, so that each
step forward was often followed by a retreat.

The correspondence between the two mystics is colored by tentative
and allusive revelations of innermost secrets. In 1929 Shapira wrote to
Alfandri that despite his poor state of health, his reluctance to interrupt
his Torah studies, and the alarming security situation in Palestine
following the Arab Revolt of 1929, he was unable to resist his desire to
meet with Alfandri. The latter replied that Shapira must not come at the
point in time, and implored him not to allow the Evil Impulse (*yetzer ha-
ra*) to get the better of him, "for reasons I cannot discuss in detail." This
comment by Alfandri should be seen as an allusion to his mystical powers
and his claim to predict future events.[44] In response, Shapira "begs and
beseeches and inquires as to the wellbeing of his teaching with all his
heart, soul and love," and urges Alfandri not to reject his request. Shapira
also reveals his own mystical prowess, revealing by way of a secret: "And
in myself [I know that] God, may His name be blessed, will help us
already in the days of this winter with the coming of the Just Redeemer."
Shapira thus predicts the imminent appearance of the messiah. In March
1930, The Holy Grandfather writes to Shapira permitting him to make
his journey. The rabbi has no time to spare, and a month later, in the
Hebrew month of Iyar, he departs with a delegation of fifteen men.
Shapira chooses to sail from Trieste to Alexandria, since the ships on this
route are faster, despite the fact that the fare is twice the usual rate.[45] Mor
Altshuler comments that for the Maggid of Zlotchov and his disciples

---

[43] Steve Weitzman, "He That Cometh Out: On the Disclosure of Messianic Secrets." In:
Michael Morgan and Steve Weitzman (eds.), *Rethinking the Messianic Idea: New Perspectives on Jewish Messianism*. Bloomington: Indiana University Press, pp. 63–92.
[44] Goldstein, *Jerusalem Travels*, pp. 24–6.   [45] *Ibid.*, pp. 27–32.

(the first Hasidic court established after the death of the Ba'al Shem Tov, the founder of Hasidism, in the eighteenth century), the month of Iyar was believed to hold special messianic properties and the Jewish people was destined to be redeemed in this month.[46] The date of Shapira's journey may have been influenced by this tradition.

Goldstein describes the fervent prayers that were offered during the voyage, which was a period of religious endeavor and hope of imminent salvation. In Alexandria the pilgrims boarded a train to Lod (Lydda). They were welcomed by the Kabbalist Chaim Shaul Dweck, who presented Shapira with a written note from Alfandri: "I am lovesick."[47]

The rabbi's description of his arrival at the holy sites in Jerusalem illustrates his dialectical approach. His joy on reaching the Western Wall was overshadowed by his rage at God's humiliation, as "despicable and base foxes parade" on His holy mountain – a reference to the Muslim presence. Indeed, the entire work, as well as Shapira's subsequent sermons, were full of with expressions of scorn for Islam, which is described as desecrating God's name. I believe that these attacks are to be interpreted as a supplication to God to end the disgrace by sending the true messiah.[48]

During the course of his visit, Shapira met three times with Alfandri. On the first day, immediately after visiting the Western Wall, Shapira went to Alfandri's apartment. As the two men met, Goldstein declares that they "made love, and anyone who did not see their joy has never seen the true joy of the pious." Shapira made a toast and declared: "May we be worthy, with our Rabbi the Holy Grandfather, to see the revelation of the light of the Messiah King [...] on the upcoming festival of Shavuot [approximately one month later], may it come to us for good." Alfandri replied with an Amen, adding: "We shall yet speak more of this matter, God willing."[49]

The visit was timed to enable Shapira to participate in the celebrations in memory of Rabbi Shimon Bar Yochai, whose death is associated with the festival of Lag Ba'Omer. Bar Yochai, a Tannaitic sage, is traditionally credited with authoring the Zohar, the central work of Jewish mysticism, and has even been depicted as a messianic figure.[50] According to

---

[46] Mor Altshuler, *The Messianic Secret*, p. 18.   [47] Goldstein, *Jerusalem Travels*, p. 50.
[48] *Ibid.*, p. 58.   [49] *Ibid.*, pp. 62–3.
[50] Yehuda Liebs, "The Messiah of the Zohar – On the Messianic Image of Rabbi Shimon Bar Yochai." In: Yair Zakowitz (ed.), *The Messianic Idea in Israel*. Jerusalem: Israel National Academy of Sciences, 5742 – 1982, pp. 87–236 (in Hebrew).

Goldstein, Shapira's participation in the celebrations was intended to awake Bar Yochai on the anniversary of his death.[51] In his sermon on the evening of the festival Shapira explained that the purpose of his visit to the tomb was "that he [Bar Yochai] should awaken now and stand as an angel pleading on behalf of all Israel to expedite our exile and redeem our souls, that we might yet offer the Second Passover sacrifice, may it be a blessing for us, on the mount of our Temple in Jerusalem." The messianic nature of the celebration is thus overt. Shapira continued: "Thanks to study of the Kabbalah, may we be worthy for our true messiah to come speedily and in our days."[52] Accordingly, study of the Kabbalah in general, and the Lag Ba'Omer celebration in particular, serve as a catalyst for bringing nearer the End Times.

After the Sabbath the delegation again visited Alfandri's home, this time for the fateful meeting. On their arrival, Shapira asked all those present to leave the room so that he could hold a private meeting. Goldstein testifies that he left, since the purpose of the meeting involved the subject of complete redemption. He reports that the meeting lasted some two hours, "and those of us standing outside were seized by shaking and fear."[53]

According to Goldstein, Shapira read out to the Holy Grandfather a letter he had brought with him from his father-in-law, Yaacov Moshe of Komarno. In the letter, written in 1914, the rabbi revealed that Shapira's late father, Zvi Hirsch, had appeared before him in a dream. "With tears in my eyes," the Komarno rabbi wrote, "I asked him why there is this delay in our exile? And he [Zvi Hirsch] replied, "Believe me, in the upper world there is much sorrow at this, they are merely waiting for the lower righteous one who is able to impose a ruling, and so forth." The implication of this dream is of critical importance: the delay in redemption, which is also the subject of sorrow in the upper spheres, is due to a lack of leadership. God expects a righteous man to emerge who will be able to declare himself the messiah. This argument is based on the Kabbalistic tradition that in every generation there is a "founding Tzadik of the world," a leader of the generation who is the incarnation of Moses and can potentially be the messiah. The character of this righteous man who

---

[51] According to Moshe Idel, the Hasidic Tzadik is perceived as holding magical powers that can channel cosmic energies for his court and disciples, and even for the Jewish people as a whole. Moshe Idel, *Hasidism: Between Ecstasy and Magic*. Albany: State University of New York Press, 1995, pp. 149–70.

[52] Goldstein, *Jerusalem Travels*, pp. 89–90.   [53] *Ibid.*, p. 95–6.

carries the world on his shoulders is identified in the book of Zohar with Rabbi Shimon Bar Yochai; as noted, much of Shapira's visit was devoted to celebrations in Bar Yochai's memory. In the Habad Hasidic movement, for example, this title was used to crown their leader Menachem-Mendel Schneerson as the King Messiah in 1992.[54]

Thus the purpose of Shapira's visit was revealed: He had rushed to Jerusalem in order to persuade Alfandri to accept the messiah's crown. The Hasidic leader asked the Holy Grandfather to make an explicit ruling that he was the righteous one, but the later replied: "I am not a righteous one." Goldstein was unable to provide any further details about their conversation, except to note that it was protracted.

Goldstein does not report that Shapira fell into depression and despair after the failed meeting. However, his intolerance toward the Arab presence in the Land of Israel intensified during these days, and he also savagely criticized Zionist celebrations of Lag Ba'Omer at which men and women danced together. He consoled himself by declaring that "the Tannaitic Sage Rabbi Shimon Bar Yochai [or, perhaps, his latter-day reincarnation?] will surely wreak vengeance on all their rabble, speedily and in our days."[55] Shapira did not abandon his attempts to persuade Alfandri to declare his messianic nature. Indeed, he may well have been unsurprised by Alfandri's rejection of his initial approach. The coming out of the closet of the messiah, a process of which Shapira was absolutely certain, would surely require further exhortations.

Rabbi Yeshayah Asher Zelig Margaliot includes an even more remarkable account of the encounter in his autobiography. Margaliot relates that he heard Shapira ask the Holy Grandfather in Aramaic "When will my Lord arrive?" According to Hasidic tradition, this is the question the Ba'al Shem Tov asked the messiah when his soul ascended to heaven. The Holy Grandfather turned round and pointed to the wall behind him, saying, "Here it stands..." This was an allusion to a verse from the Song of Songs (2:9) implying that messiah is "just behind the wall" and redemption is imminent. Shapira asked:

"Why does he stand 'behind' our wall and not enter?" And the Holy Grandfather replied that there are those who are stalling him (viz. the wicked ones who in each generation who stand at the entrance and do not let him in). In a voice choked

---

[54] Samuel Heilman and Menachem Friedman, *The Rebbe: The Life and Afterlife of Menachem Mendel Schneerson*. Princeton: Princeton University Press, 2010.

[55] Goldstein, *Jerusalem Travels*, 126. On the role of revenge in Jewish messianic drama, see: Yisrael Yoval, "Vengeance and Curse, Blood and Libel," *Zion* 58 (5753 – 1993), 33–90.

with tears, our Rabbi, may his memory protect us, asked: "Am I among those who are stalling him, God forbid?..." The Holy Grandfather replied, "God forbid, God forbid."[56]

The first purpose of this quote is to justify Shapira's fierce struggle against modernism as the reason for the delay in the coming of messiah. The Holy Grandfather's reply can also be interpreted as a statement by the messiah. In other words, according to Margaliot's testimony, Alfandri accepted the messianic appointment but merely argued that the time was not yet ripe to make a declaration.

The delegation continued with its planned schedule, visiting the tombs of Tzadikim (sages) and attending the celebrations in Meron. On the twelfth day of the visit, however, alarming news arrived: The Holy Grandfather had fallen ill. The delegation rushed to his bedside and, before their astonished eyes, he breathed his last breath. They estimated that he was around 120 years old at the time of his death.[57]

Goldstein describes Shapira's immediate response to the death of the potential messiah. With terrifying shouts, Shapira mourned "the messiah of the God of Jacob!" He tore his clothes in the traditional sign of mourning and wept almost to the point of fainting. The next day Shapira cut short his visit and decided to return immediately to Munkacs. On the ship, he leveled bitter accusations at God: "I went away full, but the Lord has brought me back empty" (Ruth 1:21).[58] He had come to the Holy Land to sanctify God's name and crown the Lord's messiah, but God shattered his hopes. A letter sent by Moshe Goldstein to Rabbi Yeshayah Asher Zelig Margaliot after Goldstein and Shapira returned to Munkacs depicts Shapira as raging and embittered about the course events had taken. While giving a sermon on the festival of Shavuot, he reportedly struck his head with his hands, crying out "Woe!"[59]

To make matters worse, the passengers on the ship on Shapira's return journey included Zionists and supporters of Agudat Yisrael. The rabbi was irritated by their presence and was particularly angered when he saw a Zionist pioneer publicly desecrating the Sabbath. He reprimanded her and she responded insolently. Yet before the journey was over, Shapira had found the explanation for the death of the intended messiah: he had been summoned by God to act in the heavens in order to promote the redemption of the Jewish people.[60]

---

[56] Shimon Margaliot, *Azamer bi–Shvahin*, p. 70.
[57] Goldstein, *Jerusalem Travels*, p. 169.   [58] *Ibid.*, pp. 169–80.
[59] Margaliot, *Azamer bi-Shvahin*, p. 71.   [60] Goldstein, *Jerusalem Travels*, pp. 190–1.

Before continuing our exploration, it is worth taking a moment to consider Alfandri's qualities that led the Hasidic leaders to consider him a potential messiah. The laudatory work *Article of a Life of Fire* offers a biography of the man. Alfandri was born in Constantinople, Turkey; his date of birth is unknown, but the Hasidim assume that it was between 1810 and 1815. He is said to have gained a reputation as a genius in his religious studies and was offered the position of head of the religious court of the Constantinople Jewish community, though he declined to accept the honor. From a young age he developed a reputation as a forceful and uncompromising figure. He imposed particularly strict rules of Kashrut, lashing out at butchers whom he accused of failing to observe the ritual laws of slaughter and thereby damaging their livelihood. The Hasidim recall an incident when he questioned the validity of a couple's marriage and prevented them from consummating their union. He did not hesitate to turn to the religious court when he believed that the sanctity of marriage was being threatened. He insulted Rabbi Chaim Falaji and criticized his religious rulings. He predicted an earthquake in Constantinople, and the ground indeed shook while he was still speaking. He had no interest in honor or money. He was a fervent supporter of the Old Yishuv in Jerusalem. Alfandri later moved to Damascus, where he served as a chief rabbi. In 1920 he moved to Safed, marking his entry into the world of mysticism. During his time in the city, Alfandri is credited with prophecies and miracles. His zealotry led him to refuse to accept treatment from Zionist physicians, and he managed to cure his ailments by magical means. In 1925 he traveled to Jerusalem to receive medical attention and decided to stay in the city.[61]

A less idyllic depiction of Alfandri's life is offered by the researcher Yaron Harel, who focused on the period when Alfandri served as the *Hakham Bashi* (chief rabbi) of Damascus. According to Harel, Alfandri came to Damascus after serving as the rabbi of a neighborhood in Constantinople. Immediately after arriving in the city (in 1894), he became embroiled in disputes with all sides of the community due to his inflexible and excessively strict nature. This led to his isolation and eventually (in 1908) to his dismissal from the position. He fought particularly virulently against the plans to update the curriculum at the schools of the Alliance Israélite Universelle. However, he was forced to compromise and eventually even accepted an appointment as honorary

---

[61] Ibid., pp. 199–240.

president of the organization's schools in Damascus, where Jewish children studied in Arabic. After his dismissal, he remained in Damascus for five years without any means of livelihood before receiving an offer of a position from the Jewish community of Safed in 1913. Harel states that Alfandri received his appointment in Damascus while he was in his fifties. If this is the case, he would have been almost ninety years' old at the time of Shapira's visit.[62]

The general portrait painted by the stories of the Hasidim is of an elderly man who possesses magical and mystical powers and is capable both of imposing curses and of prophesying the future. He is a scholarly man who has issued religious rulings. He has lived in the Holy Land and the Holy City. Above all, he is a zealot and unafraid of controversy.

After Shapira returned to his followers in Hungary his messianic anticipation remained as potent as ever. However, since it was apparent that Alfandri could not fulfill this role, the fateful question was who might emerge as the "founding Tzadik of the world?" Who could assume the throne of leadership? As this question resonated, the similarity between Alfandri's attributes and those of Shapira himself could not have been more glaring.

THE DISPUTE WITH THE GERRER REBBE

Agudat Yisrael was officially founded in 1912 in order to unite all the Orthodox streams against the growing trend toward secularization in the Jewish world. Although Agudat Yisrael was originally a German movement it established branches among the Old Yishuv in the Land of Israel and, in 1918, the Polish branch was founded, under the name Association of the Loyal Faithful of Israel. Although the movement was originally hostile to Zionism, it moderated its stance from the 1930s against the background of the worsening persecution of the Jews in Poland and the rise of Nazism in Germany.[63]

Avraham Mordechai Alter (1866–1948), the Gerrer Rebbe, was one of the strongest Hasidic leaders of Orthodox Jewry during the interwar period. Alter was a pragmatic leader who used new tools to protect his

---

[62] Yaron Harel, *Intrigue and Revolution: The Appointment and Dismissal of Chief Rabbis in the Communities of Baghdad, Damascus and Aleppo,1744–1914*. Jerusalem: Ben Zvi Institute, 2007, pp. 203–35 (in Hebrew); Binyamin Brown, "The Eastern Sages and Religious Zealotry," *Akademot* 10, 5761 – 2001, 289–324 (in Hebrew).

[63] Yosef Fund, *Separation or Integration: Agudat Yisrael Confronts Zionism and the State of Israel*. Jerusalem: Magnes Press, 1999 (in Hebrew); Gershon Bacon, *The Politics of Tradition: Agudat Yisrael in Poland, 1916–1939*. Jerusalem: Magnes Press, 1996.

community against changing realities. Thus, for example, he favored the political involvement of his followers in the Polish parliament and in Palestine under the framework of Agudat Yisrael, despite the fierce criticism this decision evoked from the Munkacser Rebbe and the Belzer Rebbe. The Gerrer Rebbe was appointed president of the Council of Torah Sages, established by Agudat Yisrael as the spiritual authority for its operations. He encouraged his followers to emigrate to Palestine as a pragmatic solution to economic deprivation and persecution, and he himself fled from Poland to Palestine following the Nazi occupation. He also encouraged his followers to engage in secular vocations in Palestine, contrary to the practice of the Old Yishuv, which had relied on donations from overseas and devoted itself solely to Torah study. The Old Yishuv and conservative circles strongly criticized the rabbi for this decision. Agudat Yisrael even established a network of private schools for boys and girls. In order to receive official recognition in Poland, the curriculum included secular subjects and foreign languages.[64]

The curricular changes enraged Chaim Elazar Shapira, who wrote to Alter in 1922 to oppose his affiliation to Agudat Yisrael. His most potent wrath, however, was seen in response to a rumor that the Metivta – the rabbinical seminary in Warsaw – was also teaching secular subjects and foreign languages, something he found completely unacceptable and referred to as "a pig prepared with all the trappings of sanctity." He expressed his amazement at the Gerrer Rebbe's willingness to sanction such an abomination.[65]

The Gerrer Rebbe responded by pointing out that he was neither the founder nor the director of Agudat Yisrael. This reply also enraged Shapira, who felt that Alter was evading the central issue: the introduction of secular studies at the rabbinical seminary in Poland. Shapira suggested that he visit the seminary, and, in the interim, asked the rabbi to withdraw his patronage of the institution. The Gerrer Rebbe sent a curt reply: "I have visited the Metivta myself and there is not the slightest impropriety in it [. . .] I hope that as a bearer of the dignity of the Torah, [you] will see that there 'are no bears and there is no forest' [a saying implying that an allegation is completely false]."[66]

[64] Arthur Green, "Ger Hasidic Dynasty," *YIVO Encyclopedia of Jews in Eastern Europe*, 9 August 2010 (accessed in 24 February 2012). www.yivoencyclopedia.org/article.aspx/ Ger-Hasidic_Dynasty.

[65] Moshe Goldstein, *Tikkun Olam*, Mukacevo: Druck H. Guttmann, 5696–1936, pp. 7–8.

[66] *Ibid.*, p. 11.

Shapira accepted Alter's suggestion that he visit Warsaw. The visit went ahead in May 1922 and profoundly shocked Shapira. Goldstein's book *Tikkun Olam* ("Repairing the World") includes a record of the conversation between the Munkacser Rebbe and the Gerrer Rebbe. I am unconvinced that this record faithfully reflects Alter's comments. While Goldstein quotes long, eloquent speeches by Shapira, his rendition of Alter's replies are almost telegraphic in their brevity. Moreover, there is no similarity between the summary of the meeting as presented in Goldstein's book and its actual outcomes. Accordingly, the report may well have been distorted, and I shall draw on a different source in order to present the meeting from the perspective of the Gerrer Rebbe.

Shapira began the meeting by referring to Alter's assertion that there "are no bears and there is no forest," claiming passionately: "I found bears there, and a forest there, and all the animals of the forest [...] and I was exceedingly alarmed."[67] His examination revealed that the Metivta was indeed teaching foreign languages. Indeed, the entrance sign itself included the Polish inscription "Seminar of Rabbis of Poland." Shapira expressed his disgust at the expansion of the impure values of innovation and progress expounded by Agudat Yisrael and declared that it was no longer possible to remain silent. How could such an abomination take place under the patronage of the Gerrer Rebbe? Shapira acknowledged that it was necessary to teach the local language in order to receive state recognition, but argued that this should take place in private and not publicly.[68]

Shapira also claimed that he had realized during the course of his visit that the students were not thoroughly versed in religious law. In response to his question, a teacher explained that this was due to the secular studies, which distracted the students and limited the time available for Torah studies.[69]

Further reasons quoted by Shapira for opposing the approach of Agudat Yisrael included his objection to the founding of the Beis Yaacov educational network, which provided a general and religious education for girls – something he considered to be forbidden. Shapira based

[67] *Ibid.*, p. 12.

[68] The Yad Vashem website includes an unsigned article claiming that Chaim Elazar Shapira was himself obliged to learn Hungarian in order to secure recognition from the authorities for his appointment as head of the religious court in Munkacs. www.yadvashem.org/yv/en/exhibitions/communities/munkacs/rabbi_shapira.asp. (accessed March 8, 2012).

[69] Goldstein, *Tikun Olan*, pp. 33–4.

his position on the teachings of Maimonides: "Whosoever teaches his daughter the Torah is as one who teaches her frivolity."[70] Another subject of criticism was the fundraising campaign launched by Agudat Yisrael for the settlement of the Land of Israel, which led to a reduction in donations to the Old Yishuv in Jerusalem and encouraged the prohibited act of settling the Land before the arrival of messiah.[71] He also criticized the fact that, during the Gerrer Rebbe's visit to Palestine, he met with Rabbi Avraham Yitzhak Kook, a well-known supporter of Zionism.

In conclusion, Shapira suggested that rather than Agudat Yisrael, the organization should adopt the name "Assembly of the Pious." Financial support for settling the Land of Israel should be diverted to the Old Yishuv; the Metivta should no longer provide secular studies; and no changes should be made to the education provided in the Talmudei Torah.[72]

According to this source, the Gerrer Rebbe replied that he had no authority to change the regulations of Agudat Yisrael. Accordingly, he proposed that a committee of twenty rabbis, ten from each side, be formed to formulate agreed rules. This response implies that Alter agreed, in principle, to Shapira's proposed changes, and that the latter's mission was a success. However, it soon transpired that Alter was procrastinating in the implementation of their agreement and was doing nothing to advance the idea of the rabbinical meeting.

In response, Shapira decided to strengthen his Assembly of the Pious as a counterweight to the Council of Torah Sages of Agudat Yisrael. The assembly duly ruled against the "progressive" rabbinical seminar; against the settlement of the Land of Israel; against the channeling of donations for settlement at the expense of the Old Yishuv; and against affiliation to Agudat Yisrael. Shapira collected dozens of rabbinical approbations for his position, and these were published in the book *Tikkun Olam*.[73] These included approbations from the Lubavicher Rebbe, Yosef Yitzhak Schneerson, who was also considered a senior leader in the Hasidic world of the time.[74] Interestingly, Yoel Teitelbaum, who after the Second World War came to lead the radical wing of ultra-Orthodox Judaism, did not send an approbation for the book, though the book includes a letter of support from his brother, Chaim Zvi Teitelbaum. This may suggest that there was tension between Shapira and Yoel Teitelbaum.

---

[70] *Ibid.*, p. 34.   [71] *Ibid.*, pp. 13–4.   [72] *Ibid.*, p. 20.   [73] *Ibid.*, p. 41.
[74] *Ibid.*, pp. 45–54.

In a letter to Asher Lemel Spitzer the Gerrer Rebbe explained his version of the events. He claimed that his comments had been brazenly distorted to suggest that he had called for the abolition of the seminary. Alter described Shapira's three demands and addressed each one in turn. He stated that he was willing to change the name of the association if this would unify the faithful. As for secular studies in the Metivta, Alter explained that, according to the law of the land, a class could not be opened unless at least two hours were devoted to the national language and one to mathematics. He claimed that the Munkacser Rebbe had argued that agreeing to these two hours of studies would eventually lead to ten hours. The Gerrer Rebbe responded that secular studies had also been introduced at the higher yeshivah in Ger, attended by five hundred students, and that "no-one had spoken out or complained." Thus he rejected the validity of the claim. As for the donations to the Old Yishuv, Alter emphasized that the Agudat Yisrael fund must not damage other funds, and he was willing to undertake that this would be the case. Lastly the Gerrer Rebbe noted his satisfaction at the strengthening of Agudat Yisrael; while it might have its disadvantages, it was a worthy enterprise.[75] This response reflects a pragmatic approach that seeks to promote Torah study while accepting constraints that do not ultimately damage the traditional content. Alter was open to new tools, such as political parties and modern education, in order to preserve the foundations of the faith. Shapira, by contrast, was resolutely opposed to any change, even it was tactical in nature.

The dispute between the two rabbis took place in 1922, before Shapira's visit to Jerusalem, but the book was published in 1936, after the unsuccessful visit to the city. I would offer the hypothesis that the timing of the publication was not coincidental. As noted, following Alfandri's death the path was clear to seek a new "founding Tzadik of the world." The Gerrer Rebbe was one of the strongest Hasidic leaders of the time and, accordingly, he may have been considered the most natural candidate for this role. In addition, a well-known tradition in the Ger Hasidic movement, with which Shapira may have been familiar, argued that the messiah might come from the seed of the leaders of that dynasty.[76]

Shapira's leadership, and his willingness to condemn Alter publicly as a conciliatory figure whose approach was liable to lead to the destruction of

---

[75] Avraham M. Alter, *Collection of Letters from the Admor Shlita of Ger*. Augsburg: self-publication 5707 – 1947, pp. 32–6 (in Hebrew).

[76] Mark, "Messianic Hopes," 305–11.

Orthodox Jewry, may have been designed to serve two purposes: to refute the possibility that Alter was the concealed Tzadik and to point to an alternative leader. I wish to suggest that the public dispute with the Gerrer Rebbe was intended to mark Shapira as Alfandri's successor not just on the mystical level but also in the public domain. It also "corresponds" with alternative messianic traditions existent in the Ger Hasidic dynasty. The publication of this affair in 1936 should also, I believe, be seen against the background of the messianic tension within the Munkacs Hasidim. This was also the last year in Shapira's life, when the messianic activity he initiated through the use of magic prayer reached its peak.

THE REDEMPTION PRAYERS, 1929–1937

Shapira used the High Holyday prayers and the Hoshanah Rabbah service on the seventh day of the festival of Sukkot to further his messianic agenda. He sought to take advantage of the fact that the Jews came to the synagogues in their masses on these days in a spirit of repentance in order to expedite the coming of the messiah. The unique sermons he gave were dominated by a sense of siege and impotence that could be healed only when the messiah came. Shapira hoped that the collective plea for repentance would serve as a catalyst for the coming of the messiah, and called on God to complete the period of the birth pangs of messiah, which he associated with his generation, and to end the exile.

Shapira's sermons followed a fixed pattern. They began with a detailed and pessimistic description of the condition of the Jews, conveying a sense of hopelessness. Shapira rejected any possibility of mundane Jewish activism in order to solve this distress, emphasizing the negative consequences of such an approach. He then identified God as the only source of salvation through supplication, prayer, and the maintenance of the religious way of life. The demands for salvation included a forceful reprimand directed to God, the patriarchs of the Jewish people, and Tzadikim of previous generations for remaining silent and allowing the situation to deteriorate to such a nadir.

These sermons drew their rationale from the statement by Maimonides that "Israel is deemed only through repentance, and the Torah has already promised that Israel will repent at the end of its exile, and will immediately be redeemed" (*Mishneh Torah*, Laws of Repentance, chapter 7, Halakhah E). Shapira interpreted this rule as implying that, since the messiah is "just behind the wall," only a small additional effort is needed in order to bring him. A mass supplication for repentance could meet the Divine requirement and, accordingly, Shapira demanded that those who gathered at his Beit Midrash repent. At the same time, he demanded that God end the period of the "footsteps of messiah" – the tribulations that precede the coming of salvation. He also sought to use his mystical powers in order to influence the upper worlds to send the messiah. In short, Shapira's sermons served two purposes: he demanded passive obedience on the part of the public and action on the part of God.

According to Moshe Idel, a new model for messianic activities had developed among Jewish mystics in the fifteen century – the *magico-Kabbalistic model*. The background of its development was the deterioration in the condition of the Jews in Spain that eventually led to their explosion. Here, for the first time, Idel says, the Kabbalists argued that the advent of the messiah is to be accomplished by magical procedures enacted by a group of mystics that will disrupt the continuum of history and will cause a radical change in the natural order.

The heart of this model lies in the conviction that the time of the messiah is fixed and imminent. The only impediment to the final advent is the presence of forces of evil. The way to destroy evil is by magical acts. The strong messianism of this model, which forms the heart of *Sefer ha-Meshiv*, drew mixed reactions in the century after the expulsion from Spain. Kabbalistic circles in Safed later condemned the use of magic for religious and messianic ends.[77] I argue that Shapira used the magical tools kit in order to try to expedite the End.

Turning to a more detailed examination of the content of his sermons, we may begin with a sermon he gave at Hoshanah Rabbah in 1929. He described the woes of the time, including a lack of opportunities to make a livelihood and rising taxes. Those who considered sending their sons to America should know that they would surely be doomed (that is to say – they would depart from the ways of the Torah). Girls were insolent to their parents and wore immodest dress. This growing infidelity and the resurgence of evil were also manifested in the Land of Israel, where an apostate university (the Hebrew University) had just been built in the Holy City. Agudat Yisrael preferred to establish new colonies in the Land rather than support the Old Yishuv. The simple masses of Jewry, faithful in their belief in the coming of the messiah, were being persecuted and oppressed. Shapira claimed that, according to Hasidic tradition, God has already issued the command to send the messiah, but a herald

---

[77] Idel, *Messianic Mystics*, pp. 126–32.

subsequently left heaven to postpone the time of redemption. The reason for the delay was the lack of faith in God's power and the presence of humans who declared "I shall rule" (a reference to those who promoted the physical settlement of the Land of Israel). Shapira emphasized that only faith can bring salvation, and, accordingly, called on God to save His people.[78]

By 1933 Shapira's depiction of reality was even more pessimistic. He noted that deprivation and confusion were impeding the will to repent. What, for example, is a boy to do when he has no money for a dowry? What will become of the girl who longs to travel to America, where she will desecrate the Sabbath and fall victim to evil? In the Soviet Union two million Jews live under the murderous edicts of the Bolsheviks. In Germany Jews are being beaten in the street. Only the Land of Israel is a refuge, yet there colonies are being built, sanctity is being desecrated, and faith in the coming of the messiah is being eroded. It is important to appreciate that Shapira views every action taken in the Land of Israel that is not for the purpose of Torah study as irrelevant. Furthermore, the tradition of Exile dictates that no action should be taken to conquer the Land of Israel and to rebuild the Temple, since these are duties of the king messiah. Therefore, the Exilic custom is "all that is new is prohibited by the Torah." Even a prophet is not permitted to introduce changes. Shapira's conclusion is that Zionism is a forbidden change.[79] Refugees fleeing infidelity in Europe arrive in the Land of Israel only to trample on the Sabbath in public. Shapira turns accusingly to God: "Master of the Universe – will you remain silent in the face of such evil? In the face of the burning of holy Tefillin (in the Soviet Union) and the desecration of Your name there? Woe betide us! How can this be tolerated?" Shapira promised his audience that these deprivations were signs of the coming of Messiah. The only action to take against them was repentance: not political organization, not emigration to the Land of Israel, and not the desecration of the Land through its agricultural use.[80]

During the Hoshanah Rabbah service in the same year, Shapira discussed the persecution of the Jews in Germany. The lesson he drew from these events was the need for political passivity. He declared that the

---

[78] Unsigned, *Booklet of Holy Utterances*. London: self-publication, 5734 – 1974 (in Hebrew).

[79] Chaim Elazar Shapira, *Minhat Elazar* 5. Jerusalem: Emet – Or Torah Munkacz, 5756 – 1995, section 12 (in Hebrew).

[80] Chaim Falkozite, *Holy Utterances*. Munkacs: Grafia Press, year of printing unclear, pp. 3–4 (in Hebrew).

German Jews were clean shaven, desecrated the Sabbath in public, and "have already completely departed from the totality of the Jewish people." Yet due to their Jewish origin they are persecuted and beaten in a sickening manner. They are suffering purely for God's honor, despite the fact that they embody no "divine image" and no "Jewish form," and do not have the external appearance of Jews. Shapira argues that natural and mundane salvation is futile; nature cannot be relied on in any manner. Only prayer and supplication can bring salvation, not emancipation and not the assimilation of the Jews in general culture. His ultimate conclusion was simple: A Jew must engage in Torah study and raise his sons in the way of the Torah.[81]

The same conclusion emerges from his description of the developments in the Land of Israel. He quotes a sermon by Rabbi Gershon of Kitov, the nephew of the Ba'al Shem Tov, who claimed that he saw a built city and the city of God humiliated to the depths of hell. In other words, there is an inverse relationship between the building of the Land of Israel (the built city) and the destruction of ethereal Jerusalem. The building of the Land by "the Zionists and the followers of the Mizrahi and the Agudah" (all of whom he considers as indistinguishable) is leading to the "destruction of Holy Jerusalem."[82]

The impasse facing European Jewry grew steadily worse. In 1936 Shapira again discussed the persecution of the German Jews. He acknowledged that they had desecrated the Sabbath and were considered "criminals" due to their abandonment of the religious way of life, but he could not justify the Divine sentence they now faced: "Are the Hitlerists, may the name of the evil rot, better than them?!" He warned God, "Soon, there will be no-one left." The rabbi correctly sensed that Jewish existence in Europe was hanging by a thread and that they would soon be sent like lambs to the slaughter. Shapira sounded despairing in this sermon. He emphasized that the only solution was to cling to the old ways, in hope that God would send the true messiah to rescue the Jews from their distress. He likened the situation to that of a father who beats his sons so that they will behave properly: "Woe betide us that we have led the *Shekhinah* (Divine Presence) to regret and bemoan the sorrow of its sons." Again, his conclusion is that only repentance can save the Jews.[83]

In the book *The Order of the Last Year*, Shapira's disciples described his magical actions to promote redemption during the last days of his life.

---

[81] *Ibid.*, pp. 4–6.   [82] *Ibid.*, p. 8.   [83] *Ibid.*, pp. 6–10.

In his Rosh Hashanah sermon he described the deprivations facing the Jews as a mundane reflection of the war taking place in heaven between God and the *Sitra Ahra* (the "Other Side"). Just as God is involved in the ultimate battle against evil, so His believers wage a similar struggle in the mundane world. This description seeks to reinforce his followers' belief that this year will indeed be the last, and that they should conduct themselves as if they were in a war with the Evil Impulse. The time is one of repentance and, accordingly, one that embodies the opportunity for redemption.[84]

On Yom Kippur Shapira expected redemption to arrive thanks to the repentance of the masses. During the prefast meal, "the rabbi was seized by dread and fear [...] that the great and awesome day of the Lord was imminent."[85] During the prayers, he repeated several times the blessing from the traditional liturgy: "A year of redemption and salvation in the coming of the messiah, speedily and in our days, Amen." Throughout the fast day he behaved strangely, and on its conclusion he refused to greet his followers with the traditional blessing "happy new year" and refused to break his fast, seeking to extend the day in order to grant more time for the messiah to appear.[86]

A few days later, at Sukkot, Shapira again awaited the arrival of the messiah. He began his sermon on Hoshanah Rabbah by proclaiming, "I am not a preacher of sermons! Perhaps I am no more than a bad jester!" Alluding to his sense of despair, he asked, "Has God forgotten his beloved son?" He turned to God and begged for mercy and forgiveness despite the people's sins. The Tzadik's prayer sought to awaken the patriachs of the Jewish faith. Turning to Jacob, he cried out: "How can you remain silent on seeing your children in such trouble!"[87] He stood opposite the ark containing the Torah scrolls and cried: "How much longer must we wait? I am already exhausted!"[88] During the Hakafot dancing on Simchat Torah he entered an ecstatic state, danced wildly while crying, and beseeched God: "See, O Lord, who is like Your people Israel? Send us the Redeemer."[89]

Sukkot ended without the messiah appearing. In a conversation with his followers, the rabbi presented various calculations suggesting that the date of redemption would be three years later in 5701 (1940). Shapira based his remarks on a comment in the writings of the Sages that during

---

[84] Yitzhak Adler, *The Order of the Last Year*, pp. 146–7.   [85] *Ibid.*, p. 168.

[86] *Ibid.*, pp. 170–8.   [87] Goldstein, *Tikun Olam*, pp. 3–11.

[88] Adler, *The Order of the Last Year*, p. 189.   [89] *Ibid.*, p. 213.

the three hours preceding redemption, there would be terrible birth pangs of the messiah. He claimed that each of God's days comprises 1000 years. According, three hours of such a day are equivalent to 125 years. In 5675 (1815), three Tzadikim of the generation passed away: Yisrael Hopstein, the Maggid of Kozhnitz (thirteen Tishrei); Rabbi Menachem Mendel of Rimanov (nineteen Iyar); and the Visionary of Lublin, Yaacov Yitzhak Horowitz (nine Av). A reckoning of 125 years from the year of their death leads to 5701 (1940), and, accordingly, the ultimate redemption could not come later than that year.[90] Elsewhere, Shapira played with numbers and letters in order to hint that an apocalyptic event would occur in 5702 (September 1941). He claimed that if Jews in the Land of Israel failed to observe the Sabbath, it would vomit them out. According to his calculations, this dramatic event would occur in 5702 (1941/2).[91]

Shapira also defended the eschatological calculations of the Admor of Shinava, who had claimed that redemption would occur in 5666 (1906). Although many years had passed since this date, Shapira urged his followers not to despair. "The beginning of salvation came then, and, soon in our days, the good ending of true salvation will arrive."[92] Thus the messianic process began before Shapira and would soon come to completion. In his sermon at Hanukkah, Shapira promised his followers that the hidden light of the King Messiah would be revealed during the Festival of Lights. Immediately after completing his sermon, Shapira died.

Rachel Elior argues that the ideal leadership of the Tzadik as presented in Hasidic writings includes four key elements: charisma, mutual devotion and responsibility, embodiment of the divine dialectic, and the linking of the divine and the material. On the basis of these elements, I will attempt to describe Shapira's sermons as an effort to expedite the End.

According to Elior, charisma – the Divine grace granted to the Tzadik – is characterized by the transformation of the Tzadik into a tool and conduit for converting concealed Divine bounty into overt bounty and for converting abstract Divine grace into tangible grace that meets human needs. This process can be seen in Shapira's actions: He sought to serve as a conduit for bringing the King Messiah, who would put an end to the deprivation and persecution of the Jews. "Mutual devotion and responsibility," Elior explains, refers to the double-edged perception of the Tzadik's leadership, from the perspective of his flock and from God's perspective. She claims that the Tzadik is superior to the masses due to his

---

[90] *Ibid.*, p. 227.   [91] Shapira, *Mashmia Yeshua*, p. 66.
[92] Adler, *The Order of the Last Year*, pp. 285–6.

direct contact with the Divine being. He must represent his flock to God as a public emissary. The Divine bounty he enjoys must be channeled in favor of his believers – action on behalf of the collective is the condition for his receiving this gift. Accordingly, the Tzadik is dependent on his followers, who give him the strength to stand before God. Again, this can be seen in the case of Shapira: His demands that his followers repent filled him with energy, which he could then use in order to raise his demands for messiah. His status as a mediator between the lower beings (his flock) and the upper being (God) creates an awakening of the former that will lead to an awakening in the latter.

According to Elior's analysis, Hasidism attributes the Tzadik with the ability to exert a supernatural influence over the upper and lower worlds; his function is to mediate between the two. The Tzadik can embody the transition from "nothingness" (*ayin*) to "everything there is" (*yesh*) and to grant material and spiritual bounty. Through his magic prayers Shapira sought to transform the flawed world into a perfect one. The Tzadik's mystical powers to consort with God are not a goal in their own right, but are intended to enable God's bounty to be brought down and bestowed on the community. Shapira's efforts and his intimate relationship with God were intended to secure the sublime goal of expediting redemption.[93]

Shapira used the events of the Hebrew calendar in order to inspire his listeners to repent – an action that embodies a cosmic dimension. Their response was the instrument he could use to expedite the End and bring the messiah. He also used his status as the Tzadik of his generation, employing prayer in an effort to engage in magic actions that would awaken God, Rabbi Shimon Bar Yochai, and the founders of the Jewish faith to send the true messiah. This, perhaps, explains Shapira's uniqueness. While the Hasidic Tzadik bears spiritual responsibility for his congregation, and his mystical powers must provide spiritual benefit for his followers, Shapira may have seen himself as the "founding Tzadik of the world," who must play the role of the harbinger of redemption for all Israel.

SHAPIRA CONFRONTS PROPHETIC FAILURE

In his lifetime Rabbi Shapira was forced to cope with the failure of repeated messianic predictions: the full redemption did not arrive as the

---

[93] Rachel Elior, *The Mystical Origins of Hasidism*. Oxford and Portland: Littman Library of Jewish Civilization, 2006, pp. 126–51.

result of World War I; Alfandri died in front of his eyes; the messiah did not appear during the last year of his life.

The well-known work *When Prophecy Fails* presents a theory of how people deal with cognitive dissonance. The model created by Leon Festinger et al. argues that when believers are faced with facts that contradict their beliefs, they prefer to ignore the facts and to adhere to their beliefs. To do so, they require outside confirmation that they are right; accordingly, in many cases, prophetic failure creates a strong proselytizing tendency.[94] The cognitive dissonance theory is almost fifty years old and many scholars argue that its principles have not withstood the test of research. In order to unite all the knowledge accumulated in the study of cognitive dissonance, Lorne Dawson developed a model according to which, when prophecy fails, three possible reactions can result: intensified *proselytization*, sundry *rationalizations*, and acts of *reaffirmation*. Whereas Festinger and his team argued that proselytization is a key component for the movement's survival, many case studies published after *When Prophecy Fails* prove that proselytization is actually very rare. Rationalizing is the key tool used to respond to failure, and it can develop in several different ways. The use of mysticism to spiritualize prophecy is one of the main approaches; others include arguing that the prophecy was a test of faith, blaming others for the failure (on the grounds of misinterpretation), or blaming others for interfering with the fulfillment of prophecy. Reaffirmation comes through inner work to increase social solidarity through special educational activities, celebrations, and rituals.[95]

If we examine Shapira's response on the basis of these insights, his growing demand for repentance can be explained as a tool for proselytizing in order to reduce cognitive tension.

The rabbi also offered many rational explanations for failure. For example, in his responsa *Minhat Elazar*, he addressed the failure of his prophecy concerning the First World War, arguing that all the signs suggested that the war was indeed the manifestation of the birth pangs of redemption. The reason why messiah failed to appear at the end of the war, he said, was because the *Sitra Ahra* (Satan) worked to fail it with his many soldiers – "the leaders and many hypocrite Rebbes etc, etc." The

---

[94] Leon Festinger, Henry W. Reicken, and Stanley Schachter, *When Prophecy Fails: A Social and Psychological Study of a Modern Group That Predicted the Destruction of the World*. Minneapolis: University of Minnesota Press, 1956.

[95] Lorne Dawson, "Clearing the Underbush: Moving Beyond Festinger to a New Paradigm for the Study of Failed Prophecy." In: Diana Tumminia and William Statos, Jr. (eds.), *How Prophecy Lives*. Leiden and Boston: Brill, 2011, pp. 69–98.

Rebbes, who worked in Satan's service, fooled all of the Jewish people into praying for the peace of the nations, instead of praying for full redemption, and accordingly redemption was denied. The Rebbes' prayers for peace brought Satan's victory. Therefore, peace is even worse for the Jews than war itself. Another approach was to blame Jewish merchants who desecrated the Sabbath during the war.[96] From Shapira's response, we learn that his rationalization of failure focused on attempts to blame a third party. Those who are responsible, according to his analysis, are those who refused to follow his spiritual path, and prayed for peace and to the end of war, instead of praying for the collective redemption. These saboteurs include even his fellow spiritual leaders, other Hasidic Rebbes.

Alfandri's death dealt a further blow to Shapira's predictions. In this case, his coping mechanism was spiritualization. Thus, what ostensibly seemed to be a failure was recast as the realization of the prophecy of redemption in the Divine spheres. This technique enables the revival of hopes of redemption following their ostensible failure, and the expectation of imminent mundane realization.[97] While on his return journey from Palestine, the rabbi already found his explanation for the death of the intended messiah. He felt that Alfandri had died in order to speak out for the Children of Israel in heaven and expedite redemption from above. The explanation for his death came through the spiritualization of failure and its definition as realization on Divine levels invisible to mortal eyes. This explanation allowed Shapira to describe the Tzadik's death as a further step in the path toward full redemption, since Alfandri was now even closer to God and could therefore be more effective in his pleas for the messiah. Thus what may appear to be failure is actually progress. Only the mystic (Shapira) can know the concealed truth, thanks to his special powers, and thereby breathe new life into messianic expectations.

Reconfirmation activities were also apparent in the manner in which Shapira dealt with cognitive dissonance. For example, during the last year of his life, after all the dates he had mentioned had passed, he pushed the date of redemption forward by several years through eschatological calculations. This enabled him to argue that the messianic hope had not been

---

[96] Shapira, *Minhat Elazar* 5, section 36.

[97] Gordon Melton, "Spiritualization and Reaffirmation: What Really Happens When Prophecy Fails," *American Studies* 26(2), 1985, 17–29; Lorne L. Dawson, "When Prophecy Fails and Faith Persists: A Theoretical Overview," *Nova Religio* 3(1) (1999), 6–82.

thwarted, but merely delayed. Shapira employed a similar approach in order to justify the failure of the eschatological prediction of the Admor of Shinava, and said that his calculations predicted only the beginning of the messianic process, and were therefore still valid. Shapira's sermons and pleas for the messiah, as part of his High Holiday prayers, can similarly be explained as rituals of reconfirmation of his messianic expectations, despite the growing sense of failure and despair.

DISCUSSION

The facts presented so far reflect messianic tension and growing expectation of messianic redemption. This material can be interpreted in two distinct ways. Firstly, a restrictive analysis will argue that while this review reveals messianic foment, it does not reveal personal messianic activism or the identification of a specific individual as the messiah. Even the search for the founding Tzadik of the world does not imply actual self-identification as messiah, but merely a further step toward this stage. Accordingly, it cannot be concluded that Shapira saw himself or Alfandri as candidates to be enthroned as the messiah. Secondly, a more expansive interpretation of the material will lead to the conclusion that the messianic fervor described in the material was intended to create a positive identification between the Tzadik and the messiah. According to this approach, Shapira indeed saw himself as a candidate for the role of a Tzadik who is also the messiah.

I will address each of these possible interpretations in turn. According to the restrictive interpretation, the evidence surrounding Shapira's visit to Jerusalem does not necessarily suggest that the purpose of his journey was to identify the messiah, but rather to find a Tzadik. The dream of the Komarno rabbi indeed speaks of the need to find a Tzadik and does not explicitly mention the word "messiah." Moreover, Margaliot's testimony that he approached Alfandri and asked "When will my Lord arrive?" was published decades after the actual event and should be regarded with caution. As for the debate with the Gerrer Rebbe, this can be seen as no more than a principled argument over matters of education. There is no absolute proof of any messianic dispute raging beneath the surface.

By contrast, the expansive interpretation argues that Alfandri's identification as the Tzadik also implies that he was seen as the messiah. This approach is proven in several places in the work *Jerusalem Travels*, which, as noted, was published while Shapira was still alive and received his approbation. Firstly, the exchange of correspondence between the rabbis before the delegation departed shows that there was an expectation that messiah would be revealed in the very near future – less than one month. This narrows the time gap between the Tzadik and the messiah to the point that the two are virtually synonymous. Secondly, after Alfandri's death Shapira cried out: "Oy, the messiah of the God of Jacob!" This clearly implies that he considered Alfandri to be the potential messiah. Accordingly, Margaliot's testimony merely provides further support for this narrative and its late date does not detract from its reliability. Moreover, the fusion of the Tzadik and the messiah is not an unusual approach in the Hasidic world. The scholar Yeshaya Tishbi, for example, has commented that to see the Tzadik as merely one of the steps toward the role of messiah "is not the type of statement that is common in Hasidic literature."[98] As mentioned, Zvi Mark noted the similarity between the figure of the messiah and that of the Tzadik, a role that is absolutely identified in the character of Rabbi Nachman of Breslov. During the outburst of messianism in Habad in the 1990s, the Hasidim identified their Rabbi Menachem Mendel Schneerson as the complete embodiment of both the Tzadik and the messiah.

Regarding the dispute with the Gerrer Rebbe about the methods of study in the Metivta, there is indeed no conclusive evidence that this embodied any messianic tension. However, according to the expansive interpretation, this debate cannot be divorced from the broader context of Shapira's public activities and his conviction that the revelation of the Tzadik must come through public leadership. This debate clearly presents the contrast between true leadership (Shapira) and false leadership (Alter) and, accordingly, it can be seen as vital in order to prove Shapira's suitability for the role of Tzadik/messiah. Since Alter was one of the most prominent leaders of his generation, his condemnation can be seen as an extremely important task for Shapira.

We might also propose an intermediary approach between these two positions. There is indeed no unequivocal evidence in Shapira's writings that he considered himself a candidate for the role of Tzadik in the sense of messiah; neither can this be found in his followers' writings. All the evidence that has been presented is indirect and subject to different interpretations. Due to the sensitive nature of making such a declaration in his lifetime, and due to fear of failure and disgrace (such as that which

---

[98] Yeshayah Tishbi, "The Messianic Idea and Messianic Tendencies in the Rise of Hasidism," *Zion* 22 (5727 – 1967), 35 (in Hebrew).

occurred during his visit to Jerusalem), Shapira may well have found it more convenient to adopt a vague stance on the matter. To return to the example of the messianic outburst in Habad, Schneerson never declared himself to be the messiah, although it was clear to his followers that this was his intention. This explains the caution exercised by Hasidim in raising such claims. After Shapira's death they could easily omit this aspect from their testimonies since it had never been stated explicitly.

I would add that remaining in this intermediate sphere also enabled Shapira to advance and retreat in his self-identification as messiah. It is possible that there was a retreat in his position during the last year of his life. During this year, as we noted, his earlier eschatological calculations failed to materialize, as did his prediction that messiah would appear by no later than the festival of Sukkot. After this failure, he again postponed the End by a further three or four years. Shapira was gravely ill by this stage and was aware of his condition, referring to himself as "exhausted." Thus after postponing the date for the End Times, the rabbi may have realized that this event would not come during his own life. In his final sermon, Shapira stated that the hidden light of messiah had been revealed at Hanukkah – the first stage in the messianic process. Thus, he clearly did not believe by this stage that he was the messiah.

My conclusion is that Alfandri's death enabled the identification of a new founding Tzadik of the world. In my opinion, it is certainly possible that Shapira saw himself as a candidate for the role of the concealed Tzadik. Such a conclusion could be based on the following factors: Shapira's personal qualities were similar to Alfandri in terms of his zealotry and forcefulness; his struggle against the Gerrer Rebbe showed that he was the type of leader awaited by the "upper worlds" according to the dream of the Komarno Rabbi; his prayers and spiritual beseeching for the coming of messiah could be seen as a reflection of his special status, above that of any other Hasidic Tzadik. As he approached death, however, it is possible that Shapira was less inclined to identify himself as a candidate for this role.

CONCLUSION

The description of Shapira's messianic tension illuminates a broader phenomenon regarding messianic expectations in Orthodox Judaism during the period preceding the Second World War. These expectations did not wane with Shapira's death, and later, in the 1990s, they would reemerge in full force in the Habad movement, whose leader Menachem Mendel Schneerson was crowned as the king messiah. Several interesting similarities can be noted between the two instances:[99] Both Hasidic leaders were the subject of messianic tension during their years of activity, but in both cases the dramatic eruption came as they neared the end of their life. Neither leader had a son to inherit their leadership position: Shapira had a daughter but no sons, while Schneerson was childless. Both leaders hinted at their own messianic status but did not unequivocally externalize this claim. Both instances had a leadership style that embodied many of the expected traits of the "founding Tzadik of the world," and both were particularly careful to promote the strict observance of the Sabbath as a magical action with eschatological force. The main difference between the two is that while the messianic eruption in Munkacs was confined to the inner circle around Shapira, the eruption in Habad encompassed the entire movement and was widely exposed to the general public. Since his death, Schneerson has had no successor.

Shapira's successor as the head of the Hasidic radicals, Rabbi Yoel Teitelbaum, also expounded an acute form of messianic expectation. However, the background against which he acted was radically different, dominated by the Holocaust and the establishment of the State of Israel. Shapira and Teitelbaum operated in the same geographical domain and had similar views. Teitelbaum was a generation younger than Shapira, having undergone his education and early rabbinical experience at a time when Shapira was already the leader of the radical camp in Hungary. The two leaders shared an antimodernist approach and a profound opposition to Zionism. They both negated any Jewish activism in the Land of Israel that was not devoted solely to Torah study. Like Shapira, Yoel Teitelbaum also believed that he was living through the days preceding the arrival of messiah and that his generation had reached such a nadir that the only rational conclusion was that the just Redeemer was about to appear. However, the differences between the two figures are striking. Teitelbaum based his anti-Zionist approach on the Talmudic legend of the Three Oaths and thus claimed that the Holocaust was a divine punishment for the sin of Zionism (see Chapter 6). He opposed any action to expedite the End, even on the

---

[99] For further discussion of the Habad case, see: Heilman and Friedman, *The Rebbe*.

spiritual plane. Shapira, by contrast, did not quote the Three Oaths and did not employ this rhetoric in his opposition to Zionism. Moreover, his entire life was devoted to a spiritual endeavor to expedite redemption and bring the End.

The scholar Benjamin Brown interestingly noted that by the nineteenth century all the Hungarian rebbes had adopted a highly nomistic approach: Hasidic leaders defended the Halakhah and adopted the radical ultra-Orthodox approach. The most radical of these figures was Tzvi Elimelech of Dinow, Shapira's great-great-grandfather. However, among these rabbinical circles a doctrine of "holiness of sin" had also developed and Tzvi Elimelech was one of the advocates of this approach. He argued that actions undertaken for the sake of Heaven, even if they constituted a transgression, would nevertheless count as good deeds. This approach was also found among the members of the Teitelbaum dynasty and was noted by Yekutiel Yehuda (Yetev Lev) Teitelbaum (1808–1883), Yoel's grandfather.

Brown describes this as a "soft antinomism" and emphasizes that he was unable to find any "smoking gun" instance in which a specific transgression was recorded and then justified as a sin for the sake of Heaven. However, he suggests that these actions were concealed and does not believe these discussions were merely theoretical. Brown offers several explanations for the use of this doctrine, suggesting that it may have provided a convenient excuse for delays in prayers; the use of extreme means against rivals; and the appointment of nonobservant Jews to key positions in various Orthodox communities.[100]

On the basis of our earlier discussion, I would like to offer another explanation for the use of this doctrine. According to the rabbinical literature, actions that are intended to hasten the End are forbidden. However, Rabbis Tzvi Elimelech of Dinow and Yekutiel Yehuda Teitelbaum were known as keen eschatologists (see Chapter 6). Based on the research on Chaim Elazar Shapira, who continued his ancestor's radical traditions and was also a keen eschatologist, it might be hypothesized that taking action to draw the redemption closer could be understood as a "holy sin." It is possible that his fervent belief in the imminence of redemption, combined with his deteriorating state of

---

[100] Benjamin Brown, "The Two Faces of Religious Radicalism: Orthodox Zealotry and 'Holy Sinning' in Nineteenth-Century Hasidism in Hungary and Galicia," *Journal of Religion* 93(3) (2013), 341–74.

health and his deep conviction that his own intentions were pure and sublime, pushed him to transgress the explicit prohibition against hastening the End.

The biography of Chaim Elazar Shapira offers insight into the early roots of a stream that would assume central importance in the Hasidic world following the Second World War. Messianic tension is a vital component in understanding his life, and in understanding the development of radical ultra-Orthodox Hasidism.

5

The life and work of Rabbi Yoel Teitelbaum, founder of the Satmar Hasidic court in New York

We now turn to an examination of the biography and character of Rabbi Yoel Teitelbaum (1887–1979), the Satmar Rebbe. Over the course of his life, Teitelbaum was involved in dramatic events in spanning different countries and continents. He first gained prominence as a young Hasidic rabbi in Hungary during the last years of Jewish life in this region before the Nazi occupation. During the Second World War, Teitelbaum managed with great difficulty to escape and save his life. After the war he became a central figure in the revival of the Hasidic world in the United States. He served as the spiritual leader of one of the largest Hasidic courts, which he rebuilt almost from scratch, and he also headed the most extreme faction within the Haredi community in Jerusalem.

Teitelbaum gained a reputation as a strict, zealous, and uncompromising religious leader. His appointment as head of the religious court (*Gaon Av Beit Hadin*) of the Haredi community in Jerusalem and his fierce struggle against Zionism certainly contributed to this image. However, a careful examination of his biography and the paths he chose, against the backdrop of the Hasidic world and the options open to him, paints a more complex picture. Even the greatest of zealots found that compromise was sometimes unavoidable on various issues, such as the status of women and education; even the fiercest opponent of the State of Israel adopted a de facto stance that was far more nuanced and may even have approached that of Agudat Yisrael at a certain point in his life, as we shall see. And although Teitelbaum headed HaEdah HaHaredit, a community based on outside donations, he supported the idea that young men from the community should participate in the work force.

Teitelbaum is acknowledged as a key figure in contemporary Haredi Judaism; several scholars have examined his spiritual outlook[1] and the Hasidic court he founded in New York.[2] I will discuss the rabbi's ideology in the next chapter and offer some new lines of thought relative to the existing research. Until recently, however, academic works have not addressed Teitelbaum's life story or examined the manner in which his spiritual world influenced the paths he chose and the Hasidic court he founded.[3]

Unsurprisingly, an external researcher who seeks to explore Teitelbaum's biography encounters an objective problem: a closed religious community that advocates ideological isolationism will inevitably be reluctant to open itself to outsiders. This may explain why many researchers have refrained from examining Teitelbaum's life story, concentrating instead on his readily available written thought. While the Blau Archive has opened a window into the world of the Jerusalem zealots, I did not enjoy access to any similar source illuminating the world of the Satmar Rebbe. Accordingly I was obliged to rely on the hagiographical sources. The disadvantage of such sources by way of historical documentation is obvious: they are selective, prone to adulation, and on occasions descend into flights of fancy. A comparison of different hagiographic works helped me identify nuances and differences and raised several key issues regarding Teitelbaum's biography. Even when all the sources present a united front, however, this cannot be regarded as the absolute truth. The

---

[1] Refael Kadosh, *Extremist Religious Philosophy: The Radical Religious Doctrines of the Satmar Rebbe*. PhD Dissertation, The University of Cape Town, 2011 (in Hebrew); Norman Lamm, "The Ideology of the Neturei Karta: According to the Satmarer Version," *Tradition* 12(2) (1971), 38–53; Zvi Jonathan Kaplan, "Rabbi Joel Teitelbaum, Zionism, and Hungarian Ultra-Orthodoxy," *Modern Judaism* 24(2) (2004), 165–78; Allan L. Nadler, "Piety and Politics: The Case of the Satmar Rebbe," *Judaism* 31(2) (1982), 135–52; and David Sorotzkin, "Building the Earthly and Destroying the Heavenly: The Satmar Rebbe and Radical Orthodox School of Thought." In: Aviezer Ravitzky (ed.), *The Land of Israel in 20th Century Jewish Thought*. Jerusalem: Ben Zvi Institute, 2004, pp. 133–67 (in Hebrew).

[2] Israel Rubin, *Two Generations of Urban Island* (2nd edition). New York: Peter Lang, 1997; Jerome Mintz, *Hassidic People: A Place in the New World*. Cambridge: Harvard University Press, 1992; Solomon Poll, *The Hassidic Community of Williamsburg* (2nd edition). New Brunswick: Transaction Publishers, 2006.

[3] After the completion of this research, a doctoral dissertation was approved by the Senate of Tel Aviv University on the biography of the rabbi. The dissertation has a much more detailed narrative, however on the questions relating to the Holocaust a different position is presented than that I adopt here. See: Menachem Keren-Kratz, *R' Yoel Teitelbaum – The Satmar Rabbi (1887–1979): Biography*. PhD Dissertation, Tel Aviv University, 2013.

weakness of these sources is particularly apparent regarding the period 1944–1946, during the Holocaust in Hungary and the year that followed.

The historical facts relating to this period are ostensibly uncontroversial: The rabbi's life was saved thanks to the intervention of the representatives of the Zionist movement in Hungary, who enabled him to board the Kastner Train as part of the "blood for goods" deal between the representatives of the Budapest ghetto and the Nazi leadership. Since the rabbi later became the fiercest Jewish Orthodox opponent of Zionism, biographers from within the Satmar were forced to confront the ethical ramifications of the fact that he owed his life to Zionist activists.

I will present the Satmar narrative regarding the Holocaust period shortly, while noting significant gaps, internal contradictions, and different versions. I will also propose alternative hypotheses based on various allusions in the sources.

A valuable resource was published in English in 2011: the bibliography of Teitelbaum by Dovid Meisels,[4] one of the Rebbe's closest associates, particularly during his latter years. The level of detail in this work revealed new nuances and refined my overall assessment of Teitelbaum. This bibliography joins an earlier work by Alexander (Sander) Deitsch, a prominent figure in Satmar.[5] These two works present different positions on certain questions and their authors are identified with different factions within the movement. Accordingly, they highlight the divisions within Satmar and cast light on the different narratives regarding the Rebbe's biography. Each biographer seeks to justify his position on the basis of the revered leader's actions. Another important source is *Moshian shel Yisrael*, an extremely comprehensive Hasidic biography on which I draw in order to illuminate various aspects of the Rebbe's life. This biography contains copies of many useful primary sources.[6]

This chapter discusses three periods. The first section examines Teitelbaum's life through the outbreak of the Second World War, while the second describes his escape from Hungary, arrival in Switzerland, and emigration to Mandatory Palestine, as well as the circumstances that later led him to emigrate to the United States. The final section discusses the

---

[4] Dovid Meisels, *The Rebbe – The Extraordinary Life and Worldview of Rabbeinu Yoel Teitelbaum the Satmar Rebbe*. Lakewood, NJ: Israel Book Shop, 2011.

[5] Alexander Deitsch, *Butzina Kadisha*, 1–2. New York: Tiferes Publishing, 1998, 2000 (in Hebrew).

[6] Shlomo Yaacov Gelbman, *Moshian Shel Yisrael*, vol. 1–9. Kiryas Yoel: Ohel Torah Publishers, 1989–2008 (in Hebrew).

reconstruction of the Satmar Hasidic court in the United States and the founding of the Hasidic enclave.

THE EARLY PERIOD: 1887–1944

The Teitelbaum family settled in the Marmaros area in 1808 after Moshe Teitelbaum (1758–1841) was appointed rabbi of the Jewish community in Ujhely. After visiting the Tzadik of Lublin, Teitelbaum was convinced by his approach and adopted a Hasidic identity. Teitelbaum established a new school of Hasidic leadership that was scholastic and strict. He sought to install his son Eliezer Nissan (1785–1855) as rabbi of the community of Sziget in the Marmaros region, but Eliezer Nissan resigned after five unsuccessful years in the position. Shortly before his death Teitelbaum appointed his grandson Yekutiel Yehuda Teitelbaum (1803–1883), also known as Zalman Leib, as his successor in Ujhely. After his death, however, the community removed Yekutiel Yehuda from his position. Many years later, in 1858, the grandson managed to secure the position of rabbi of Sziget after his father's unsuccessful experience in the community had been forgotten.[7] His appointment came at the height of the crisis in Hungarian Jewry that would lead to the split between the Orthodox and Neolog movements. Yekutiel Yehuda viewed any innovation, without exception, as a threat to traditional Judaism and his response was uncompromising and extreme. He was only willing to compromise on the question of modern education when state coercion made this inevitable. Menachem Keren-Kratz argues that the opposition to modern education on the part of the Teitelbaum dynasty in the late nineteenth century led to widespread ignorance and illiteracy in Marmaros, where their influence was at its strongest. He also notes that Yekutiel Yehuda Teitelbaum adopted the enclave model, rejecting any sense of responsibility for the public as a whole and focusing solely on preserving his own narrow community.[8]

Yekutiel's death led to a protracted leadership struggle. Eventually his son Hanania Yom Tov Lipa Teitelbaum (1834–1914) was appointed rabbi of Sziget and went on to become one of the leaders of Hungarian

---

[7] David Shen, *Lovers of G-d in the Carpathian Mountains*. Jerusalem: Shem Publishers, 5765 – 2004, pp. 11–119 (in Hebrew).

[8] Menachem Keren-Kratz, *Marmaros–Sziget: "Extreme Orthodoxy" and Secular Jewish Culture at the Foothills of the Carpathian Mountains*. Jerusalem: Carmel, 2013, pp. 77–80 (in Hebrew).

Hasidism. Hanania became involved in the anti-Zionist struggle from an early stage. In 1898 he launched a public campaign to promote women's modesty and oppose new fashions in clothing. Evidence also suggests that he used violent agents to attack those who disobeyed traditional norms in a manner similar to the current-day "modesty patrols."[9]

Yoel Teitelbaum was the younger son of Chananiya Yom Tov Lipa and Hannah Teitelbaum. His elder brother was called Chaim Zvi, and he also had three sisters: Sarah, Esther, and Hessa. The Teitelbaum family was active in the towns of Sziget and Ujhely in Hungary, and he later established a presence in Krohle and Satmar,[10] both towns with a significant Jewish population.[11] The Jewish community in the Carpathian Mountains was divided into various factions and the Hasidic community itself included three major dynasties: Vizhnitz, Teitelbaum, and Spinka.

Yoel Teitelbaum was engaged to his wife Chava when he was just seven and the couple married when he reached the age of eighteen. The wedding was brought forward as Yoel's father, Chananiya Yom Tov Teitelbaum, was gravely ill; he passed away some two weeks after the event.

After the death of the father, his elder son Chaim Zvi, who was based in Sziget, was appointed his successor.[12] The eldest son was usually considered the natural heir in Hasidic dynasties and the Teitelbaum family was no exception to this rule. Chaim Zvi was married to the granddaughter of Chaim Halberstadt, the Sanzer Rebbe and one of the most important Admors (Hasidic leaders) of Hungarian Jewry, underscoring the high prestige in which the Teitelbaum dynasty was held.[13]

When one son inherits his father's position as Rebbe his married brothers usually leave the city in order to prevent rivalry and competition. Yoel and his wife duly moved to Satmar, where he joined the local yeshivah as a regular student. According to the biographer Alexander Deitsch, Satmar was not a Hasidic center at this time (1904) and most of the leaders of the community belonged to the opposing scholastic stream of Orthodox Judaism.[14] Yoel does not seem to have made a particularly good impression on some of the communal leaders during his first stay in Satmar: years later, when his name was first raised as a candidate for the

---

[9] *Ibid.*
[10] The name of the city also appears as Satu Mare and Szatmár; the spelling Satmar is standard in the Jewish context.
[11] Avraham Fuchs, *The Admor of Satmar*. Jerusalem: self-publication, 5740–1980, p. 17.
[12] *Ibid.*, pp. 31, 63.   [13] Cf. Deitsch, *Butzina I*, p. 42.   [14] *Ibid.*, p. 51.

position of Av Beit Din (head of the Jewish religious court) in the city, the proposal provoked fierce opposition and his candidacy was delayed for almost six years.[15]

In order to understand why Teitelbaum aroused such strong negative reactions, two aspects should be considered: Issues relating to the development of the Hasidic movement at the time, and Teitelbaum's personality as reflected in his followers' descriptions.

In his important study on Hasidism in Poland, Mendel Piekarz argues that a process of degeneration was seen in the seventh and eighth generations of the movement; this process was particularly apparent in the case of the Hungarian Hasidic movement. Piekarz explains that Hasidism was founded as a radical movement that sought to change the religious way of life, emphasizing spiritual experience rather than the scholasticism, which had been the supreme value of Rabbinical Judaism. However, the classic values of Hasidism could not withstand the growing pressure of secularism. The writings of Hasidic leaders show that they reached the conclusion that an essentially personal spiritual experience did not provide a sufficiently strong bulwark against the tide of secularization. Accordingly, these leaders believed that religious life must once again be grounded in the strictest observance of the traditional way of life and in study of the Torah. In the generations preceding the Second World War the leaders of European Hasidism clung zealously to Jewish tradition and opposed any change. The way to cope with the challenges of secularism, they argued, was to adhere to Torah study as the foundation of the religious way of life: a position that was diametrically opposed to the original goals of Hasidism.[16]

There is a personal aspect of this question. It emerges that Yoel Teitelbaum (also known by the nickname "Yoelish") showed an excessive attention to cleanliness even as a young boy. The Hasidic biographer Dovid Meisels claims that he was seen washing his body and face obsessively as a child, and various teachers and acquaintances claimed to have observed this behavior since Yoel was as young as two. His mother was apparently disturbed by this character streak and expressed her unhappiness. As the years passed, Teitelbaum's obsession with cleanliness seems

[15] In more details about the campaign to win the Satmar community see: David Myers, "'Commanded War:' Three Chapters in the 'Military' History of Satmar Hasidim," *Journal of the American Academy of Religion*, 81(2) 2013, pp. 1–46; Keren-Kratz, *R' Yoel*, pp. 95–174.

[16] Mendel Piekarz, *Ideological Trends in Poland during the Interwar Period and the Holocaust*. Jerusalem: Bialik Institute, 1990, pp. 37–49 (in Hebrew).

only to have become more extreme. Meisels relates that in winter the Rebbe would wash himself in ice-cold water before the morning prayers; as he prayed, the other worshippers could see his blue lips and shivering body. Meisels claims that "this was a practice he continued his entire life."[17] Meisels portrays this behavior as a positive trait reflecting a desire on Teitelbaum's part to purify himself before attending to sacred matters. According to the biographer Shlomo Yaacov Gelbman, Teitelbaum suffered from constipation from an early age; his followers recall that he would spend hours a day on the toilet. The Hasidic biographers saw this as further evidence of his desire to purify his body.[18] From a modern perspective, however, the descriptions seem to be consistent with an obsessive compulsive disorder. Throughout his life the Rebbe placed great emphasis on cleanliness and purity, and wherever he exerted his influence he was concerned to encourage the construction of ritual baths and related matters.

It is possible, then, that the opposition to Teitelbaum was the result of two factors: The Hasidic tendency to conservatism and insularity, on the one hand, and the Rebbe's personality traits and obsessive quest for purity, which complemented and highlighted the conservative nature of the movement, on the other.

Teitelbaum's first rabbinical appointment was in 1911 in the city of Orshiva, which at the time was within the borders of Carpatho-Russia. Orshiva was a small, poor city whose religious life was in a state of degeneration. Yoel's brother Chaim-Zvi recommended him to a delegation from the community. Some of the communal leaders opposed Yoel's candidacy but he overcame the hurdle and secured the appointment. Orshiva suffered badly during the battles of the First World War and many of its residents fled; Teitelbaum himself returned to Satmar.[19] After three years the Rebbe returned to Orshiva, where he remained until 1926. Toward the end of his period of office, Orshiva became a Zionist stronghold. Teitelbaum's main contribution to Jewish life in the city appears to have been the establishment of ritual baths.[20] As his own letters show, he was unable to halt the trend to secularization and the support for Zionism in the city.[21] Indeed, Menachem Keren-Kratz noted that Teitelbaum was unable to stop the growth of the Zionist movement in all the places in which we worked prior to the Second World War.[22]

---

[17] Meisels, *The Rebbe*, p. 23.   [18] Gelbman, *Moshian Shel Yisrael 1*, pp. 80–82.
[19] Deitsch, *Butzina 1*, pp. 54–9.   [20] *Ibid.*, pp. 58–9.   [21] Meisels, *The Rebbe*, p. 37.
[22] Keren-Kratz, *R' Yoel*, p. 162.

In 1926, while Teitelbaum was still in Orshiva, his elder brother died suddenly. His eldest son, Zalman-Leib, was fourteen at the time. Given these circumstances, Yoel Teitelbaum asked to serve as the rabbi of Sziget and to replace his brother as head of the dynasty. However, the leaders of the community rejected his candidacy, preferring instead to appoint the late Rebbe's young and inexperienced son.[23] However, the space created in the leadership of the dynasty allowed Yoel to gain prominence and to attract many of his father's followers. The same year he was appointed rabbi of Krohle in Romania, a larger and more important city than Orshiva.[24]

Teitelbaum visited Mandatory Palestine for the first time in 1932. During his stay in Jerusalem, Rabbi Yosef Chaim Sonnenfeld died and a search began to appoint a new leader for the community in the city. According to the Satmar sources Teitelbaum was offered the position of chief rabbi of the Haredi community in Jerusalem.[25] Keren-Kratz claims that the purpose of Teitelbaum's visit to Jerusalem was to promote his candidacy as Sonnenfeld's successor, and that he enjoyed the support of the members of Kollel Ungarin, the most extreme faction of the Haredi community in the city. However, Agudat Yisrael favored Rabbi Zvi Yosef Dushinsky from Khust in Ukraine, who was a well-known and prestigious rabbinical figure, though too flexible for the zealots' taste. Teitelbaum's supporters were unable to overturn the decision.[26]

Although Dushinsky received the appointment, Teitelbaum's supporters nevertheless issued a letter of appointment and invited him to come to Jerusalem, apparently in an attempt to split the ranks of Agudat Yisrael in the city.[27] Teitelbaum rejected the offer, citing two reasons. Firstly, he did not wish to leave his community. Secondly, "Even putting all this side there are all types of trials that cannot be detailed in letters and documents, and a number of difficult and tremendous obstacles standing like walls."[28] In any case, as noted, he had never been a serious contender for the position. However, his response suggests that he had a spiritual

[23] Rubin, *Satmar*, pp. 29–38.   [24] Deitsch, *Butzina 1*, p. 69.

[25] Meisels, *The Rebbe*, pp. 40.

[26] Menachem Keren-Kratz, "Maharitz Dushinsky: 'A Guard for the Guard,' – Thwarting the Rapprochement of Agudat Yisrael to Zionism." In: Benjamin Brown and Nissim Leon (eds.), *Hagdolim: The People who Shaped Haredi Judaism in Israel: A collection of Essays in Honor of Professor Menachem Friedman*. Jerusalem: Van Leer, (forthcoming) (in Hebrew).

[27] Shlomo Yaacov Gellman, *Moshian Shel Yisrael* 5. Kiryas Yoel: Ohel Torah Publishers, 1997, pp. 467–70 (in Hebrew).

[28] Deitsch, *Butzina 1*, p. 73.

difficulty in accepting the position in Jerusalem that he was not willing to discuss in detail. An examination of his attitude to Jerusalem throughout the course of his life suggests that he was reluctant to associate himself too closely with the city. Although he moved to Jerusalem after the end of the Second World War, he stayed in the city for less than a year before continuing to the United States. At a later stage, when he was offered the position of *Av Beit Din* of HaEdah HaHaredit, he conditioned his acceptance on an understanding that he would not be required to live in the city, but merely to visit it once every four years. My personal hypothesis is that his reticence regarding the holy city can be explained by his obsessive approach to issues of ritual cleanliness; it is possible that he felt that he was insufficiently pure to live in such a sacred place.

In 1928, Eliezer David Greenwald, the rabbi of the city of Satmar, passed away. Teitelbaum was offered the position and agreed. To his surprise, however, his appointment provoked fierce opposition within the community and was delayed until 1934. As mentioned, the residents of Satmar should have been well acquainted with Teitelbaum, who had spent at least seven years in the city as a yeshivah student and as a refugee from Orshiva. His visit to Jerusalem and the mention of his name as a possible candidate to lead the Haredi community had also raised his profile in Satmar. Although this "candidacy" was essentially artificial and self-initiated, it eventually enabled his supporters to placate the opposition to his appointment among the scholastic Orthodox population and among the Sanzer Hasidim.[29] Accordingly, in 1934 Teitelbaum assumed the position of the Rabbi of Satmar, a city with a population of some 50,000, of whom approximately 13,000 were Jews. The city was home to a large yeshivah with several hundred students.[30] He would remain in his position as head of the community until its annihilation in 1944.

Yoel Teitelbaum did not have any sons and therefore lacked a natural heir. He had three daughters from his first marriage to Chava: Chaya-Roiza, Rachel, and Esther. In 1921, his youngest daughter Esther passed away and was buried in Satmar. Another daughter, Rachel, died in 1931 after a protracted illness and did not leave any children. His eldest daughter survived the Holocaust but did not produce any heirs.

[29] Shlomo Yaacov Gelbman, *Moshian Shel Yisrael* 6. Kiryas Yoel: Ohel Torah Publishers, 1999, pp. 10–107 (in Hebrew).
[30] www.yadvashem.org/odot_pdf/Microsoft%20Word%20-%207459.pdf viewed on December 24, 2012

The death of the couple's two daughters profoundly scarred Chava; after Rachel's death she spent months crying for her child. Chava herself died in 1936. According to the Satmar biographer Dovid Meisels, she probably suffered from depression aggravated by her sorrow at the loss of her daughters.[31]

A year after Chava's death Teitelbaum married Alta Feiga, who was twenty-five years younger than the Rebbe. It eventually emerged that she was unable to have children. According to the Satmar Hasidim, Teitelbaum spent little time with his wife and their daily contact was confined to half an hour when they took tea and spoke together.[32] It should be noted that this pattern of minimal contact with the spouse was typical among the scholastic elite of the Haredi streams at the time.[33] The substantial age gap and the fact that the couple had no children may also have caused a degree of remoteness between the couple.[34] Nevertheless, the Rebbetzin (rabbi's wife) eventually emerged as the strongest figure in the movement after her husband suffered a stroke in 1968.

Toward the end of the 1920s the financial situation in the Marmaros region deteriorated, with a concomitant rise in anti-Semitism. This situation drove many Jews to express a desire to immigrate to Palestine and Orthodox leaders realized that unless they took action the masses would turn to Zionism. Therefore, many Orthodox rabbis in the region changed their opposition to settling the Land of Israel. In 1933 a major convention attended by some one thousand people was held in Sziget to discuss Haredi settlement in the Land of Israel. Yoel Teitelbaum agreed to support this activity and even sent a letter of support for the idea to be read at the conference. In 1935 several hundred Jews from Marmaros emigrated to Mandatory Palestine.[35]

THE HOLOCAUST

The rise to power of the Nazis and the outbreak of the Second World War completely destabilized the position of the Jews in Europe. Polish Jewry,

---

[31] Meisels, *The Rebbe*, pp. 55–56.   [32] *Ibid.*, pp. 57–60.

[33] Margalit Shilo, *Princess of Prisoner? Jewish Women in Jerusalem, 1840–1914*. Massachusetts: Brandeis University Press, 2005.

[34] Menachem Keren-Kratz argues that the relationship between the two was actually very good. He found that due to the marriage, the rabbi's relationship with his daughter Chaya Roiza deteriorated dramatically due to rivalry between the daughter and the wife, who was actually younger than the daughter. Keren-Kratz, *R' Yoel*, pp. 151–2. I disagree with Keren-Kratz's assessment of the relationship.

[35] *Ibid.*, pp. 122–5.

the largest community, was the first to be affected. Hungary remained an island of relative stability almost until the end of the war. Since the 1930s Hungary had been governed by a pro-Nazi party that had introduced anti-Jewish legislation. In 1940 Hungary joined the Fascist axis alongside Germany, Italy, and Japan. Due to its pro-Nazi tendencies, Hitler refrained from occupying Hungary, with the result that the condition of the Jews was better than in the countries that fell under direct German occupation. There were no ghettoes in Hungary, religious life and Zionist activities continued, and Hungarian Jews were not sent to the concentration or extermination camps (although several labor camps were established for Jews).

As the gates of the world remained closed to the European Jews, the only possibility for emigration, albeit on a limited scale, was to Mandatory Palestine. After the British published the "White Paper" which drastically cut the number of visas available for immigration, "certificates" allowing migration were given only to those who declared their support for Zionism. Haredi opponents of Zionism found themselves trapped.

Before entering into the discussion regarding Teitelbaum's actions during the Holocaust of Hungarian Jewry, it is worth pausing to examine the attitude of the Hasidic rabbinate in Hungary toward Zionism and Agudat Yisrael. As we have seen, the legend of the Three Oaths was interpreted as prohibiting any rebellion against the state of Exile of the Jewish people. On the basis of this source, some Hasidic rabbis were opposed to Zionist activities, which they considered an outrage against God's authority.[36] After the First World War and the Balfour Declaration, some Hasidic courts began to moderate their opposition to Zionism. However, this moderation was less apparent in Hasidic circles in Hungary, which continued their fierce opposition to the movement.[37] Agudat Yisrael became increasingly moderate in its attitude toward Zionism in the 1930s and adopted a de facto position of cautious cooperation with the movement.[38] As a result, the Hungarian Hasidic leaders opposed Agudat Yisrael and most of the Hasidic movements refused to support the new framework.

The Hasidic biographer Dovid Meisels claims that in 1940 Agudat Yisrael attempted to persuade the Hungarian leadership to take

---

[36] Aviezer Ravitzky, *Messianism, Zionism and Jewish Religious Radicalism*. Chicago and London: University of Chicago Press, 1993, pp. 40–78.
[37] Piekarz, *Polish Hassidism*, pp. 232–64.   [38] *Ibid.*, p. 259.

advantage of its quota for emigration to Palestine and to remove the senior rabbis from Hungary.[39] Agudat Yisrael argued that they should accept this proposal in accordance with the religious imperative to save lives (*pikuach nefesh*). At this time – shortly after the start of the war – many of the Hungarian religious leaders rejected this suggestion, presumably under the illusion that Hungary would continue to provide a relatively safe haven.

Menachem Keren-Kratz claims that in 1942 the Mizrahi movement offered Teitelbaum an immigration certificate but the movement's representatives were expelled from town in disgrace. Later Teitelbaum himself tried to obtain a certificate from Agudat Yisrael, but he was unwilling to sign a declaration of support to Agudat Yisrael and his application was duly rejected.[40] Teitelbaum instructed his followers to resist Agudat Yisrael's attempts to persuade them to emigrate. According to Meisels, his reasoning was as follows:

One may not join the Agudah because Agudah cooperates with the Zionists, working alongside with them to achieve a Jewish state. That state, once achieved, will certainly be ruled by heretics and non-believers who will use it as a vehicle to wipe out Torah and Emunah (faith) from the holy land...

As to the argument that Jews needed somewhere to flee, the Rebbe responded that the Zionist goal was not to save Jews! They could have saved many more Jews in Palestine by refraining from pressing for a state... And even if some lives could be saved by going to Palestine, one cannot save Jews by subjecting them to a danger to their belief in Hashem (God) and His Torah.[41]

Teitelbaum argued that it was preferable to remain in Hungary rather than strengthen the supporters and partners of Zionism. It must be emphasized that at this time the Jews of Hungary were not facing imminent and mortal danger. However, it is impossible to ignore the historical fact that the Rebbe was ultimately saved due to the opportunity he was given by Zionist activists in Budapest. He was not the only Hasidic rabbi to be saved in this manner. There is no evidence that Teitelbaum ever publicly expressed gratitude to those who helped him.

In March 1944 Hitler ordered his forces to occupy Hungary. This move had tragic consequences for the Jewish community: almost the

---

[39] Meisels, *The Rebbe*, p. 94.

[40] Keren-Kratz, *R' Yoel*, pp. 202–3. His daughter Chaya Roiza and her husband signed such a declaration and duly received certificates (*ibid.*, p. 203). Later they escaped from Satmar, and after arriving in Mandatory Palestine they worked hard to obtain a certificate for the father.

[41] Meisels, *The Rebbe*, p. 95.

entire Jewish population of the country – some 450,000 souls – perished in the extermination camps. By July 1944, there were no Jews in Hungary.

In the face of their worsening military defeats, the Nazis accelerated their policy of concentrating and annihilating Jews. Initially all the Jews were concentrated in ghettoes in the provincial cities. Later they were moved to Budapest, where some 100,000 Jews lived. After the German occupation, strict laws were enforced against the Jews with the goal of preventing them from moving around the country or from escaping. The goal was to concentrate the Jews in the ghettoes and then send them to their death.

Satmar was a five- or six-hour journey from the border between Hungary and Romania, which was not under Nazi occupation. Thus the border offered a chance for survival, though the journey was anything but straightforward. Those wishing to flee were forced to pay large sums and found themselves at the mercy of smugglers and criminals.[42] A few days before the Jews were concentrated in the ghetto, from which it was impossible to escape, Teitelbaum sent his daughter to Romania, assuming that if she managed to cross the border he would join her. His daughter and her husband indeed managed to cross into Romania. The evening before the Jews of Satmar were herded into the ghetto, Teitelbaum set out for the border. He was less fortunate than his daughter, however. The truck driver who took him, together with a large group of Jews, was unfamiliar with the route. Due to his error the Jews did not reach their desired destination but were seized by German soldiers and sent to the Klausenburg/Cluj ghetto.

In March 1944, immediately after the German occupation, members of the Jewish Relief and Rescue Committee of Budapest contacted the senior Nazi leader Adolf Eichmann, who came to Hungary to plan the annihilation of the Jewish population, and Kurt Becker, the head of the SS Economic Department. During the discussions, Eichmann and his staff suggested that the Jews of Hungary could be moved outside the zone of German occupation in return for 10,000 trucks and sundry merchandise (the proposal became known as the "blood for goods" deal). Yoel Brand, a senior member of the Relief and Rescue Committee, flew to Istanbul to forward the proposal to the British. On the orders of Lord Moyne, the

---

[42] On the escape of Hungarian Orthodox Jews during Nazi occupation see: Esther Farbstein, *Beseter Hamadregah: Orthodox Jewry in Hungary Facing the Holocaust*. Jerusalem: Mosad Harav Kook, 2013 (in Hebrew).

British Minister of State for the Middle East (whose permanent base was in Cairo), Brand was placed in detention and his proposal was not even discussed.

After the failure of Brand's mission, the Relief and Rescue Committee continued to pursue their contacts with Eichmann and his staff. The main negotiator from the Jewish side was the Zionist activist Yisrael (Rudolf) Kastner. The Nazis permitted a train to leave Hungary carrying several hundred Jews and the number of passengers eventually reached 1,684. The fortunate passengers were chosen by Kastner and Otto Komoly, the chairman of the Rescue Committee, and included Kastner's own family, some 300 people from the Klasenberg ghetto, wealthy Jews (who paid $ 1,000 per person), and members of the various Zionist youth movements. Most of the Zionist leadership of Hungary boarded the train. Kastner believed that the train would be the first of many, but this did not prove to be the case. Instead of heading for Portugal, a neutral country, the train arrived in Bergen-Belsen concentration camp in Germany. Kurt Becker continued to negotiate with the Joint Distribution Committee and the Jewish Agency regarding the "blood for goods" deal. In August 1944, during the course of the negotiations, 318 of the former passengers on Kastner's train were released from Bergen-Belsen and sent to Switzerland; in December of the same year, they were joined by the remaining 1,366 inmates of the camp who had arrived on the train.[43]

Kastner's activities became the subject of a fierce controversy after the war. In a famous libel trial conducted in Israel, the district court Judge Binyamin Halevy found that Kastner had "sold his soul to the devil" and assisted the Germans in annihilating the Jews of Hungary. Kastner's reputation was partially vindicated by the Israeli Supreme Court in an appeal against the ruling, but by this time Kastner was no longer alive. He was murdered by several young men incensed by the allegations leveled against him in the libel trial.

Yoel Teitelbaum was included in the list of those eligible to board the train, together with his wife and his personal assistant. Since it was only possible to save a few hundred people out of a Jewish population of some four hundred and fifty thousand, and since the Zionist leaders determined who would be saved, an unavoidable question is why Teitelbaum secured permits despite his fierce anti-Zionist views. Why did the Zionist activists

---

[43] Yehuda Bauer, *Jews for Sale? Nazi-Jewish Negotiations, 1933–1945*. New Haven: Yale University Press, 1994.

not prefer to allocate these three places to their supporters rather than their sworn opponents? There is no clear answer to this question.

Hasidic historiography offers two possible answers to this mystery, both of which may cast some light on the actual events. Tcitclbaum's followers claim that the main reason for the inclusion of the Rebbe's name in the list was intervention on his behalf by Kastner's father-in-law, Dr. Yosef Fischer. It should be noted that Kastner and his family, including Fischer, were originally from the town of Klasenberg, where Teitelbaum and Fisher were among those forced to live in the ghetto. Dr. Fischer was an influential figure and one of the leaders of the Jewish community in the city. A Satmar source even claims that he was the head of the Neolog Jewish community in the city[44] (the Neolog movement, popular in Hungary, adopted a modernizing approach to the Jewish religion but was less radical in its innovations than the German-based Reform movement). According to the Satmar sources, after Fischer and Teitelbaum eventually reached Switzerland Fischer confessed to the Rebbe that his own mother had appeared before him in a dream and insisted that he include Teitelbaum in the list of those allowed to board the train.[45]

This explanation may contain a kernel of truth. During his libel trial Kastner stated: "I received a personal request from him [Dr. Fischer] to include Rabbi Yoel Teitelbaum in the list... Truly, I do not recall any other such request."[46]

The second claim is that the Orthodox community in Budapest paid the required ransom for Teitelbaum's place.[47] This was certainly the case after the train departed: its progress was halted several times by Eichmann, who each time demanded more money in order to allow the train to reach a safe destination. As mentioned earlier, the passengers were initially sent to Bergen-Belsen concentration camp, and only after five months of additional negotiations and payment of a further ransom were all the passengers released.[48] According to Gelbman, "Our Rebbe was included in the list of railroad passengers thanks to the activities of the Haredi activists, and not out of any generosity on the part of the Zionists."[49] The problem with this assertion, however, is that the Haredi activists in Budapest had no influence over Yosef Fischer in Klasenberg,

---

[44] Meisels, *The Rebbe*, p. 109.
[45] Deutsch, *Butzina* 1, p.127; Meisels, *The Rebbe*, p. 114.
[46] The quote from the ruling appears in Avraham Fuchs, *The Admor*, p. 116.
[47] Gelbman, *Moshian Shel Yisrael* 8. Kiryas Yoel: Ohel Torah Publishers, 2004, p. 351 (in Hebrew).
[48] Meisels, *The Rebbe*, p. 114.   [49] Gelbman, *Moshian Shel Yisrael* 8, p. 351.

and it was he who acted on Teitelbaum's behalf. My own conclusion is that the decision to allow Teitelbaum to board the train was not influenced by the requests of the Haredi activists in Budapest but was a personal decision on Fischer's part.

Teitelbaum's decision to board the train raises a principled question as to why he agreed to be included in the list of passengers on the train. Two aspects are at stake in this context. The first is the abandonment of his followers to their fate at the mercy of the Nazi oppressor. The flight of rabbis from Europe was a general phenomenon that was later the subject of considerable criticism. After the war, for example, a document was found in Auschwitz extermination camp bearing the testimony of the Rebbetzin of Stropkov against Aharon Rokach, the Belzer Admor. Rokach, one of the most important Hasidic leaders of the time, took advantage of a precious "certificate" three months before Hungary fell and emigrated to Mandatory Palestine. The Rebbetzin wrote: "They themselves fled to the Land of Israel the last moment, saving their own lives and leaving the people to go as lambs to the slaughter. Master of the Universe! In the last moments of my life I beg you, forgive them for this terrible desecration of your name!"[50]

The second aspect is why the rabbi agreed to board a train that was arranged by the very Zionist activists he despised and whom he saw as the source of all evil, to the point that he argued that the Holocaust itself was divine retribution for Zionist action (I will discuss Teitelbaum's ideology in greater detail in the next chapter). How did he feel able to enjoy the fruits of Zionism? As will be recalled, just a few years earlier he had opposed emigration to the Land of Israel in order to avoid strengthening the Zionist cause. By boarding the train was he not granting Zionism a victory?

According to the Hasidic biographers, Teitelbaum could not have helped his followers by remaining in Europe and chose to leave in order to "raise heaven and earth" on their behalf. They claim that Teitelbaum was forced to hide after the Nazis entered Satmar, so that he was already inaccessible to his followers and there was no point his remaining in the city. Teitelbaum reached the conclusion that he would be able to do more to save the Jews if he escaped to a free country.[51]

These versions do not explain why the Zionists went out of their way to save Teitelbaum. I would suggest that one reason could be his

---

[50] Quoted in Piekarz, *Polish Hassidism*, p. 413.
[51] Gelbman, *Moshian Shel Yisrael* 8, pp. 77, 157.

willingness to subscribe to the goals of Zionism by expressing support for Agudat Yisrael. An allusion to this possibility may be found in his main work, *VaYoel Moshe*. In a comment not repeated elsewhere, Teitelbaum writes:

Moreover the Zionist themselves, when they controlled the total number of certificates granted by the English government each year for immigration to the Land of Israel, wished to give a certificate only to those who followed their approach and agreed with their method, the method of Zionism, heresy and apostasy, Heaven forfend, and anyone who wished to travel to the Land of Israel was forced to flatter them and their ways.[52]

In this passage Teitelbaum claims that it was impossible to secure a permit to emigrate to the Land of Israel (thereby escaping mortal danger) without expressing support for Zionism. Is it possible that he, too, followed this course of action? Might Teitelbaum have given Dr. Yosef Fischer, his neighbor in the ghetto, a declaration of his willingness to support Zionism in some shape or form, and in return intervened on his behalf alone, among all the inhabitants of the ghetto? I should add that a few months later the Zionist movement again intervened to prevent Teitelbaum's expulsion to a refugee camp in Algiers and enable him to travel to Palestine. Given the highly restricted number of individuals who could be saved, what led the Zionists to go to such lengths on Teitelbaum's behalf? I should emphasize that the Zionists never claimed to be in possession of any declaration by Teitelbaum supporting this hypothesis; for the present, at least, it can be considered no more than speculation.

After the passengers from the train reached Switzerland, following a nerve-wracking period of five months spent in Bergen-Belsen, Teitelbaum was welcomed warmly by the local Orthodox community. However, the Swiss government refused to host the refugees on a permanent basis and they were forced to move elsewhere or face deportation to a refugee camp established in Algiers.[53] Once again the Rebbe faced a dilemma. As he explained in his own words, immigration to the Land of Israel was possible only with a certificate from the Zionist movement, at the price of an expression of support for the movement's goals. Accordingly, Teitelbaum asked his nephew, Yekutiel Yude Teitelbaum, who lived in America, to secure an entry visa enabling him to travel to the United

[52] Yoel Teitelbaum, *Sefer VeYoel Moshe: Kolel Shelosha Maamarim* (5th edition), Brooklyn, NY: Bet Mishar Yerushalayim, 1981 (in Hebrew), p. 184.

[53] Meisels, *The Rebbe*, p. 123. See also: Yoel Teitelbaum, *Divrei Yoel* 1: *Correspondence* (3rd edition). New York: Jerusalem Book Store Inc., 1982, pp. 192–4 (in Hebrew).

States. According to the Satmar historiography, the application was approved. However, a careful reading of Teitelbaum's correspondence with his nephew shows that the Rebbe eventually decided not to file the application, preferring to move to the Land of Israel.[54]

According to the Hasidic sources, the British government intervened on behalf of the passengers on the train and provided them with permits outside the usual quota framework. This enabled Teitelbaum to travel to Jerusalem without being obliged to express support for Zionism. Indeed, the Hasidic historiographers claim that the Rebbe received the certificate as a personal favor from a Jewish Agency official (no name is mentioned) who came from the Hasidic community of Planch (Połaniec, Poland), whose rabbi was also related to Teitelbaum.[55]

The material presented by the Hasidic biographers themselves contradicts this version of events. According to the documents they published in the biographies, the Jewish Agency issued seven hundred certificates for the survivors from Kastner's train who had been held in Bergen-Belsen. Teitelbaum's daughter Roiza and her husband Hananiya had already reached Palestine and intervened on his behalf, and accordingly his name was included in the quota allocated to Agudat Yisrael. The couple turned to every possible source of help, including the Agudat Yisrael leaders Meir Itcha Levin, Moshe Porush and even the Zionist Chief Rabbi Itzhak Halevi Herzog. All these figures sent letters of support to the Jewish Agency on Teitelbaum's behalf, and accordingly he received a precious certificate.[56] Teitelbaum himself implored his daughter to contact Agudat Yisrael on his behalf.[57] It thus emerges that he received the certificate thanks to the efforts of figures in Agudat Yisrael, and even to the intervention of the Zionist chief rabbi.

During his stay in Switzerland Teitelbaum cooperated with Zionist activities in an attempt to help Jewish refugees from Hungary. The biographer Shlomo Yaacov Gelbman presents the summary of a meeting to discuss this matter held at Teitelbaum's home with several individuals, including Yosef Fischer. The record shows that there was no hostility between the rabbi and his Zionist rescuers after he arrived in Switzerland, and they were able to meet in the Rebbe's home to consider ways to cooperate.[58] Indeed, the Hasidic reports claim that Kastner's attorney asked Teitelbaum to give testimony on his behalf during the libel trial in

[54] Teitelbaum, *Divrei Yoel* 1, pp. 192–4. [55] Gelbman, *Moshian Shel Yisrael* 8, p. 559.
[56] Gelbman, *Moshian Shel Yisrael* 9, pp. 161–2, 172–3. [57] *Ibid.*, 213.
[58] Gelbman, *Moshian Shel Yisrael* 8, pp. 612–4.

the 1950s. Teitelbaum declined to do so, but the mere fact that Kastner requested his assistance suggests that he felt that the Rebbe's testimony would be in his favor. Again, this suggests the absence of the profound hostility Teitelbaum's followers describe.[59] During his stay in Switzerland the rabbi also cooperated with activists from Po'alei Agudat Yisrael, a movement that was active in establishing colonies in Palestine – something the Rebbe would later decry as a mortal sin. Teitelbaum cooperated with them as part of the "Committee for the Child," a body formed by Po'alei Agudat Yisrael to help Holocaust orphans.[60]

Might Teitelbaum have received the certificate thanks to his cooperation with Zionist and Agudat Yisrael activists? It is important to bear in mind that at the end of the Second World War, the Zionist movement was in a strong position relative to other Jewish movements. The majority of the Jewish opponents of Zionism perished at the hands of the Nazi death machine, while many supporters of Zionism left Europe in time and embarked on the project of establishing a Jewish state in Palestine. Zionism enjoyed considerable support around the world as reports spread of the fate of the Jews in Europe, while the ultra-Orthodox at the time seemed to be a negligible minority, weak, and debilitated.

I would like to suggest that Teitelbaum's decision to emigrate to the Land of Israel at this point may have reflected a messianic conviction on his part that the Second World War constituted the "birth pangs of the messianic age" and that complete redemption was imminent. According to his belief, this was the generation of the "footsteps of messiah" – the last generation before the coming of the Redeemer – and at such a critical time he preferred Jerusalem to New York. I should emphasize that Teitelbaum was by no means the only Orthodox rabbi to interpret the events of the time in this manner; others who adopted this approach included Yissachar Shlomo Teichtel[61] and the Admor Yosef-Yitzhak of Lubavitch.[62]

---

[59] Gelbman, *Moshian Shel Yisrael* 9, p. 45, footnote 26.   [60] *Ibid.*, p. 109.

[61] Yitzhak Hershkowitz, *The Redemption Vision of Rabbi Yissachar Shlomo Teichtel, HY"D: Transitions in His Messianic Perception during the Holocaust.* PhD Dissertation, Bar Ilan University, 2009 (in Hebrew).

[62] Shalom Ratzabi, "Anti-Zionism and Messianic Tension in the Thought of Rabbi Shalom Dover," *HaTziyonut* 20 (5756 – 1996), 77–101 (in Hebrew); Menachem Friedman, "Messiah and Messianism in the Habad–Lubavitch Hassidim." In: David Ariel-Joël [et al.] (eds.), *The War of Gog and Magog: Messianism and Apocalypse in Judaism Past and Present*, Tel Aviv: Yediot Acharonot Publishers, 2001, pp. 161–73 (in Hebrew).

I have formed my hypothesis on the basis of an examination of Teitelbaum's letters, collected by his followers and published in three volumes, and after analyzing his philosophical approach (as discussed in the next chapter). In his letter to his nephew, Yekutiel Yude Teitelbaum, the Rebbe detailed the reasons that led him to prefer Jerusalem. He noted that he had managed to secure a certificate and that he was afraid he would lose this if he first traveled to the United States. More importantly, however, he stated that his "full intention now is to settle in the Land of Life and to wait there until the salvation of Israel, speedily and in our days, Amen."[63] This argument is repeated in all his letters from this period. He ends this same letter with the following sentence: "May the Lord, blessed be He, guide us in the paths of righteousness for His name's sake, blessed be He, and above all may He grant us speedy, complete, and true redemption, for there is no other way for the salvation of Israel; may the Lord, blessed be He, have mercy and heal the broken hearts, rebuild the ruins and make our hearts joyous in His salvation, blessed be He, speedily and in our days, Amen."[64] In a footnote, his editors added: "From all our Rebbe's letters from this period, it appears that he was resolute in his sacred determination to settle in peace in the Holy Land until the coming of our messiah."[65]

It might be argued that such statements can be made by way of hyperbole and do not necessarily reflect genuine messianic anticipation. However, I would note that the Rebbe employed such rhetoric during the period immediately following the Second World War, but no remnants of such content can be found in all the letters from later years published by his followers after his death. It is not unreasonable to suggest that the unfathomable destruction in Europe during the war and the mass annihilation of the Jews, combined with his own personal fortune in escaping together with several of those closest to him, may have led him to develop messianic expectations. Such expectations would certainly have provided a sound basis for his decision to travel to Jerusalem.

Be this as it may, Teitelbaum's stay in Jerusalem was relatively brief. The months he spent in the concentration camp in Germany, the inadequate diet, and the diseases from which he had suffered all took their toll on the Rebbe's state of health, both physical and mental.[66] After arriving

---

[63] Teitelbaum, *Divrei Yoel* 1, p. 193.   [64] *Ibid.*, pp. 194–5.

[65] *Ibid.*, p. 193, footnote E.

[66] "These trials and woes, Heaven forfend, which at all times do not leave my memory." Teitelbaum, *Divrei Yoel* 1, p. 195.

in Jerusalem, Teitelbaum began to suffer from severe infections in the gall bladder, liver, and lungs. According to his own testimony, he was at death's door.

I would suggest that during the period following the war, including his time in Jerusalem, Teitelbaum may have adopted an ideological position close to that of Agudat Yisrael, advocating cooperation with the Zionist movement in the task of establishing a Jewish state.

The Satmar biographer Dovid Meisels quotes a story that may offer some support for my hypothesis, I recognize may seem provocative. He reports that during Teitelbaum's stay in Jerusalem he was visited one day by the son of the leading Haredi Rabbi Zev Soloveitchik (the Brisker Rebbe), who sought to convince Teitelbaum to join the struggle against Zionism. According to Yosef-Dov Soloveitchik, Teitelbaum rejected the request. Meisels offers the following account:

The Satmar Rebbe spoke to me [Yosef-Dov] about the battle against Zionism. He tried to convince me that since a Zionist state is now inevitable, and most religious Jews are positive about the idea, perhaps it would be a better strategy for us to deal with the Zionists and fight from within so to save whatever can be saved. I [Yosef-Dov] was very surprised to see that the Satmar Rebbe has changed his tune and is no longer the zealot he once was.

According to Meisels, Teitelbaum's reply was actually intended as a test, to gauge how Yosef-Dov Soloveitchik would respond.[67] The fact that this story is included in the records of an official Satmar biographer is in itself surprising. Why would Meisels choose to reveal an episode that casts doubts on the Rebbe's zealous credentials? One possibility is that a rumor concerning this meeting may have been rife among the Haredi public, and they chose to respond to this in a convoluted manner by confirming the content of the rumor, while arguing that Teitelbaum's remarks were made not as a serious statement but in jest or as a test of Soloveitchik's zealotry. Further evidence of Teitelbaum's willingness to change his position on Zionism at this time is presented by the scholar Israel Rubin in his comprehensive study on Satmar Hasidism in New York.[68]

The Hasidic biographies provide further evidence supporting my hypothesis. For example, Gelbman reports that after Teitelbaum arrived in Jerusalem he was asked to give a sermon at Kahal Yereim Synagogue, a Neturei Karta institution. The Hasidic sources state that he "touched only

---

[67] Meisels, *The Rebbe*, pp. 132–3.
[68] Israel Rubin, *Satmar*, pp. 66–7. Rubin claims that the rumor was false.

briefly" on anti-Zionist issues and focused mainly on the need to reinforce religious piety and modesty. A footnote adds that after Teitelbaum arrived in the city Rabbi Yitzhak Sheinberger warned him not to attack the Zionists, since this could prove dangerous. Indeed, Gelbman describes two attempts by supporters of Zionism to assassinate the Rebbe. Fearing for his life, he preferred to remain silent.[69]

In reality, the quotes from the Rebbe's comments in his aforementioned sermon reveal an extreme anti-Zionist rhetoric. Teitelbaum is quoted as claiming that Zionism "... will ultimately be completely obliterated from the world, and the Holy One, blessed be He, will remove this spirit of impurity from the Land ... The entire Zionist Yishuv is to be considered as if it had already been eliminated."[70] The problem with these quotes is that Gelbman does not provide any reference or proof confirming their veracity, in contrast to all his other claims in the book, which are supported by generous references. Moreover, the biographer claims that Teitelbaum's grave illness was a Divine penalty for the insufficiently forceful nature of his sermon. Since the quotes of the Hasidism sound more than sufficiently forceful, I find these explanations implausible.

The evidence speaks for itself. The explanations offered by the Hasidic biographers as to why Zionist activists twice issued Teitelbaum with a visa to enter Palestine are unconvincing. Even the Rebbe himself admitted that it was impossible to obtain a "certificate" without expressing support for Zionism. Teitelbaum's stay in Jerusalem coincided with the emergence of the Neturei Karta. The Rebbe would later become the spiritual leader of HaEdah HaHaredit and would be renowned for his fiercely anti-Zionist stance. Yet at this time he was not involved in any activities relating to Neturei Karta and refrained from making an overly extreme attack on Zionism when he gave a sermon at one of its institutions. In my opinion, it is almost impossible to believe that Teitelbaum was not even slightly grateful to the Zionists for saving his life, particularly during the period immediately following the war. Taken together, this evidence reinforces my conviction that during this period Teitelbaum was more moderate in his opposition to Zionism, as suggested by the testimony of the Brisker Rebbe's son. This hypothesis is further supported by Teitelbaum's cooperation with Zionist elements in Switzerland.

The Hasidic biographers state that Teitelbaum left for America in order to engage in fundraising and had no intention of remaining in the

---

[69] Gelbman, *Moshian Shel Yisrael* 9, pp. 416–7.   [70] *Ibid.*, pp. 413–4.

country. The Rebbe enjoyed a rich religious life and a supportive Hasidic community in Jerusalem. However, Keren-Kratz argues that Teitelbaum had accumulated significant debts due to the mismanagement of his businesses and had to escape in order to avoid bankruptcy. He also was unable to win the support of the Jerusalem community and had only a few followers.[71] Nevertheless, the prospect of living in the United States as a strictly religious Jew was far from endearing: "His pure heart was flooded by fears and doubts as to how he could make his home in this country [...] The condition of the poor Jewish residents was miserable and bitter. Their children were not educated in Torah and the fear of God. The impurity of secular enlightenment and knowledge was voraciously eating away at their number. The impurity of the Gentile country was to their disadvantage, and they mixed with the Gentiles and learned their ways."[72] The Satmar biographers conclude that the Rebbe planned to leave Jerusalem for a short period, but that circumstances led him to change his plans: "Our Rebbe did not originally imagine that he would settle here in America."[73]

In September 1946, Teitelbaum left Jerusalem and traveled to New York. In order to enter the United States he obtained a work visa signed by the consul general of the United States in Jerusalem. Kahal Haredim Synagogue, a congregation of Hungarian Hasidim, sought to employ him and provided him with a contract.[74] This suggests that the purpose of his journey was to work and settle in the United States rather than to pursue a fundraising campaign as the Hasidic sources claim.

I believe that a pattern can be discerned. The Rebbe was not inclined to spend long periods of time in the Land of Israel, and even when he attempted to settle in the country he did not remain there for long. In an attempt to explain this behavior, I would like to offer a suggestion based on an analysis of his earlier actions.

Teitelbaum had a pedantic and purist character. As noted above, he had an obsessive tendency to dwell on thoughts of impurity and pollution on embarking on religious worship. Another characteristic was his desire to separate and isolate himself in order to avoid external influence and to refrain from coping with changing realities. This pattern was typical of large sections of the Haredi community in Hungary, which separated itself from the broader Jewish community in order to avoid contact with

---

[71] Keren-Kratz, *R' Yoel*, p. 233.   [72] Deitsch, *Butzina 1*, p. 161.   [73] *Ibid.*, p. 153.
[74] *Ibid.*, p. 154.

the modernizing streams.[75] The Haredi community continues to follow this approach to the present day, gathering in enclaves that prevent or reduce modern influence.[76] The Rebbe acted in accordance with this pattern when he established Satmar in New York (see later). Teitelbaum was opposed to outreach and prohibited his followers from engaging in efforts to influence the broader Jewish community such as those undertaken by the Habad Hasidic movement, due to his fear of exposure and counterinfluence.

Teitelbaum stayed in Jerusalem for less than a year, during most of which time he was seriously ill. He left as soon as his state of health improved. Is it possible that he feared that he was beginning to be influenced by the environment and that his opposition to Zionism was weakening? Perhaps he preferred to leave rather than to change his ways. He may have felt that the impurity of support for Zionism was taking him over, and that the only way to avoid this was to move away. The Satmar biographers even hint that he feared for his life, interpreting his illness as divine retribution for his adoption of a more moderate tone.

NEW YORK

After arriving in New York in 1946, Teitelbaum focused his efforts on rebuilding the shattered world of Hasidic Judaism and on establishing institutions similar to those he had founded in prewar Europe. He worked mainly with Holocaust orphans and refugees who longed to recreate their spiritual world on American soil after arriving in a state of mental and physical exhaustion. Much of his support and most of the donations for the institutions he established in the United States came from Holocaust survivors who had managed to rebuild their lives and who were devoted to the cause of rebuilding the world of Torah following the devastation.[77]

Teitelbaum's main project was the formation of a Hasidic enclave within New York. He acted to ensure the separation of the enclave in various fields: the establishment of separate educational institutions,

---

[75] On the division in the community, see: Jacob Katz, *A House Divided: Orthodoxy and Schism in Nineteenth-Century Central European Jewry*. Waltham: Tauber Institute Series for the Study of European Jewry, 2005.

[76] Samuel Heilman and Menachem Friedman, "Religious Fundamentalism and Religious Jews: The Case of the Haredim." In: Martin E. Marty and Scott Appleby (eds.), *Fundamentalism Observed*. Chicago: University of Chicago Press, 1991, pp. 197–264.

[77] Meisels, *The Rebbe*, p. 154.

physical enclosure in an urban enclave, and the creation of visual segregation through dress and language.

Educational institutions

The Yetev Lev D'Satmar congregation was founded in New York in 1948. At the time, it had not more than ten members, but its growth proved dramatic. Today (2015), the Satmar Hasidic movement is believed to number more than 100,000 followers. The early group of supporters was based on Hasidim who had been followers of Teitelbaum in Hungary, but those who subsequently joined the court came from diverse backgrounds.[78]

In 1951 Satmar opened a Talmud Torah seminary that became a center for Hasidic studies. This was the first institution of the kind opened in the United States and it soon became a magnet for those seeking this format of studies. The Joint Distribution Committee (known as "the Joint") sent Holocaust survivors from Europe to live in various cities around the United States, but most of them eventually gathered in New York, providing the institution with its first students.

The students who attended the Talmud Torah came from families that did not necessarily maintain the strict religious standards of Satmar. Many Hasidic Holocaust survivors who settled in the United States abandoned their former way of life. Accordingly, one of Teitelbaum's goals was to gradually reinstate the old traditions. After establishing his educational institutions, the Rebbe decided not to reject any student. There was concern that students from less observant background might lead their fellows astray, but the assumption was that those who were not suited to the institution would eventually leave, while the others would adapt the Hasidic style. With hindsight, the institutions he established served as a catalyst for the revival of Hasidic Judaism. The younger generation changed first and later influenced their parents, leading to the reestablishment of a Hasidic community.[79]

In the last generation in Europe before the Holocaust, the subject of the content of studies in Hasidic institutions was the focus of considerable disagreement. Conservatives opposed any element of secular studies in the seminaries. According to the historian Mendel Piekarz, the Admor of Sanz, one of the most prominent Hungarian rabbi, argued that the

[78] Rubin, *Satmar*, p. 40–2.   [79] Meisels, *The Rebbe*, pp. 381–2.

introduction of secular studies was tantamount to nothing less than the destruction of religion. Others adopted a more conciliatory approach, such as Moshe Yechiel Rabinowitz, who argued that the Hasidic education system must be open to the needs of the time, and should not confine itself solely to the methods and themes of the old Talmud Torah.[80]

Teitelbaum favored the latter approach. According to Meisels, he was aware of the materialistic nature of American society and recognized that economic prosperity was a vital tool in any effort to revive the Hasidic institutions. Accordingly, he ordered that secular subjects be included in the school curriculum. In the afternoons, the boys in his institutions studied English reading and writing, arithmetic, geography, and American history.

Moreover, the Satmar schools could not have followed the exclusively religious curriculum used in European institutions, since American law required them to provide core studies. The Rebbe preferred to teach these secular subjects in his own institutions rather than face demands to send the children to public schools: "Allowing the children to learn secular subjects in the Yeshivah under his close supervision was certainly a lesser evil than sending them to public schools with Gentiles for six hours a day."[81]

The Rebbe wanted his students to be successful in the world of business and recognized that the teachers needed to prepare them for a productive life could not be found within the ranks of the movement. Accordingly, he employed as his director Dr. Frankel, an active member of Agudat Yisrael in New York, who was charged with attending to the secular content of the studies and with recruiting suitable teachers from outside the Hasidic community.[82] Satmar later prepared textbooks in Yiddish that were used by Haredi educational institutions throughout the United States.

The secular studies were introduced by way of an unavoidable constraint. The studies were held in the afternoon when the students were already tired after hours of religious learning. According to the scholar Israel Rubin, the students constantly disrupted the secular classes. The students were well aware of the lack of importance attached to these subjects and showed little interest, in sharp contrast to their approach to their religious classes. At the age of sixteen the secular classes ended and very few students showed an inclination to continue their studies.

---

[80] Piekarz, *Polish Hasidism*, pp. 115–8.   [81] Meisels, *The Rebbe*, pp. 381–2.
[82] *Ibid.*, pp. 418–9.

Rubin argues that the schools functioned as a shield against acculturation. The boys studied Torah and the girls received vocational instruction.[83]

However, in the 1980s a trend began for both men and women to study electronics. The need for advanced training in this field demanded a strong technological grounding. Special institutions were opened to provide this training while maintaining a strict Orthodox lifestyle. The Satmar sector did not have any particular objection to modern technology per se and many of its members have made a living from the field.[84]

Another innovation in the field of education was the establishment of institutions for girls. In the traditional Hungarian Hasidic community girls had not attended school and were educated in the home. Agudat Yisrael established the Beis Yaacov network of girls' schools, but the network was unable to establish a presence in Hungary due to fierce rabbinical opposition. In 1950 Satmar opened a girls' school in New York to teach both religious and secular subjects and to provide vocational training enabling the girls to enter the job market. The network was called Bais Ruchel in memory of Teitelbaum's second daughter, who had died in Hungary.

In this case, too, the main motive behind the establishment of the girls' schools was to prevent girls being sent to the public system. Moreover, Jewish homes were lax in terms of religious observance, so that home schooling was a less effective tool than had been the case in Hungary. A further consideration was that given Teitelbaum's fierce opposition to the Beis Yaacov network it would be unreasonable for the community to send its girls to the very institutions it had condemned.

The religious half of the day's studies was taught in Yiddish while the second half was devoted to English, mathematics, and history. The older girls received vocational instruction in skills such as sewing. The Rebbe permitted the teaching of the sciences, including new discoveries, alongside health and nutrition classes.

The religious classes were held in Yiddish in order to prevent the women from acquiring knowledge of Hebrew that would enable them to engage in independent study. To this end, the network prepared textbooks in Yiddish, since it could not use the Hebrew scriptures themselves. There was apparently a substantial gap between the religious and secular studies. While the secular subjects were taught at a high standard the religious classes were on a low level and many of the girls found them

[83] Rubin, *Satmar*, pp. 161–89.   [84] *Ibid.*, pp. 190–9.

inadequate. The highly conservative nature of this part of the curriculum reflected pressure from the conservative wing of the movement, which was unhappy about the idea of providing women with a religious education.[85]

The girls' institutions aimed to enable women in the community to help with housework and to prepare suitable brides for the young men who were Torah scholars, in order to ensure that the family would maintain a religious lifestyle consistent with Hasidic tradition.[86] The Satmar community took a positive view of participation by women in the job market, and accordingly it was vital to provide them appropriate training.

The sector also established separate summer camps for boys and girls that emphasized strict observance of the Hasidic way of life. The camps kept young people busy during the summer and prevented their being attracted to the summer camps offered by the wider Jewish community in the United States. The camps focused mainly on studies and did not usually include recreational activities.[87]

In the field of adult education, Teitelbaum took the view that a religious lifestyle should not be a barrier to making a livelihood. After arriving in the United States, he consistently encouraged all his followers to participate in the job market and to make a decent living. The culture of the Old Yishuv in Jerusalem, which argued that Torah students should devote themselves exclusively to their studies and which called on Jewish communities to support them to this end, was not found among the Satmar Hasidim. Indeed, the Rebbe prohibited his followers from "making a living" from their studies. Instead, he encouraged them to find time to study Torah in the morning or evening without impairing their ability to make a livelihood. The same was true of the graduates of the Talmud Torah – after marrying, they were required to find work.[88] A further innovation in the field of adult education in the Hasidic community was the introduction of the Kollel, an institution for further Torah studies for married men during the first two years after their marriage. This institution was adopted from the Lithuanian tradition.[89]

Dress

One of the ways in which Teitelbaum emphasized the distinct identity of his community was through external appearance, an aspect that ensures a

---

[85] *Ibid.*, pp. 161–89.   [86] Meisels, *The Rebbe*, pp. 462–83.   [87] *Ibid.*, pp. 486–90.
[88] *Ibid.*, pp. 161–3.   [89] Rubin, *Satmar*, pp. 181–2.

sharp and immediately visible barrier between his followers and out-siders. The Rebbe waged a protracted and stubborn struggle on this matter with his followers, who did not always share his zeal on this matter.

Students in the Satmar Talmud Torah were required to wear distinctive dress. The boys were required to grow their sidelocks down to their cheeks and wore large black velvet skullcaps and long-sleeved shirts, even in summer. These rules were designed to create peer pressure and encour-age conformity.

Before the Second World War, American Jews had not been accus-tomed to dressing in this manner. In particular, the custom of growing long sidelocks had been abandoned. As a result the children who attended the Satmar institutions in New York were often ridiculed by other Jewish children in the heavily Jewish neighborhoods of the city. Teitelbaum also prohibited the boys to play ballgames due to his concern that they would become overly attached to this pastime and due to their central role in American culture. Meisels argues that the Satmar children felt that they were under attack from all sides, but that this merely served to enhance their self-esteem and their pride in their distinct identity.[90]

The desire for assimilation and the need to integrate in the general job market led many American Jews, even among the Orthodox, to modify their dress. Thus the return to Hasidic garb represented a countermove-ment emphasizing separatism and the rejection of integration.

The streimel is a fur hat traditionally worn by married Hasidic men on Sabbath and the festivals. The streimel was not universally adopted by all the Hasidic communities in Europe. Nevertheless, strict adherence to Hasidic dress throughout the week, and to the streimel on the Sabbath, became one of the hallmarks of Satmar. It might be asked why a custom should be followed in the United States that was not usual in Europe. Meisels reply: "It separates the Jew and makes him unwelcome on the Gentile street. If Gentiles avoid him he has fewer opportunities to sin."[91] As this comment suggests, the imposition of the streimel in America reflected a desire to emphasize Jewish separatism and distinction on the external level. These were the tools that enabled the creation of a Hasidic enclave within a modern metropolis.

Women's dress also served as a tool for separatism. In this case, however, the Rebbe was forced to accept certain compromises. According

---

[90] Meisels, *The Rebbe*, pp. 401–3.   [91] *Ibid.*, pp. 344.

to the custom among Hungarian ultra-Orthodoxy, married women were supposed to shave their hair and cover the head with a silk scarf without exposing the roots of their hair. The community rejected the custom of wearing a shaitel or wig. In sermons he gave in 1937–1938, Teitelbaum claimed that a woman who wore a wig would be cursed.[92]

When he attempted to impose this position on his community, however, many women refused to adopt this practice. Teitelbaum argued that this was the traditional way, that women who failed to follow the practice would be cursed, and that only families whose women shaved their hair could be close to the Rebbe. However, he realized that he could not engage in an all-out war on this matter. According to Meisels, almost all the women in the community wore wigs and regarded the demand to shave their head as an unacceptably extreme demand. The Rebbe did not want to lose such a large number of followers and preferred to drop his demand.[93]

Another focus of the modesty campaign was the demand for women to wear thick stockings. The Rebbe was concerned at the growing fashion for flesh-colored stockings, which he felt imitated Gentile practices. In 1951 he launched a modesty campaign among his followers including a mandatory dress code for women. He instructed the men in the community not to perform any religious ritual in the home, such as Kiddush (sanctification of wine on Sabbath and the festivals) or grace after meals, unless all the women of the house were modestly dressed. On Rosh Hashanah he warned the congregation that women who wore sheer stockings would not benefit from hearing the shofar. Teitelbaum demanded the use of black wool stockings. The production of these stockings was discontinued in the 1970s due to changing fashions and a shortage developed in the Satmar community. In 1973 the movement went to the length of purchasing a production line in order to ensure that suitable stockings would always be available.[94]

The girls' schools did not have a set uniform, as part of the effort to encourage modest dress. The assumption was that if the schools demanded a uniform, the girls would wear different clothes at school than at home. This concern suggests that Teitelbaum was not confident that his followers would follow the standard of modesty he demanded when dressing their daughters.[95]

---

[92] Teitelbaum, *Divrei Yoel* 1, pp. 14–15.   [93] Meisels, *The Rebbe*, p. 351.
[94] *Ibid.*, pp. 354–61.   [95] *Ibid.*, p. 473.

The religious enclave and the foundation of Kiryas Yoel

Haredi society is a voluntary entity and in theory its members are free to join or leave the community as they please. The free market of religion continued to apply in America, even among the Haredi population.

An absence of physical boundaries weakens the status of the Haredi community and the authority of its rabbis, since their followers can leave at any point. Moreover, the Jewish suburbs of New York City were open to individuals with worldviews that differed radically from those of the Satmar Hasidim, particularly in terms of the attitude toward Zionism. Teitelbaum was disturbed by this situation and sought to regain some of the coercive authority that the rabbis had enjoyed in the *Shtetls* (small towns) of Eastern Europe.[96] The Rebbe argued that the city was full of destructions and tests. As his community grew, the problem became more pronounced. His ideal was to enable the community to live in isolation, removed from the temptations of the big city. As part of his efforts to fight these temptations, he forbad yeshivah students to obtain driving licenses and expelled any student who was known to drive.

Teitelbaum's desire to leave New York City was also motivated by demographic changes in the city. Areas that were once considered strongly Jewish, such as the Bronx, Harlem, and Crown Heights, became slums. Williamsburg and Borough Park had not yet become Haredi areas. The Rebbe sought to establish a town on the shtetl model on the outskirts of New York. He was also aware that the rapid growth rate of the movement had led to an urgent need for new housing solutions.[97]

The first location he considered, in the 1950s, was Staten Island. At the time the island was not yet connected to the city by bridge. Accordingly, many of his followers were unhappy about the proposed location since they would have to use the ferry to get to and from work. The federal government eventually decided to declare the island a public park, thereby preventing the implementation of this plan.[98]

In 1973 land was purchased in the city of Monroe, some sixty miles from Williamsburg, and one hundred families moved into a compound known as Kiryas Yoel. Teitelbaum chose the families carefully and demanded that they pay particular attention to the laws of purity and modesty. The compound grew dramatically and became home to

[96] *Ibid.*, p. 531.   [97] Mintz, *Hassidic*, p. 206.   [98] Meisels, *The Rebbe*, pp. 537–8.

thousands of Satmar Hasidim. Teitelbaum himself moved to Kiryas Yoel, although the majority of the community remained in Williamsburg.[99]

The attitude to Zionism

Teitelbaum emerged as the leading Jewish figure opposed to the Zionist movement. In 1953, Zelig Reuven Bengis, the head of the religious court of HaEdah HaHaredit, passed away. At the time, HaEdah HaHaredit was a small and weak body following a split in its ranks in 1945, when the supporters of Agudat Yisrael effectively left the organization (see Chapter 2). Until 1948, Rabbi Dushinsky headed the organization's religious court and imposed his authority on the entire Haredi community. After his death, Bengis took over, but Agudat Yisrael appointed Rabbi Zev Soloveitchik as its authority. After Bengis's death, the leaders of HaEdah HaHaredit approached Teitelbaum. The organization formed the kernel of those opposed to Zionism, and Teitelbaum became its spiritual leader.

The Jerusalem zealots assumed that Teitelbaum would relocate in order to live among them, but he refused to do so. He reached an agreement that he would visit Jerusalem every four years in order to maintain contact with his supporters.

Teitelbaum authored his main anti-Zionist work – *VaYoel Moshe* – following the Sinai War of 1956, which created a sense of euphoria among most Jews. I will discuss this book in detail in the next chapter. The work lauded Jewish life in the Diaspora and rejected any manifestation of Jewish political independence in the Land of Israel before the arrival of the messiah. *VaYoel Moshe* gained recognition as the most important and systematic manifesto of Haredi anti-Zionism.

Following Israel's victory in the Six-Day War of 1967, the Jewish world was swept by an even greater wave of euphoria and amazement. Many saw the outcome of the war as the result of miraculous and divine intervention. The Habad Hasidism launched a mass campaign to encourage Jewish men to put on Tefillin (phylacteries),[100] while the euphoria in the Religious Zionist camp led to the emergence of Gush Emunim.[101]

---

[99] *Ibid.*, pp. 531–50.

[100] Samuel Heilman and Menachem Friedman, *The Rebbe: The Life and Afterlife of Menachem Mendel Schneerson.* Princeton: Princeton University Press, 2010, pp. 183–90.

[101] Motti Inbari, *Messianic Religious Zionism Confronts Israeli Territorial Compromises.* New York: Cambridge University Press, 2012, pp. 15–36.

Satmar was apparently not immune to these trends: Meisels reports that Teitelbaum was shocked to see that even those who came to his Beit Midrash were swept away in the enthusiasm.[102]

One of the reasons for the excitement that followed the war was the fact that Israel had regained access to the Jewish holy places, and particularly the Western Wall. Jews could once again visit the remnant of the Second Temple and many Haredim began to come to the site to pray.

For Teitelbaum, however, Israel's success in the war was merely further evidence of the strengthening of Satan, reinforcing his belief that the messianic End was imminent. He ordered his followers not to visit the Western Wall, since anyone who did so could not avoid a sense of gratitude toward the Zionists for occupying the site.

In 1968 Teitelbaum published a second book, *On Redemption and Change*, in which he explained why the war was not a manifestation of "overt miracles" and why it was vital to maintain the opposition to Zionism. The book was actually written by Teitelbaum's students on the basis of his sermons; the Rebbe himself merely provided the introduction.[103]

Despite his anti-Zionist fervor Teitelbaum was concerned about the image of the movement, as the following two incidents illustrate. In 1968 Democratic presidential candidate Herbert Humphrey visited Teitelbaum. Presumably unaware of the Rebbe's complex attitude to Zionism, Humphrey warmly praised the State of Israel during their meeting. Teitelbaum's subsequent comments to his followers may seem surprising:

Had he spoken to me in support of the state, it wouldn't have bothered me in the least. We Jews have the Torah which forbids us to have a state during exile, and therefore we cannot ask the Americans to support the state. But the non-Jew has no Torah, and by supporting the state he feels he is helping Jews. And on the contrary: if an American non-Jew is against the Zionist state, he shows he is an anti-Semite.[104]

This quote emphasizes the nuanced nature of Teitelbaum's position and his desire to show his devotion to the interests of all Jews. His position was that while Jews must not support the State of Israel, it was permissible and even desirable for non-Jews to do so.

From 1954 onward Satmar Hasidim began to organize protests outside the Israeli consulate in New York on various issues. One demonstration sought to highlight Israel's policy on the subject of autopsies. It emerged

[102] Meisels, *The Rebbe*, p. 449.   [103] *Ibid.*, pp. 497–516.   [104] *Ibid.*, p. 243.

that pro-PLO demonstrators were planning to join the protest and to change its character and goals. When the Hasidim informed the Rebbe of this he ordered them to cancel the demonstration: "The world must not gain even the incorrect impression that we are demonstrating for the same reason and on the same grounds as the Arabs."[105]

The rejection of zealotry

In an earlier chapter, I discussed Blau's ambivalent attitude toward the phenomenon of zealotry, as manifested in spontaneous acts of violence against alleged examples of the "desecration of God's name." The position of Neturei Karta was one of a priori rejection of such zealotry but a posteriori support for individual actions.

Satmar was also forced to consider its position on this issue. In the spring of 1967, just before the war, a number of yeshivah students decided to take the law into their own hands. They broke into a Religious Zionist synagogue, tore the Israeli flag from the wall, and hung signs expressing the hope that the Arab states would win the war and kill the Zionists. Others prepared rubber stamps bearing anti-Zionist slogans and defaced dollar bills, contrary to American law.

Teitelbaum's response to this phenomenon differed from that of Blau, who as will be recalled supported the young men who torched a sex shop in Tel Aviv. Teitelbaum condemned the zealots in his community, apologized to the board of the synagogue that was vandalized, and even temporarily suspended the students involved from his yeshivah.

He argued that the independent action by the Hasidim damaged the good name of the yeshivah and harmed the movement's campaign against Zionism. Due to the students' actions Satmar would now be perceived as an extremist group of self-hating Jews. In a speech in the Beit Midrash, Teitelbaum explained:

There are a few *bachurim* (students) who act independently, without asking the staff ... They don't have *derech eretz* (good manners) for anyone, and they think they know everything ... They are the emissaries of the *Sitra Ahra* (Satan); they are the worst of all.

If someone here is not happy with my approach, if someone here thinks I am mistaken, I am not forcing anyone to listen to me. Let him leave and not come to our yeshiva anymore! We can't run things like this. Even if it's a few people doing these actions, the end result is destruction.[106]

---

[105] Deitsch, *Butzina 1*, p. 322.   [106] Meisels, *The Rebbe*, pp. 518–9.

These comments highlight Teitelbaum's demand for complete conformity and his intolerance of any deviation from his leadership. However, it should be noted that the Rebbe enabled the existence of a conservative wing within the movement. According to Israel Rubin, two camps may be discerned within the Satmar sector – a moderate wing and a conservative wing. The moderates have sought to promote reform in education and in the community's lifestyle while the conservatives opposed any such innovations. Rubin argues that Teitelbaum identified with the conservative camp on the personal level, but preferred to adopt an intermediate position and to play the role of mediator. He points out that although the Rebbe rejected zealotry, the penalties he imposed on those who deviated from his line were relatively mild and were later interpreted as tacit approval.[107]

The death of the Rebbe and the inheritance struggle

In 1968 Teitelbaum suffered a stroke and was left partly incapacitated. He appointed one of his associates as head of the yeshivah and his wife emerged as the dominant figure in the court.

Some remarks regarding Teitelbaum's wife are appropriate at this juncture. As will be recalled, he married Alta Feiga in 1937 and it later emerged that she was barren. According to tradition, a man could divorce his barren wife after ten years and remarry. An absence of heirs creates a particularly acute crisis in a Hasidic dynasty. The possibility of a divorce was raised during the 1960s and Alta Feiga herself fought bitterly against this possibility. Teitelbaum eventually decided not to divorce his wife, explaining that he felt unable to do so after all the suffering the couple had endured together.[108]

Following Teitelbaum's stroke his wife became the main liaison between the Rebbe and the Satmar community and her power increased dramatically. Over a period of eleven years the Rebbetzin was the strongest figure in the court. After Teitelbaum passed away in 1979, she was asked to relinquish her powers but refused to do so.

During the Rebbe's lifetime the movement did not make any decision regarding his future heir, preferring to believe that the messiah would arrive before this became necessary.[109] After his death the leaders of the community identified Rabbi Moshe Teitelbaum as his heir. Moshe was

---

[107] Rubin, *Satmar*, pp. 80–2.   [108] Mintz, *Hassidic*, pp. 89–90.
[109] Rubin, *Satmar*, pp. 236–7.

the son of Yekutiel Yehuda Teitelbaum, the late Rebbe's nephew. Moshe Teitelbaum had served as the rabbi of a small Hasidic community in the Borough Park section of New York and referred to himself as the Sziget Rebbe, after the Hungarian town that was the original home of the Teitelbaum dynasty. Although he was not a member of Satmar he agreed to accept the appointment.

The transition from the charismatic leadership of Yoel Teitelbaum to Moshe's very different style was far from easy. The first step taken by the new Admor was to dismiss all the Rebbetzin's allies from key positions in the court and to install his own children in their place. Such nepotism is accepted practice in Hasidic movements, but the defeated camp resented the move, eventually leading to a schism in Satmar. The Rebbetzin and her small circle of supporters argued that no heir should be appointed since the Rebbetzin visited her husband's grave every day and communicated with him, so that Yoel's leadership could continue even after his death. The truth was that the Rebbetzin had already effectively run the court for eleven years with little involvement on her husband's part and saw no reason to change the situation. Keren-Kratz argues that the Rebbetzin had acquired the status of a "saint."[110]

The mainstream of the movement opposed the Rebbetzin's subversive actions. The Rebbetzin and her supporters eventually founded a separate Hasidic court known as Bnai Yoel. They established their own educational institutions, Batei Midrash, and ritual baths. A fierce struggle ensued regarding access to Yoel Teitelbaum's grave and Moshe's leadership. The dissenters accused Moshe of running a business and trading on the stock exchange, something that is considered unacceptable for a Hasidic rabbi. It was also alleged that he had made unreasonable financial demands for his services as rabbi and leader. Bnai Yoel remained a small and relatively uninfluential faction. After the death of Moshe Teitelbaum in 2006, Satmar split between his two sons, Zalman Leib and Aharon. The Bnai Yoel faction joined the followers of Zalman Leib.[111]

CONCLUSION

I shall conclude this chapter by offering a comparison between the Satmar Rebbe and two figures who had similar beliefs and worldviews:

---

[110] Keren-Kratz, *R' Yoel*, p. 358.   [111] Mintz, *Hassidic*, pp. 126–38.

Menachem-Mendel Schneerson, the seventh Rebbe of the Habad-Lubavitch,[112] and Amram Blau, the leader of Neturei Karta.

Menachem-Mendel Schneerson (1902–1994) served as the leader of the Habad dynasty and was one of the most influential figures in the post-Holocaust Haredi world. Although Habad now has a global presence, its headquarters are still situated in the suburbs of New York City, in close proximity to the Satmar community. Habad and Satmar are the two largest Hasidic movements in the United States.

An examination of the biographies of Teitelbaum and Schneerson raises both similarities and differences. While Teitelbaum served as a rabbi and arbiter from an early age and filled rabbinical positions in Europe, Schneerson only reached a leadership position after the Holocaust. Indeed, he initially considered various fields of pursuit and aspired to become an electrical engineer, gaining a secular education in Berlin and Paris before the Second World War.

Habad had been uprooted from its center in Russia following the Bolshevik revolution and the subsequent antireligious campaigns. The sixth Admor, Rabbi Yosef Yitzhak Schneerson, was forced to flee Europe at the beginning of the Second World War, reaching New York in 1940. The members of the movement used their influence to extricate his daughter and her husband Menachem-Mendel from France in 1941. After Yosef Yitzhak Schneerson died in 1950 a fierce inheritance struggle erupted, since he left no sons. His two sons-in-law, Shmariyahu Gurary and Menachem-Mendel Schneerson, fought for the leadership position. While Teitelbaum lived in the ghettoes and concentration camps of Europe and only escaped the Holocaust thanks to extraordinary good luck, Menachem-Mendel was saved from such traumatic experiences.

Schneerson and Teitelbaum each built a Hasidic empire almost from scratch. They both married barren wives and did not have sons to inherit their positions after their death. In his leadership battle, Schneerson based his authority on the claim that he was communicating with the dead Admor, so that his leadership was ostensibly a manifestation of the sixth Admor's will. This is reminiscent of the tactic employed by Teitelbaum's widow on the basis of her daily visits to his grave.

The two rabbis had dramatically different ideological approaches. While the Satmar Rebbe imposed a policy of introspection and isolationism, the Lubavitcher Rebbe placed great emphasis on outreach to the

---

[112] The information about Schneerson is taken from: Heilman and Friedman, *The Rebbe*.

general Jewish public. In order to appreciate this difference it is worth looking briefly at the different views within the Hasidic world regarding Jews who reject the authority of Torah. According to the historian Mendel Piekarz, most Hasidic rabbis in the interwar period argued that all Jews carry an inner spark: even if they sin they are still Jews, and even the worst offenders have nevertheless performed countless commandments. This interpretation served to soften hostility toward those seen as religious offenders. The opposite approach, expounded by Rabbi Elhanan Bonim Wasserman, rejected the importance of the genetic factor and argued that membership of the Jewish people was conditional on observance of the commandments. He claimed that the modern secular parties constitute "Amalek," and their descendants are to be considered "the seed of Amalek."[113]

Like Neturei Karta, the Satmar Rebbe tended to follow the view that secular Jews lay beyond the legitimate boundaries of Judaism. Accordingly, he believed in the need to separate his community from their power and influence.[114] According to this approach the Haredi enclave should separate itself from its surroundings in every facet of life; they had no interest in engaging with Jews who followed different worldviews. By contrast, the Habad movement is characterized by a desire to draw the sinners closer and to recruit supporters for the movement from outside the Haredi enclave. Habad has developed an extensive network of emissaries who operate throughout the Jewish world to draw Jews closer to its version of Jewish heritage.

These different approaches are also evident when we turn to the issue of Zionism. Habad never adopted a pro-Zionist stance, and Menachem-Mendel Schneerson never visited Israel. Nevertheless, Lubavitcher Hasidim have been profoundly involved in developments in Israel, including political issues. In particular, they are renowned for their uncompromising support for the entire Land of Israel. In 1996 Habad supporters played an active role in Benjamin Netanyahu's successful bid for the premiership, financing his campaign under the slogan "Netanyahu is good for the Jews." As mentioned earlier, Habad launched a campaign after the 1967 War encouraging Jews to put on Tefillin in acknowledgment of the apparent miracles that had occurred during the war.

By contrast, the Satmar Rebbe was extremely suspicious of Zionism. He prohibited his followers to take part in the Israeli elections, refused to

---

[113] Piekarz, *Polish Hassidism*, pp. 122–53.
[114] For detailed discussion of the position of Neturei Karta, see Chapter 2.

accept government funds for his educational institutions, and interpreted Israel's successes as evidence of the growing strength of Satan.

The two rabbis also occupied opposite ends of the spectrum in terms of their attitude to messianism, despite the fact that they both argued that the messianic End was close or even imminent. Yosef Yitzhak Schneerson, the sixth Admor of the Habad movement, claimed that the horrors of the Holocaust and the collapse of the religious Jewish world were both manifestations of the "birth pangs of messiah" that precede the End Times. He saw the devastation as proof of the approaching End.[115] The Satmar Rebbe espoused a similar approach. This is a pessimistic form of premillenarian catastrophic messianism that anticipates colossal devastation as part of the "birth pangs of messiah." By contrast, the seventh Admor of Habad saw the successful rehabilitation of the movement and the flourishing State of Israel as evidence of the approaching End Times. This is a more positive approach: though devastation is still a required element, it is followed by revival. Schneerson claimed that redemption could be brought nearer if Habad Hasidim devoted themselves to spreading the light of Judaism throughout the Jewish world (a postmillenarian position).[116] During the last two years of his life, messianic tension in Habad erupted in a personality cult and Schneerson was declared the King Messiah by his followers.

Habad has its headquarters in Crown Heights, New York, while Satmar is based in Williamsburg. The ideological tensions between the two movements led to tension and even to violent incidents between their respective followers.[117] Habad was generally successful in its goal of engaging in outreach with the broader public, and the exposure of its emissaries to secular culture did not, in most cases, lead to desertion or secularization. Satmar, meanwhile, preferred to isolate itself from general culture in order to avoid unwelcome influences. With hindsight both approaches appear to have been successful, and both Habad and Satmar have expanded their circles of influence considerably. Habad has become a leading force within American Jewry as a whole. Satmar is an important player within the Haredi world in and around New York, and Teitelbaum served as head of the religious court of HaEdah HaHaredit in Jerusalem.

---

[115] Ratzabi, "Anti-Zionism."

[116] Aviezer Ravitzky, "The Messianism of Success in Contemporary Judaism." In: Stephen Stein (ed.), *The Encyclopedia of Apocalypticism*, 3: *Apocalypticism in the Modern Period and the Contemporary Age*. New York and London: Continuum, 1998, pp. 204–29.

[117] Mintz, *Hassidic*, pp. 154–65; Deitsch, *Butzina* 2, pp. 295–7.

Amram Blau and Yoel Teitelbaum shared a similar ideological approach, but significant differences can be seen between the two leaders. Blau was a somewhat unidimensional figure. He did not bear responsibility for an entire community and essentially functioned as a benchmark for right-wing Orthodox zealotry. By contrast, Teitelbaum was the leader of a Hasidic community. He was a more multidimensional character and his position required him to attach greater weight to pragmatic considerations before reaching a decision.

Blau was no Don Quixote, however, and before launching a campaign he was careful to make sure that he enjoyed adequate support. His character was also reflected in his insistence on marrying Ruth Ben-David against the wishes of the rabbis of HaEdah HaHaredit. Once he made a decision he was completely unwilling to compromise, even on the tactical level. As an extremist figure he was better placed to insist on his position even if this entailed the risk of failure (as, e.g., in his campaign against mixed swimming pools, which proved a resounding failure). Teitelbaum was forced in some instances to adopt more moderate positions. Thus, for example, he abandoned his demand for women to shave their heads in order to avoid the loss of supporters. He was forced to open girls' schools, contrary to the traditional ways. He was also more moderate than Blau in his attitude toward the State of Israel. The image of his movement was more important to him than participation in every anti-Zionist initiative, and he had no desire to be portrayed as a self-hating Jew.

The relationship between Teitelbaum and Blau might appear to be similar to that between a commander and a soldier, but the reality is more complex. In some instances Neturei Karta and the Satmar Hasidim found themselves at loggerheads. In 1970, for example, a number of Satmar Hasidim participated in an anti-Israeli demonstration in New York together with Fatah activists. The Satmar Rebbe, who had been unaware of the planned demonstration, expelled the Hasidim from the Beit Midrash. In response, Neturei Karta organized a demonstration against the Satmar Rebbe in Jerusalem.[118] The Rebbe also disagreed with Neturei Karta regarding participation in the elections to the Jerusalem city

---

[118] Arguably, in the last decade of his life, Teitelbaum served as Neturei Karta's leader only by title. See: Special correspondent, "Satmar Hasidim Who Demonstrated with Fatah in New York Expelled by the Rebbe, but Defended by Neturei Karta," *Ma'ariv*, March 13, 1970, 20; Yuval Elitzur, "Neturei Karta Declared Its Independence," *Ma'ariv*, August 24, 1979, 1 (in Hebrew).

council. While Teitelbaum favored participation in municipal elections, Neturei Karta was opposed to involvement in any electoral process in the State of Israel, even on the local level. More recently, as noted in the introduction to this book, representatives of Neturei Karta attended a conference of Holocaust deniers in Teheran in 2006. Rabbi Yekutiel Yehuda Teitelbaum, one of the leaders of the sector following the death of his father Moshe, fiercely condemned those who attended the event.[119] It would seem that concern for the reputation of the sector has a moderating effect on the anti-Zionist campaigns of Satmar, whereas Neturei Karta is free of such concerns. Moreover, each side has been shown to be willing to attack the other in public.[120]

In closing, I would like to focus on the second wives of Yoel Teitelbaum and Amram Blau – Alta Feiga and Ruth. Both were unusually strong women against the background of the Haredi world. Ruth's "entrance examination" to this world was her involvement in the kidnapping of Yossele Schumacher and his smuggling out of the State of Israel.[121] This is an unusual course of action in the Haredi world, which usually tends to respect law and authority, and the involvement of a woman in such criminal activity is even more exceptional. After Teitelbaum's stroke Alta Feiga became the strongest figure in the Satmar, which she effectively ruled for the following eleven years. After her husband's death she refused to abandon her leadership role and led a dissident Hasidic court – an almost unthinkable action in the Hasidic world.

Teitelbaum refused to divorce his wife despite pressure on him to do so when it emerged that she was barren. Amram Blau also refused to break off his engagement to Ruth, and his stubborn loyalty effectively led to his removal as leader of Neturei Karta.[122]

What made Teitelbaum so successful? Although he was aggressive, stubborn, and aloof, he was also wise enough to understand the American life style and to reinvent Hasidic Judaism in the new country, while

---

[119] Yekutiel Yehuda Teitelbaum even issued a Torah opinion stating that the representatives who visited Teheran were "committing an act of insanity" that weakened the community and its zealous struggle. See: www.yoel–ab.com/data/ upload_images/docs/ 4581bc19075add6b.jpg (accessed September 1, 2013).

[120] Menachem Keren-Kratz even argues that the loudest attacks on the Rebbe came from the ranks of Neturei Karta. Keren-Kratz, *R' Yoel*, p. 297.

[121] Ruth Blau, *Guardians of the City*. Jerusalem: Idanim, 1979 (in Hebrew).

[122] Kimmy Caplan, "'An Insolent, Dirty Convert Woman:' The Scandal of the Marriage of Amram Blau and Ruth Ben-David," *Iyyunim bitkumat Yisrael* 20 (5770 – 2011), 300–35.

making many changes. Unlike the experience in Hungary, where there were many communities that were associated with radical ultra-Orthodoxy, he was almost the only anti-Zionist rabbi on American soil, and accordingly he enjoyed a unique position. His theology was clear and sharp; he was even able to provide a response to the theological dilemma regarding the role of God during the Holocaust. His extreme version of Orthodoxy was appealing to some Holocaust survivors who immigrated to the United States after the war. The fact that he encouraged his followers to go to work also helped him to generate income for the movement's institutions. His patronage of the Jerusalem radicals further enhanced his prestige.[123]

Teitelbaum was an unusual character who secured remarkable achievements. He was a controversial leader and many opposed his positions. On the personal level, he survived the Holocaust and managed to rebuild his own life and to lead a new era of growth in the Hasidic world on an unprecedented scale. Despite his much-flaunted zealotry he was a complex character and he underwent many changes over the course of his life. The fact that the Nazis were unable to eradicate Hasidic Jewry and that people such as Teitelbaum were able to overcome enormous suffering is an achievement that should not be overlooked. Teitelbaum revived a unique branch of the diverse world of Judaism and became one of the most interesting figures in contemporary Jewish history.

[123] Keren-Kratz, *R' Yoel*, pp. 363–9.

6

Eschatology, dualism, and the decline of the generations

The world view of radical ultra-Orthodoxy

This chapter discusses the ideological worldview of radical ultra-Orthodoxy, beginning with the schism in the Hungarian Jewish communities in the 1860s. I will base my examination on the positions advocated by Rabbi Akiva Yosef Schlesinger at this time and the similar views espoused decades later in Jerusalem and New York by Rabbis Yeshayah Asher Zelig Margaliot and Yoel Teitelbaum. Schlesinger, Margaliot, and Teitelbaum operated in different times and places (Hungary, Jerusalem and New York) but can nevertheless be regarded as representatives of a similar ideology. In particular, I will emphasize the antimodernist tendencies in these circles, their firm assertion of eschatological theories, and their tendency to view deviations from tradition in a dualist and demonological manner. David Sorotzkin had demonstrated that the roots of radical ultra-Orthodoxy were planted in the seventeenth century, with the rise of modern era. I believe that these ideas matured on a larger scale after the schism in Hungary at the nineteenth century, where I start my discussion in this chapter.[1]

I present each of the three rabbis individually. I begin with Schlesinger, basing my examination of his beliefs on his treatise *Lev Ha'ivri* ("The Heart of the Hebrew.") Although Schlesinger presented the founding principles of this ideology, his followers were uncomfortable about quoting him directly due to his in-principle support for the establishment

---

[1] I will refer to Sorotzkin's arguments at greater length further in the chapter as part of the discussion of the teachings of Rabbi Yoel Teitelbaum. See: David Sorotzkin, *Orthodoxy and Modern Disciplineation: The Production of Jewish Tradition in Europe in Modern Times*. Tel Aviv: HaKibbutz HaMeuhad, 2011 (in Hebrew).

of a Jewish state in the Land of Israel.[2] I shall then proceed to examine the thought of Rabbi Margaliot, with his strongly dualist and apocalyptic approach. Lastly, I will present the worldview of Yoel Teitelbaum, which blends dualism and eschatology to create an extremist and antimodernist ideology that has its roots in acute messianic tension.

The rabbis viewed the modern era as so degenerate that the advent of the messiah must be imminent. All these religious leaders adopted a dualistic approach according to which the only proper Jewish way of life is radical ultra-Orthodoxy, while any deviation from it represents the rise of Satanic powers, which are expected to grow prior to the End Times. They all viewed their opponents – moderate Orthodox Jews as well as the secular – as the reincarnation of the mixed multitude: an unauthentic segment of the Jewish nation.

AKIVA YOSEF SCHLESINGER

Akiva Yosef Schlesinger (1837–1922) is a paradoxical and unusual character. The historian Jacob Katz commented: "Some have claimed that Akiva Yosef Schlesinger was both the grandfather of Zionism and the grandfather of Neturei Karta, and there is some truth in this claim ... I do not know who takes more pride in him, but both drew elements from his philosophy, or if they did not draw them – then at least both show aspects that are close to his approach."[3]

Schlesinger was born in Pressburg, Hungary and received a strictly traditional Jewish education. His father was part of the circle of Moshe Sofer (the "Hatam Sofer,") the founder of Hungarian Orthodoxy,[4] and he raised his son in keeping with Sofer's worldview. Akiva was ordained to the rabbinate in 1857 in Pressburg by Rabbi Avraham Shmuel Binyamin Sofer (the "Ktav Sofer,") the son of the Hatam Sofer. In 1860 he married Liba, the daughter of Rabbi Hillel Lichtenstein. Schlesinger and Lichtenstein would become the twin pillars of radical Orthodoxy.

---

[2] Michael Silber, "The Emergence of Ultra-Orthodoxy: The Invention of Tradition." In: Jack Wertheimer (ed.), *The Uses of Tradition*. Cambridge: Jewish Theological Seminary, 1992, pp. 23–84.

[3] Quoted in Michael Silber, "A Hebrew Heart Beats in Hungary: Rabbi Akiva Yosef Schlesinger – Between Ultra-Orthodoxy and Jewish Nationalism." In: Avi Sagi and Dov Schwartz (eds.), *One Hundred Years of Zionism*, 1. Ramat Gan: Bar Ilan University Press, 5763 – 2003, p. 226 (in Hebrew).

[4] Jacob Katz, "Towards a Biography of the Hatam Sofer," *Divine Law in Human Hands: Case Studies in Halakhic Flexibility*. Jerusalem: Magnes Press, 1998, pp. 403–43.

In 1870 he emigrated to Palestine where he was involved in Jewish settlement activities; he was among the founders of the colony of Petach Tikva.[5]

In 1863 Schlesinger published his treatise *Lev Ha'ivri* ("The Heart of the Hebrew"), which fiercely criticized the phenomenon of religious reform and the neo-Orthodox stream's support for acculturation. This book was dedicated to the teachings of the Hatam Sofer, of whom Schlesinger considered himself a rightful heir.[6] The book was very popular and appeared in five editions. Schlesinger wrote the book against the background of the crisis in Hungarian Orthodoxy during the nineteenth century. Jews who adhered to traditional values and life style faced a series of challenges during this period: the requirement by the state that educational institutions provide secular studies; growing linguistic acculturation; pressure to adopt a Magyar identity; and widespread religious reforms in the synagogues. By the 1870s Orthodox Jews realized that they would soon become a minority within the Jewish population of Hungary.[7]

Schlesinger opened *Lev Ha'ivri* with an attack on the teaching of Jewish scriptures to Gentiles and the growing openness of Jews to study non-Jewish texts. This phenomenon had begun with the famous project initiated by Moses Mendelssohn (1726–1786) to translate the Hebrew Bible into German. Mendelssohn is considered one of the fathers of the Enlightenment movement that swept German Jewry.[8] Schlesinger regarded the study by Jews of nonrabbinical texts (which he referred to as "exterior books" and "Gentile knowledge") as the greatest threat to the Jewish world. He argued that those who read such books are considered "evil" and believed that attempts to return them to the fold were futile.[9] Mendelssohn advocated various changes to the Jewish way of life, with an emphasis on the adoption of Gentile culture. He called for the abandonment of the Yiddish language and opposed distinctive Jewish dress. He also advocated the abandonment of traditional Jewish names.

[5] Michael Silber, "Schlesinger, Akiva Yosef," *YIVO Encyclopedia of Jews in Eastern Europe*, 2010. www.yivoencyclopedia.org/article.aspx/Schlesinger_Akiva_Yosef (accessed March 4, 2013).

[6] Meir Hildesheimer, "The Attitude of the Ḥatam Sofer toward Moses Mendelssohn," *Proceedings of the American Academy for Jewish Research* 60, (1994), 141–87.

[7] Silber, "The Emergence," pp. 24–5.

[8] David Sorkin, *Moses Mendelssohn and the Religious Enlightenment*. Berkeley: University of California Press, 1996.

[9] Akiva Yosef Schlesinger, *Lev ha'ivri*, Jerusalem: Zuckerman, 5784 – 1924, p. 3.

However, the real point of concern to Orthodoxy was that Mendelssohn did not seek to abandon Jewish tradition in its entirety, but rather to create a hybrid version of Jewish and German culture. Accordingly, Schlesinger considered neo-Orthodoxy to be an even greater threat to Judaism than the Reform movement that deliberately introduced changes into the synagogue structure and in Jewish rituals. He dubbed the neo-Orthodox "Sadducees,"[10] referring to the sect from the Second Temple period that rejected rabbinical authority and the Oral Law.

As a counterweight to Mendelssohn's plan of acculturation, Schlesinger emphasized the distinctive identity of Judaism, which should be manifested in individuals' names, language, and dress. He referred to these three elements by the Hebrew acronym *shale'm*, which also means "complete," and argued that following the ways of the past and highlighting particularistic Jewish identity was a reflection of authenticity. His model of the ideal course to be followed by Jews was the mirror image of that promoted by Mendelssohn. He opposed changing Jewish first names (the process by which Aharon became Adolf or Moshe Martin). He rejected the call for the Jews to adopt the language of their Gentile environment and argued that Jews must remain separate from their neighbors and must not speak the Gentile languages. In the area of dress, too, Schlesinger prohibited such innovations as the shortening of the beard and sidelocks and growing long hair on the top of the head.

Schlelesinger had to respond to the enlightened critiques who argued that the "Jewish" languages (primarily Yiddish) were dialects of Gentile tongues. Moreover, Maimonides himself wrote his works in Judeo-Arabic, and the Bible had been translated into Greek and Aramaic. Schlesinger's response was that the Jewish languages were corrupted versions of Gentile tongues, thereby maintaining their distinctive character. He argued that the translation of the Bible into Greek was an example of the Biblical rule presented in Psalm 119: "It is time to act for the Lord: they have broken your Torah." In other words, this act of translation was the exception that proved the rule, rather than an attempt to replace the Torah with alien teachings.[11]

Schlesinger saw the dramatic changes in the condition of the Jews, and particularly the collapse of the world of traditional Judaism, as a manifestation of the approaching messianic age. I will refer to his approach as "catastrophic millennialism," which is marked by belief in an imminent

---

[10] Silber, "The Emergence," pp. 27–9.   [11] Schlesinger, *Lev ha'ivri*, pp. 23–8.

transition to the millennial kingdom. Catastrophic millennialism involves a pessimistic view of human nature and society. Humans are so evil and corrupt that the old order has to be destroyed violently to make way for the perfected millennial kingdom. This approach adopts a radical dualistic worldview: reality is seen in terms of good and evil, reflected in an adversary perception of the relations between true believers and those outside the fold.[12]

Schlesinger refers to the discussions in the Babylonian Talmud concerning the period preceding the coming of the messiah. In the Rabbinic literature the "footsteps of messiah" are described as a miserable period characterized by spiritual and material decline. For example, the Babylonian Talmud states that the messiah Son of David will come only in a generation that is either entirely guilty or entirely innocent (Sanhedrin 98a). Accordingly, Schlesinger argues, the emergence of the "Reform sect" is proof of impending redemption, based on his characterization of this movement as one devoted to the desecration of the Sabbath, intermarriage, rejection of the idea of miraculous redemption through the king messiah,[13] the selective observance of the commandments, and the eating of forbidden foods in public.[14] He attacked the Reform as "Satan . . . a wolf in sheep's clothing," and warned his follows to separate themselves from Reform Jews.

Schlesinger's eschatological and dualist perspective led him to the conclusion that isolationism and an internal schism in the Jewish world were unavoidable and even desirable. He argued that the Talmudic vision of a generation that is entirely guilty and a generation that is entirely innocent in the premessianic period demands a sharp distinction: "Those who remain in the Jewish people will be absolutely righteous or absolutely evil." Accordingly, the best course of action is to divide the synagogues between the heretics and the faithful.[15]

---

[12] Catherine Wessinger, "Catastrophic Millennialism." In: Richard Landes (ed.), *Encyclopedia of Millennialism and Millennial Movements*. New York: Routledge, 2000, pp. 61–3.

[13] The Reform movement consistently rejected the anticipation of an individual messiah Son of David, just as it rejected the concept of the formation of the Kingdom of the House of David in the End Times. Reform Judaism saw redemption as a gradual and infinite process achieved through human efforts to "repair" the world. See: David Ariel-Joël, "Messianism without Messiah: The Messiah Who Will Not Come." In: David, Ariel-Joël and others (eds.), *The War of Gog and Magog: Messianism and Apocalypse in Judaism, Past and Present*. Tel Aviv: Hemed Publishers, 2001, pp. 161–73 (in Hebrew).

[14] Schlesinger, *Lev ha'ivri*, p. 3.   [15] *Ibid.*, p. 5.

Schlesinger found further evidence of the imminence of the messianic era in the teachings of the mystical book of the Zohar, applying the term *erev rav* ("mixed multitude") from the Kabbalistic treatise to those Jews who introduced innovations. The "mixed multitude" is mentioned in the Book of Exodus (12:38): "A mixed multitude (*erev rav*) went up with them, and also large droves of livestock, both flocks and herds." The traditional Jewish literature defines the "mixed multitude" as non-Jewish Egyptians who joined the exodus from Egypt, assimilated into the nation, and were later responsible for various problems, particularly incitement against Moses and God. In the Kabbalistic literature (particularly the *Ra'aya Mehemana* and *Tikunei Hazohar*), this group receives particular attention, and the radical ultra-Orthodox leaders base their teachings on these mystical sources.

Two leading scholars in the field of Jewish thought, Yitzhak Baer and Yeshayah Tishbi, claimed that the epithet "mixed multitude" was attached to the leaders of the Spanish Jewish communities in the thirteenth century after they were accused of offending Jewish morality and forming alliances with Gentiles in order to harm the Jewish people and distance the Divine presence. The Kabbalistic works claim that when the messiah comes the "mixed multitude" will be eliminated from the world. This formed part of their anticipation of the End Times as an imminent event in which God would reward the righteous and punish the wicked, including the "mixed multitude," for their countless offenses.[16]

Rabbi Chaim Vital, who lived in the sixteenth century and was close to Rabbi Yitzhak Luria, offered a different interpretation of the "mixed multitude," which he defined as an intermediate group between Jews and Gentiles. In the End Times, said Vital, this group would be converted and brought fully into the Jewish fold. He viewed the *Conversos* – Jewish converts to Christianity who returned to Judaism in this period – as an example of this positive phenomenon.[17] However, the negative perception of this term based on the Zohar has since become universally accepted. During the Sabbatean controversy in the seventeenth century, both followers and opponents of Shabtai Zvi denigrated each other as the mixed multitude.[18]

---

[16] Yitzhak Baer, "The Historical Background of the *Ra'aya Mehemena*," *Zion* 5, 1 (1940), 1–44 (in Hebrew); Yeshayah Tishbi, *The Teaching of the Zohar*, 2. Jerusalem: Bialik Institute, 1949, pp. 686–92 (in Hebrew).

[17] Shaul Magid, "The Politics of (un)Conversion: The 'Mixed Multitude' (*erev rav*) as Conversos in Rabbi Hayyim Vital's Ets ha–da'at tov," *Jewish Quarterly Review* 95(4) (2005), 625–66.

[18] Pawel Maciejko, *The Mixed Multitude: Jacob Frank and the Frankist Movement, 1755–1816*. Philadelphia: University of Pennsylvania Press, 2011.

The identification by ultra-Orthodox circles of modern Jewish trends as the "mixed multitude" is also based on the writings of Rabbi Zvi Elimelech Shapira, the founder of the Dinov-Munkacs Hasidic dynasty. In his essay *Ma'ayan Ganim* ("The Spring's Gardens") he labeled Reform and Enlightenment as the reincarnation of the mixed multitude.[19] Like Shapira, Schlesinger argues that the current days are of the beginning of the premessianic days where the last selection between good and evil is about to be made.[20]

According to Schlesinger, in order to ascertain whether the messiah's time has truly come, God presents tests to examine the Jews' faith. He saw his period, with the destabilization of past ways and the great temptations facing the Jews to integrate in general culture, whether by way of assimilation or acculturation, as a Divine test presented by God to His faithful. He declared that it was preferable to live in poverty, suffering, and hunger than to enjoy popularity and wealth at the expense of changing the old ways and turning to "external books."[21] Schlesinger wrote: "And you, Sons of Zion who are truly faithful to the Lord … if you wish you and your seed to have a portion and inheritance with the Lord, do not veer from your forefathers' ways … let not your feet follow the paths of evil."[22]

For Schlesinger, joining Reform was equal to conversion into a different religion. It was preferable, he suggested, to "deliver one's soul" rather than join the Reform, which he considered a sin to be avoided even on pain of death.[23] He adopted a zealous approach, arguing that no mercy should be shown toward the sinners since the Bible did not offer a model of such forgivingness. Moses, for example, showed no mercy when he killed those who persecuted the Children of Israel, and the Prophet Samuel showed no mercy when he beheaded the Amalekite King Agag. These examples, he concluded, suggest that the proper response to sinners is violence. The zealous behavior of Pinchas in the Bible also lauds the use of violence: Pinchas murdered Zimri and Cozbi after they sinned in public.[24]

---

[19] David Sorotzkin, *The Supratemporal Community in an Era of Changes: Sketches on the Development of the Perception of Time and Collective as a Basis for the Definition of the Development of Jewish Orthodoxy in Modern Times*. Jerusalem: PhD Dissertation, The Hebrew University of Jerusalem, 2007, pp. 193–203 (in Hebrew); Zvi Elimelech Shapira, *Maayan Ganim*. Zolkeiw: S. Meyerhoffer, 1848 (in Hebrew).

[20] Schlesinger, *Lev ha'ivri*, p. 27.   [21] *Ibid.*, pp. 5, 23.   [22] *Ibid.*, p. 45.

[23] *Ibid.*, p. 37.

[24] Schlesinger's opinions are over simplistic. For the Bible's approach toward violence see: Robert Eisen, *The Peace and Violence of Judaism*. New York: Oxford University Press, 2011, pp. 15–64.

Nevertheless Schlesinger moderated the Biblical message somewhat, emphasizing that individuals must not turn to violence as this is forbidden by the law of the land: "However, we are not permitted to actually kill and to wreak the Lord's zealous vengeance, since the law of the land is the law ("*dina d'malchuta dina*"); we are bound by the Three Oaths not to rebel against the nations."[25] Regarding the principle "Love your neighbor as yourself" (Leviticus 19:18), which would seem to mandate a peaceful approach, Schlesinger responded that this applies only if the sinners repent. As long as they refuse to do so, there is a religious commandment to struggle against them: "They are Sadducees, and they must not be pitied whatsoever."[26] For him, the identification of the sinners as the *erev rav* and as Sadducees removes them from the circle of Jews to whom one must remain committed, since this approach argues that there is a genetic distinction between proper Jews and the descendants of the *erev rav*; the obligation to behave peaceably does not apply in their case.

Schlesinger's adherence to the principles of zealotry led him to reject any change or modification in response to new realities, even if the changes were tactical rather than substantive. He rejected any revision in the structure of the synagogue, quoting Talmudic and Kabbalistic sources in support of his position.[27] He also prohibited the use of the local language, rather than Jewish languages as Yiddish or Hebrew, for sermons: "And on this matter our rabbi, may his memory be a blessing [i.e., Moshe Sofer], established a great rule prohibiting any change, whatever its nature, for we have only that which we inherited from our forefathers."[28]

Schlesinger engaged in a separate discussion on issues relating to women; here, too, he rejected any possibility of change. He called for the rejection of new fashions prevalent among women on the grounds of modesty. He also expressed his fear that a more moderate approach to women's dress would prove a slippery slope leading to the mass abandonment of the old ways: "Our forefathers were redeemed thanks to pious women and now, for our abundant sins, they are collaborating and causing licentiousness in our generation."[29] He advocated reprimands and demonstrations against women who exposed their hair, and

---

[25] Schlesinger, *Lev ha'ivri*, pp. 47, 49. For a discussion of the effects of the Three Oaths on Jewish memory and practice, see: Aviezer Ravitzky, *Messianism, Zionism, and Jewish Religious Radicalism*. Chicago and London: University of Chicago Press, 1993, pp. 211–34.

[26] Schlesinger, *Lev ha'ivri*, p. 48.   [27] *Ibid.*, pp. 63–4.   [28] *Ibid.*, p. 73.

[29] *Ibid.*, p. 79.

even forbad women to wear wigs: "I absolutely forbid this for you."[30] He opposed the provision of religious or secular education for girls and advocated the maintenance of traditional gender roles.[31] He later moderated his position regarding women's education, and in the Utopian society he depicted in an essay from 1873, he advocated teaching women Hebrew in order to strengthen its use as a spoken language in the home.[32]

Schlesinger argued that the situation was so bad that his supporters should not send their sons to the yeshivot due to the dangers they would face: "Happy is he who can protect his soul and his seed and not send them away from his home and his supervision until their time comes to marry." He believed that boys should study Torah for several years and then learn a trade, quoting a verse from the Ethics of the Fathers: "All study of the Torah which is not accompanied by work is destined to prove futile." However, boys must recognize that Torah study is the most important act, while work is of secondary importance.[33]

On the basis of these insights, Schlesinger advocated a retreat into an ultra-Orthodox enclave: "Save your infants and children." A place of refuge must be prepared that is free of spiritual dangers, avoiding the need to live with the heretics. This approach reflects a desire to respond actively to change rather than remaining passive. This is a form of zealotry that does not resort to violence, but calls for the removal of the wicked from the community of the faithful and rejects any changes in the structure or language of prayer in the synagogue.

Schlesinger anticipated that Orthodoxy would be defeated in its struggle against modernism, and therefore perceived an urgent need to create the ultimate ghetto. His reading of the direction events were taking led him to conclude that the only safe place for faithful Jews was the Land of Israel, a remote and isolated land. Accordingly, in 1870 he emigrated to Palestine, and three years later he published a detailed essay advocating the establishment of a Jewish state to operate on the basis of Orthodox principles, organized around agricultural colonies.[34] His proposed colonies were to be managed in accordance with quasidemocratic principles, including decision making by majority rule, and boys and girls would learn Hebrew, which would serve as the language of speech. Schlesinger

---

[30] *Ibid.*, p. 81.   [31] *Ibid.*, pp. 84–5.   [32] Silver, *Pa'amei lev*, p. 9.

[33] Schlesinger, *Lev ha'ivri*, p. 67.

[34] Michael Silber, "Alliance of the Hebrew, 1863–1875: The Diaspora Roots of an Ultra-Orthodox Proto-Zionist Utopia in Palestine," *The Journal of Israeli History* 27(2) (2008), 119–47.

called for an end to the system of charitable donations from the Diaspora used to support the Old Yishuv, and urged that Diaspora resources be redirected to financing the mass emigration of Jews to the Land of Israel (a position that incurred the wrath of the Old Yishuv rabbis). He even advocated the formation of military units to protect the agricultural colonies.[35]

Schlesinger's struggle against acculturation, particularly in the fields of language and dress, motivated him to leave Hungary and to develop a Utopian approach embodying nationalist ideas that predated the Jewish national movement.[36] As a result, some Zionist thinkers later came to see him as the harbinger of Zionism. Later ultra-Orthodox figures found it difficult to identify with Schlesinger and showed an ambivalent and suspicious attitude toward his thought. They readily adopted his diagnosis of the situation, but his adoption of a solution based on Jewish nationalism met with reservations and confusion.[37] The model of retreat into a religious enclave was enthusiastically adopted by the entire ultra-Orthodox world. However, the enemy to be combated was identified as the Zionist movement in addition to Reform. Radical ultra-Orthodox leaders were fiercely critical of any Orthodox support for Zionism, whether a priori (as in the case of Religious Zionism) or a fortiori (as with Agudat Yisrael).

RABBI YESHAYAH ASHER ZELIG MARGALIOT

Yeshayah Asher Zelig Margaliot (1894–1968) was born in Chelm (at the time part of the Austro-Hungarian Empire) to a Belz Hasidic family. In 1906 he was sent by his father to Palestine to join the ranks of the Old Yishuv. His first teacher was Rabbi Avraham Simcha Horowitz of Baranov, who was an enthusiastic eschatologist. According to the hagiographic sources, he calculated that the end of the world would come on the eve of Passover (the sources do not state in which year); accordingly, he set out on this particular eve of Passover for the Western Wall in order to prepare to make the Pascal sacrifice on the Temple Mount after the

[35] Rachel Elboim–Dror, "The Ultimate Ghetto: A Subversive Ultra-Orthodox Utopia," *Jewish Studies Quarterly* 7(1) (2000), 65–95.

[36] Schlesinger follows here the Hatam Sofer's approach to immigration to the Land of Israel. See: Moshe Samet, *Chapters in the History of Orthodoxy*. Jerusalem: Carmel, 2005, p. 26 (in Hebrew).

[37] Silber, "The Emergence," pp. 81–2.

messiah arrived and the Temple was miraculously reconstructed.[38] Margaliot engaged in messianic calculations and formulated a plan for the establishment of the Third Temple.[39]

After Horowitz's death, Margaliot joined Rehovot Ha-Nahar Yeshivah and became a student and close associate of the Sephardic Kabbalist Rabbi Chaim Shaul Dweik. Rehovot HaNahar became the leading institution devoted to Lurian Kabbalistic studies based on the interpretation of Rabbi Shalom Sharabi.[40] After Dweik's death, a schism occurred and the Sha'ar Shamayim Yeshivah was established alongside the original institution. Sha'ar Shamayim supported Jewish nationalism, and Rabbi Avraham Yitzhak Kook was given the honorary title of "senior officer" in the yeshivah. Margaliot regularly attended the new yeshivah.[41] His decision to attend a yeshivah along with supporters of Zionism is certainly surprising – the division between the religious supporters and opponents of Jewish nationalism was profound and often personal. Jerusalem zealots fiercely attacked Kook and the Chief Rabbinate institutions he headed. Margaliot himself composed an entire book, *Ashre ha-ish* ("Happy is the Man"), criticizing Kook. Kook's supporters evidently decided to fight back and sought to damage Margaliot's livelihood, to the extent that he considered leaving the country.[42] After Dweik's death, Margaliot became a follower of the "Holy Grandfather" Rabbi Shlomo Eliezer Alfandri. He also helped organize the meeting between Admor Chaim Elazar Shapira of Munkacs and the "Holy Grandfather" with the goal of expediting redemption (see Chapter 4).

Margaliot authored some thirty books on various themes relating to the Kabbalah, such as the qualities of Rabbi Shimon Bar Yochai, who has traditionally been considered the author of the Zohar and an incarnation of king messiah. Other topics covered by his works included the merits of circumcision, the importance of external appearance, and the struggle against Zionism and its proponents.

Yehuda Liebes has noted the surprising similarities between Margaliot's approach to Zionism and the philosophy presented in the writings

---

[38] Shimon Margaliot, *Azamer bi-Shvahin: The Life of the Hasidic Kabbalistic Rabbi Yeshayah Asher Zelig Margaliot, May a Sage's Memory Be a Blessing.* Jerusalem: self-publication, 5763 – 2003, pp. 32–5 (in Hebrew).

[39] Margaliot, *Azamer,* p. 20.

[40] For a detailed description of this institution, see: Yonatan Meir, *Rehovot ha–Nahar: Kabbalah and Esotericism in Jerusalem (1896–1948).* Jerusalem: Ben Zvi Institute, 2011 (in Hebrew).

[41] *Ibid.,* p. 20.   [42] *Ibid.,* p. 191.

of the Judean Desert sect. Margaliot cannot possibly have read the Hidden Scrolls or even been aware of their existence, since they were only discovered in the early 1950s, decades after he wrote his books. Liebes comments that it is interesting to see how similar ideas can emerge from such different periods and situations in the development of Jewish tradition.[43] (In the following chapter I will discuss at greater length the similarities between ancient and modern patterns of zealotry).

In 1927 Margaliot published his dogmatic work *Ashrei Ha'Aish* ("Happy is the Man"), which will form the main basis for my analysis of his thought. The work was intended as an ideological manifesto of the Old Yishuv in Jerusalem in the context of its struggle against Zionism. At the time, as will be recalled, Agudat Yisrael was hostile to Zionism. Accordingly, Margaliot could aim to produce a text that presented the ideological stance of the entire Haredi population in the Land of Israel. Agudat Yisrael later distanced itself from its original opposition to cooperation with the Zionist movement,[44] and Margaliot's position then became a platform of the minority group of HaEdah HaHaredit and Neturei Karta (see Chapter 2). Margaliot's approach was based on three central elements: eschatology, demonology and an extreme form of dualism.

One of the main issues in early twentieth-century Hasidic discourse was the attitude that should be adopted toward Jews who abandoned the Torah and commandments. Most Hasidic rabbis, including the Ger and Alexander rabbis, argued that such offenders nevertheless continued to form part of the Jewish people, despite their offenses. Accordingly, they continue to bear a Jewish essence and efforts should be made to bring them back to the fold.[45]

Margaliot could not deny that Jewish tradition recognizes the continued presence of such a "Jewish essence" even among those who transgress. He was familiar with Talmudic statements emphasizing the value of all Jews, such as "The offenders are as full of commandments as a pomegranate" (*Babylonian Talmud, Sanhedrin* 37a) and "A Jew remains a Jew, even though he has sinned" (*Babylonian Talmud, Sanhedrin* 44a).

[43] Yehuda Liebes, "HaEdah HaHaredit in Jerusalem and the Judean Desert Sect," *Jerusalem Research in Judaic Studies* 3 (1981), 135–52 (in Hebrew).

[44] Yosef Fund, *Separation or Integration: Agudat Yisrael Confronts Zionism and the State of Israel.* Jerusalem: Magnes Press, 1999 (in Hebrew); Gershon Bacon, *The Politics of Tradition: Agudat Yisrael in Poland, 1916–1939.* Jerusalem: Magnes Press, 1996.

[45] Mendel Piekarz, *Ideological Trends of Hassidism in Poland during the Interwar Period and the Holocaust,* Jerusalem: Bialik Institute, 1997, pp. 122–56 (in Hebrew).

However, Margaliot refused to interpret such verses as implying that efforts should be made to reach out to the offenders. He based his position on the exclusion of the offenders from *Klal Yisrael* (the Collectivity of Israel) and their identification as part of the *erev rav* (the "mixed multitude.") The more lenient Talmudic verses therefore no longer applied to them, and no merit should be seen in their actions.

According to Margaliot, those Jews who cast off Torah and the commandments belong to the Satanic forces, and their growing strength is paradoxically evidence of the impending End Times. For him, in the period before the messianic End, the strength of the *erev rav* increases. Like Schlesinger, Margaliot also believed that God had presented the true believers with a test of their resolve to separate themselves from the *erev rav*. The mass abandonment of the religious way of life, referred to by the rabbi as "heresy and apostasy," would be the final and greatest test. Against this background, the objective of *Ashrei Ha'aish* was to emphasize the need for the faithful to steel themselves for this final battle: "The time is one of war." The faithful must be armed so that they could withstand the forces of impurity. Accordingly, Margaliot opposed any tendency to compromise; any achievement the offenders secured would only strengthen them: "Someone who should protest against them and fails to do so is called a sinner."[46]

Margaliot explained that the *erev rav* are the descendants of the Egyptians and their sorcerers who mixed in with the Israelites as they left Egypt. Thus the offenders of our own generation are the reincarnation of these souls. He went on to propose a test of faith to determine who was of holy origin and who was a descendent of the *erev rav*. He suggested that there are three categories of religious deviation: apostate (*min*), heretic (*epikoras*) and infidel (*kofer*), and argued that while the first two categories cannot repent, infidels may yet return to the true fold. The test lies in the observance of the Sabbath: "He who observes [the verse] 'keep and remember' on the Sabbath remains in our image as ourselves."[47] In other words, those supporters of Zionism who continue to observe the tradition may yet repent and be saved. He added that a person whose parents are proper Jews but who rejects the Torah thereby shows that his soul stems from the *erev rav*, and he is not of proper Jewish descent.[48]

---

[46] Yeshayah Asher Zelig Margaliot, *Ashrei Ha'Aish*. Jerusalem: Breslav Press, 5681 – 1921, pp. 1–7 (in Hebrew).

[47] *Ibid.*, p. 39.   [48] *Ibid.*, p. 40.

The obligation to separate oneself from the *erev rav* imposes a prohibition on association with them; one should not even look at them, in case this sparks curiosity and damages the pure soul.[49] They should not be greeted and it is permissible to malign them. It is a positive commandment to hate them.[50] It is permissible to pray for their repentance, and it is prohibited to pray for their death.[51] Accordingly, Schlesinger negates the use of the Kabbalistic *pulsa dinura* ceremony, which beseeches God to cause the death of a wicked person. Such ceremonies were used by Neturei Karta activists (see Chapters 2 and 3).

According to Margaliot, our age is particularly confusing. Alongside infidels who reject religion, there are others who have the external appearance of proper and innocent Jews who observe tradition and faith, yet whose actions strengthen the secular Zionists. This comment referred to the supporters of Religious Zionism. He was particularly enraged by the position of Kook, although he avoided mentioning him by name: "He wraps himself in the prayer shawls of the just and sits with them, and his goal is to drag their prayer shawls and remove them from the communality of Israel."[52]

Margaliot lashes out at the supporters of Religious Zionism, whom he describes as "wicked." He claims that the religious commandment to seek peace does not apply to relations with them, and the faithful should have no concerns about condemning them and separating themselves from them. One must not marry them or hold marriage ceremonies with their rabbis. One must not maintain commercial relations with them or include them in one's quorum for prayers. One must not allow one's children to become friendly with their association for fear of corruption.[53]

Those who adopted a more tolerant view of Zionism presented two key arguments, both of which Margaliot utterly rejected. The first was that the religious commandment to seek peace requires an effort to reach a compromise with the sinners. The second was that the Zionists deserved some credit for their actions since they were fulfilling the Biblical commandment to settle the Land of Israel. Activists in Agudat Yisrael used both these arguments to justify their efforts to engage in partnership with the Zionist movement.[54] Regarding the requirement to seek peace, Margaliot retorted: "We must choose truth before peace."[55] In other words, the sins of the Zionists make it impossible to act peaceably toward them. He argued that the Torah takes precedence over peace, and that it is

---

[49] *Ibid.*, p. 27.   [50] *Ibid.*, pp. 38–9.   [51] *Ibid.*, pp. 33–5.   [52] *Ibid.*, p. 79.
[53] *Ibid.*, p. 18.   [54] Yosef Fund, *Separation.*   [55] Margaliot, *Ashrei*, p. 12.

forbidden to pursue peace at the expense of keeping the laws of the Torah. The prohibition against divisiveness relates to mundane matters, he claimed, and not to substantive questions concerning the observance of the Torah.[56] As for the commandment to settle the Land, Margaliot noted the adage that "a commandment that is observed through a transgression leads to a transgression." In other words, the settlements that were being built by the Zionists had no value if their residents desecrated the Sabbath and they were not founded on the basis of the observance of the Torah and the commandments.[57] Similarly, he suggested that the Talmudic injunction to "love your fellow as yourself" does not apply to heretics, whom the faithful are actually enjoined to hate.[58]

Margaliot saw the obligation to confront the wicked as a sacred value. He sharply criticized Torah students who justified their passive approach by claiming that they did not want to take time away from their studies: "Even if he himself studies and prays and follows the Lord's way, how can he look on and remain silent as Jewish souls are burnt and the Torah and Judaism are burnt?"[59] Under the values system of the Old Yishuv, Torah study was supreme, and interrupting studies in order to participate in a protest was considered a transgression. Margaliot countered that silence and passivity came from Satan, who sought to quell protests. He declared: "This is a commandment observed through a transgression; it is time to act for the Lord, for they have nullified Your Torah; and sometimes setting aside the Torah is actually a way to maintain the Torah."[60] Margaliot's paradoxical approach is evident here: he claims that it is sometimes advisable to violate religious law when it serves a higher cause.[61] Protesting against the actions of the Zionist movement falls under this category. However, once such an approach is permitted, why should it not also be used by others? This stance weakened the force of the objection to the Religious Zionist argument that the settlement of the Land by nonobservant Jews was another example of the concept of a "commandment observed through a transgression."

Margaliot also discussed a practical issue that gained significance with the rising importance of the Chief Rabbinate: the role of this institution as a source of livelihood. He rhetorically asked whether, in the name of making a livelihood, it is permissible to sell the Lord's Torah. He meant to

---

[56] *Ibid.*, pp. 63–4.   [57] *Ibid.*, p. 18.   [58] *Ibid.*, pp. 42–7.   [59] *Ibid.*, p. 47.
[60] *Ibid.*, p. 48, footnote 1.
[61] This position provides a further example of the doctrine of the "holiness of sin" as discussed in Chapter 3.

argue against making religious compromises for the sake of making a living. His solution was that the faithful should believe that God would "nourish and provide for them" (the phrase is taken from the Grace after Meals), and that following in God's path would ensure a livelihood. Accordingly, he urged his readers not to accept positions offered by the Chief Rabbinate. While there were those who argued that the possibility of escaping a life of abject poverty was almost a matter of life and death, Margaliot presented the issue as a test of faith. For him, the desire to earn money and grow rich is the result of the "evil impulse" (*yetzer ha-ra*) that seeks to seduce the faithful, to dissuade them from combating evil and even to persuade them to argue that the transgressors have merits.[62]

In his treatise Margaliot sought to defend the economic interests of the Old Yishuv. This objective is reflected at several points in the book. For example, he strongly urged his readers to purchase meat slaughtered by HaEdah HaHaredit and not to rely on any other slaughtering system (i.e., that of the Chief Rabbinate). He did not make any claim that the Chief Rabbinate's slaughtering system was insufficiently strict in its religious observance. Rather, his argument was economic: "We must not join and help those wicked and we must not eat that which they have slaughtered."[63] He did not encourage Orthodox Jews to emigrate to the Land of Israel, since the resources of the Old Yishuv were limited and inadequate for this purpose.[64] He also fiercely opposed the employment of religious instructors who came from outside the circles of the Old Yishuv in order to defend the livelihood of those who were faithful to this course. He ended his treatise by demanding that no changes be made to the system of donations. Jews should not give to any charities other than those of the Old Yishuv.[65] Margaliot referred here to the economic structure of the Old Yishuv, which had always been based on the collection of donations from Diaspora Jews. Now, however, competition over donations had led to the impoverishment of the Old Yishuv.[66] As will be recalled, Amram Blau attempted to tackle this problem by establishing an agricultural settlement in Nabi Samwil, and Schlesinger himself served as patron of the association (see Chapter 2).

Margaliot sought to raise the status of the Old Yishuv in the donors' eyes by virtue of their struggle against Zionism. As mentioned earlier, he saw the supporters of Zionism as the descendants of the *erev rav* whose

[62] *Ibid.*, p. 55.   [63] *Ibid.*, p. 82.   [64] *Ibid.*, p. 89.   [65] *Ibid.*, pp. 132–9.
[66] Menachem Friedman, *Society and Religion: Non-Zionist Orthodoxy in the Land of Israel.* Jerusalem: Ben Zvi Institute, 1978, pp. 1–2 (in Hebrew).

souls are reincarnated in each generation. By the same principle, the soul of Moses is also reincarnated in every generation to fight the *erev rav*. "Accordingly, all the geniuses and righteous men who stand firm against the *erev rav* are analogous to Moses, and we should honor and respect them and listen to all they say as if it were from Moses' mouth."[67] Since he saw them as no less than the reincarnation of Moses, Margaliot argued that those who struggled against Zionism deserved respect and awe.

Margaliot believed that Torah study and religious observance in the Land of Israel enjoyed a special status superior to that of the same actions in the Diaspora. Indeed, he argued that the entire religious structure of Diaspora Judaism was dependent on the presence of Torah students in the Land of Israel. Prayers offered outside Israel ascend to the Heavens thanks only to the righteous Jews who dwell in the Land of Israel. This provided further justification for defending the income base of the Old Yishuv. Margaliot claimed that the Land of Israel amplifies positive virtues, so that worship of God is rewarded by greater privileges than are enjoyed by worshippers elsewhere. However, the converse was also true: evil acts committed in the Land of Israel will have particularly bitter and dramatic consequences. If Jews are to educate their sons to hate God and abandon the Torah, what is the purpose of emigrating to the Land of Israel, Margaliot asked rhetorically.[68]

Margaliot attacked the Religious Zionist argument, identified particularly with Kook, that messianic redemption was being realized in the mundane sphere by the Zionist activists. On the contrary, he asserted: their actions were false and were actually delaying the coming of the messiah. Redemption would enable Jews to live a complete religious life (in sharp contrast to the Zionists' heresy), and the Land of Israel would serve as an instrument for observing the commandments of the Torah. Moreover, redemption would be realized by God, and not by humans, and it would come by way of a miracle. Any attempt to pursue mundane redemption by settling the Land and building colonies was the product of Satanic actions. Margaliot briefly recalled the traditional prohibition against "ascending the wall," which was interpreted as prohibiting any collective immigration to the Land of Israel, as distinct from the actions of discrete individuals.[69]

Before messiah arrived, Margaliot believed, there would be an ultimate test of loyalty. Falsehood would gain enormous strength and enjoy the

---

[67] Margaliot, *Ashrei*, p. 79.   [68] *Ibid.*, p. 120. See also: Ravitzky, *Messianism*, pp. 48–51.
[69] Margaliot, *Ashrei*, p. 72.

assistance of fools and liars. The tool for identifying falsehood was change: Any change to the pattern of traditional Jewish study was proof of falsehood. Such falsehood might well appear in the guise of righteous men or Torah scholars (like Kook) in an attempt to mislead the Jewish people.[70] Accordingly, he claimed, Satanic forces had managed to establish schools that sought to reeducate the Jewish people in order to "steal and usurp boys and girls from their parents' home." These schools abandoned faith in the eternal God. The Zionists imbued young people with lust and evil properties. They disregarded modesty and humiliated the righteous Jews of the generation. They referred to themselves as "national Jews" in order to rebel against the Torah. Some rabbis sell their souls to the Zionists and refer to their heresy as "redemption." Satan amplifies their voices and innocent Jews fall into their trap and divert their donations.

The following paragraph illustrates Margaliot's belligerent approach and the direction in which he sought to lead his community:

We will adhere to the name of the Lord our God and the Holy Torah.... We will cloak ourselves in the spirit of heroism to humiliate those who act in falsehood and to explode and dismantle arid rocks, and we will declare and announce to all our fellow Jews wherever they may be, and to the entire world, that all these types of sects ... They and those who assist them are of the *erev rav* and came from Egypt. They have no affinity to the Jewish people; they have no right to speak anywhere in the name of Israel, and accordingly to refer to themselves as the guardians and redeemers of Israel.[71]

Margaliot's theological and ideological stance can be summarized as follows:

1. Eschatology – the identification of the present time as the era preceding the coming of messiah, a time characterized by a sharp decline in religious observance.
2. Demonology – the identification of Jewish nationalism and secularism as Satanic forces that seek to thwart and trick redemption. On the basis of this perception, Margaliot refused to see any merit in Zionism and indeed argued that they were not part of the Collectivity of Israel. This enabled him to circumvent the traditional statements, embodied in Hasidic tradition, that every Jewish soul has inherent merit.

---

[70] *Ibid.*, p. 88.   [71] *Ibid.*, p. 118.

3. Dualism – the demonization of Zionism led to a fierce desire for separation and isolationism.

4. Preserving the way of the Old Yishuv and defending its sources of income – Margaliot fought a rearguard action against the economic changes in the livelihood of the Old Yishuv, and particularly the decline in donations from overseas. For the purpose of this struggle he adopted a demonizing rhetoric against Zionism and its supporters in an attempt to dissuade Jews from donating to them. He also urged renewed support for the services provided by the Old Yishuv, such as education, the rabbinate and provision of kosher meat, in the face of the growing competition these services faced from the Zionist Chief Rabbinate.

YOEL TEITELBAUM – THE SATMAR REBBE

Even though Yoel Teitelbaum, the Satmar Rebbe, represents a relatively small community (I would estimate the total number of followers as around 100,000 as of 2013), his importance exceeds the movement's numerical strength. Above all, Teitelbaum has gained the reputation of the fiercest opponent of Zionism among post-Holocaust Orthodox Jews.

Previous works examining the ideology of the Satmar Rebbe have emphasized the anti-Zionist motif and the significance Teitelbaum attached to the oaths that prohibit Jewish activism in the Land of Israel.[72] I will focus on an additional aspect of his ideology, namely the messianic and apocalyptic element. The Satmar Rebbe saw the hallmarks of the modern age as proof of the coming End. He formed this conclusion on the basis of several Talmudic statements that characterize the time prior to the coming of the messiah as decadent and corrupt. These statements portray a generation that has no merits and can only be saved through

---

[72] Refael Kadosh, *Extremist Religious Philosophy: The Radical Religious Doctrines of the Satmar Rebbe*. PhD Dissertation, The University of Cape Town, 2011 (in Hebrew); Norman Lamm, "The Ideology of the Neturei Karta: According to the Satmarer Version," *Tradition* 12(2) (1971), 38–53; Allan L. Nadler, "Piety and Politics: The Case of the Satmar Rebbe," *Judaism* 31(2) (1982), pp. 135–52; Zvi Jonathan Kaplan, "Rabbi Yoel Teitelbaum, Zionism, and Hungarian Ultra-Orthodoxy," *Modern Judaism* 24(2) (2004), 165–78; David Sorotzkin, "Building the Earthly and Destroying the Heavenly: The Satmar Rebbe and Radical Orthodox School of Thought." In: Aviezer Ravitzky (ed.), *The Land of Israel in 20th Century Jewish Thought*. Jerusalem: Ben Zvi Institute, 2004, 133–67 (in Hebrew).

collective redemption.[73] He also drew on late Hasidic traditions arguing that the current generation had reached such a low point that the only possible conclusion was that the modern era is the last before the apocalypse. However, the traditions add that the messianic End cannot come to the world due to the actions of the Jewish people, whose sins delay its arrival. According to Teitelbaum, this grave offense is caused by the Zionist movement that promotes natural redemption and demands political action. Accordingly, the Rabbi defined Zionism as a rebellion against God.[74]

Teitelbaum adheres to a dualistic approach based on a constant battle between good and evil inclinations. Whenever one of these faces defeat, it becomes stronger in order to prevent its final elimination. Accordingly, the success of Zionism should be understood as the rise of diabolical powers: "Samael (Satan) gave us a Zionist State and a kingdom of heresy to abolish the redemption, and the Holy One will have mercy on us and will expedite our redemption and the salvation of our soul."[75]

Teitelbaum also blames rejection of the Torah for the destruction of the Third Temple. According to Jewish tradition, the First Temple was destroyed due to idolatry, while the Second Temple was destroyed due to baseless hatred. Since the Third Temple has never been built, it is not unreasonable to ask how Teitelbaum can blame unbelievers for its destruction. In order to explain this point, the rabbi presented an early Kabbalistic idea, which stated that in every generation, through the actions of the righteous, a Temple is built in heaven, while the wicked are destroying it with their evil actions.[76] This tradition was neglected for many years until it was renewed in the late nineteenth century by the Hasidic leaders Zvi Elimelech Shapira and Chaim Halberstam. According to David Sorotzkin, the background for the renewal of the tradition was the rise of the modern state, which caused the rabbis to oppose secular governments and the ideas of the Enlightenment era. This Kabbalistic

[73] Ephraim Urbach, *The Sages: Their Concepts and Beliefs.* Jerusalem: Magnes Press, 1975, pp. 649–92 (in Hebrew).

[74] Yoel Teitelbaum, *Sefer VeYoel Moshe: Kolel Shelosha Maamarim* (5th edition), Brooklyn, NY: Bet Mishar Yerushalayim, 1981 (in Hebrew), p. 9.

[75] *Ibid.*, p. 10.

[76] Haviva Pedaya, "Eretz: Time and Place – Apocalypse of End and Apocalypse of Beginning." In: Aviezer Ravitzky (ed.), *The Land of Israel in 20th Century Jewish Thought.* Jerusalem: Ben Zvi Institute, 2004, pp. 560–623 (in Hebrew).

tradition represents a tension between building foundations and destroying foundations, an idea of constant destruction.[77]

The Satmar Rebbe quotes a discussion between the Sanz Rebbe Chaim Halberstam and his followers, in which the rabbi explained his *Aliyat neshama* (the rise of the soul to higher worlds). He told them that he saw an almost completed heavenly Temple, therefore the full redemption is imminent, and all that is missing is the Temple's curtain, an insignificant part. The followers responded that they were sure the rabbi had the powers to prepare the curtain in his prayers and good actions, but he did not respond. In a different talk the rabbi said that he indeed prepared the curtain, but "a great villain ripped it in his actions."[78] The meaning of this statement, according the Satmar Rebbe, is that evil and Satan have the power to touch the very heart of the heavenly temple with their immense destructive powers. The messianic End had already begun, but "a great villain" – meaning the Zionist movement who wishes to built the mundane Land of Israel – brought destruction into the upper worlds and the heavenly Temple. Therefore there is an inversely proportional connection between those who are building the earthly land and the destruction of heavenly Jerusalem.[79] As mention, Chaim Elazar Shaipra, the Munkacser Rebbe, used a similar analogy in his magical prayers.

According to the Babylonian Talmud (*Sanhedrin* 97a) the generation before the coming of the messiah will have no values and will reject the Torah and commandments. The sages stated that "the face of the generation would be like the face of the dog," where illusion is great and the truth is missing. In the Babylonian Talmud (*Sanhedrin* 98a) it says: "in its time – I shall expedite." The meaning is that if the Jews have merits justifying their redemption then "I shall expedite" this, and redemption will come speedily; and if not – redemption will still come, but only "in its time" as appointed. In that same chapter there is another statement on the messiah: "Ben David [The messiah] comes only in a generation that is either entirely worthy or entirely guilty" (Babylonian

---

[77] David Sorotzkin, *The Supra-Temporal Community in the Era of Change: The Emergency of Perceptions of Time and Collective as the Basis for Defining the Development of Jewish Orthodoxy in Modern Times.* PhD Dissertation, The Hebrew University of Jerusalem, 2007, p. 152 (in Hebrew).

[78] Teitelbaum, *Sefer*, pp. 11–12. See also Sorotzkin's discussion on the topic: David Sorotzkin, *Orthodoxy and Modern Disciplination: The Production of Jewish Tradition in Europe in Modern Times.* Tel Aviv: HaKibbutz HaMeuchad, 2011, pp. 365–77 (in Hebrew).

[79] Ravitzky, *Messianism*, p. 47

Talmud, *Sanhedrin* 98a). According to this statement, the redemption can flower in a generation that is completely wicked.

From these descriptions the rabbi wished to find an analogy for his times: "we see in our eyes that many of these horrific things are being fulfilled in our generation due to our many sins," and the signs are testifying that we are living in that disintegrating generation. According to the rabbi, the messiah will not come because this is the worst generation ("entirely guilty") but because this is the last one ("in its time"). Therefore one can see a strong trend to predestination – this generation has to be the last one. However, in order to make redemption happen all the Jews have to do is repent, a call which allows some level of free will.

For him, one of the strongest proofs for the times of the *Akvta demeshicha* (literally, the footsteps of the messiah. This term is used to identify the last days before the coming of the End), is the strong support for Zionism in the general public. This is a takeover of evil inclinations and it is hard to resist.[80] In his writings he established a strong dichotomy between his community, which is called "Israel," and all the rest who are "wicked." For him, the current evil leadership is labeled as *erev rav* – the "mixed multitude."

According to the rabbi, more proof that the generation had reached its lowest, came with the comparison of Zionism with Shabtai Zvi and his movement. Shabtai Zvi was the seventeen-century self-proclaimed Jewish messiah. He had gathered a large group of followers, but eventually converted to Islam, while most of his followers returned to normative Judaism.[81] For Teitelbaum, the biggest difference between Shabtai Zvi and Zionism lies in the fact that the former started his mission in a traditional way; he showed great knowledge in the Talmud and in the Lurianic Kabbalah, and brought many into repentance. At the beginning it was impossible to see that he would lead his people into heresy and conversion. When people learned about his heretic statements, many decided to stand against him. Teitelbaum goes on to say that in the case of Zionism, there is not even pretence for the support of religion: "from the beginning to the end, their actions are for the ruin of religion, heaven forbid." The current generation is so wicked, Teitelbaum argued, that there is not even an attempt to build illusions, as it was with Shabtai Zvi. Since the people are so low in their religious observance, Satan gets

---

[80] Teitelbaum, *Sefer*, p. 226.
[81] Gershom Scholem, *Sabbatai Sevi: The Mystical Messiah, 1626–1676*. Princeton: Princeton University Press, 1973.

stronger, and wickedness prevails.[82] Teitelbaum was influenced by Jacob Emden, one of the biggest opponents to Shabtai Zvi. Emden declared that he would warn against Zvi even if Emden would remain the last man on earth. Teitelbaum, while making the analogy, compares his anti-Zionist enterprise to that of Emden's.

Traditional perspectives on the final days claim that redemption can be achieved with full repentance. Teitelbaum stood firmly against the opinion that redemption can come before repentance, as some Religious Zionist rabbis argued, among them Rabbi Zvi Yehuda Kook.[83] "Whoever thinks that there is an existence to redemption without repentance is holding an opinion that is contrary to the Bible and this is heresy, heaven forbid."[84] He opposed the apologetic stand of messianic religious Zionism, which expects communal repentance at the end of the messianic process, not at the beginning.

A central element in the Satmar Rebbe's ideology prohibits the transgression of the Three Oaths. Rabbi Teitelbaum believed that the establishment of any Jewish state violates the Jewish law, and he was particularly concerned by the formation of the State of Israel. As discussed in Chapter 2, the Babylonian Talmud prohibits any human initiative on a collective level to restore Jewish sovereignty to the Land of Israel before the coming of the messiah. Accordingly, for the Rebbe, Zionism and the State of Israel are tantamount to a rebellion against God, and must not be recognized in any manner. Teitelbaum sought to identify reward and punishment in all human acts, and viewed the Holocaust as the grave penalty for the rebellion by Zionism against the Three Oaths. Those Zionists who sought to "expedite the End," immigrating to Palestine and rebelling against the familiar world order, were responsible for the terrible Divine penalty that emerged in the form of the Holocaust. It was not Exile that collapsed in the Holocaust; rather, it was Zionism that led to the abandonment of Jewish flesh and blood.[85]

Teitelbaum argued that there is no obligation to immigrate to the Land of Israel at this time,[86] and indeed that this is actively prohibited in accordance with the Three Oaths. He argued that observing these oaths is a guarantee for Jewish existence. This implies also that the Gentiles

---

[82] Teitelbaum, *Sefer*, pp. 259–60.

[83] Motti Inbari, *Messianic Religious Zionism Confronts Israeli Territorial Compromises.* New York: Cambridge University Press, 2012, pp. 15–36.

[84] Teitelbaum, *Sefer*, pp. 93–4.   [85] Ravitzky, *Messianism*, pp. 40–78,

[86] Teitelbaum, *Sefer*, p. 33.

must protect the Jews as long as the Jews are under Gentile patronage. For him, even if the Gentiles do not keep their part and do not protect the Jews, as it happened during the Holocaust, it should not mean that the oaths expired. Even if the Gentiles forced the Jews to immigrate to the land of Israel, the rabbi concluded, it would be better to give your life and not to transgress the oaths.[87] Norman Lamm was right to present the paradox of this opinion, which implies a rebellion against the will of the nations.[88]

Based on Maimonides the rabbi argued that the gathering of Israel is the mission of the messiah, therefore humans are not allowed to perform it themselves. Even more, "as much as there is no world without winds so there cannot be a world without Israel."[89] Thus the scattering of Israel is for the benefit of the entirety of humanity. The rabbi stated, based on Lurianic Kabbalah, that the role of Israel is to release the divine sparks from all over the world. When this task would be completed, the messiah would come and miraculously gather the people of Israel and deliver them into their land.[90]

The idea of segregation and dualism, which is very prominent in the Satmar Rebbe's teachings, is based on the teachings of Rabbi Judah Loew, who is called the Maharal of Prague (1529–1609). According to David Sorotzkin, The Maharal was aware of the dynamics of the foundation of the modern state, and he feared its influence over the Jewish community; therefore, he rejected changes in the Jewish way of life. He developed a theology that argues that the Jewish people are unique and separate, beyond the laws of nature: They are supernatural and distinct. Jews should stay out of Christian culture and politics.[91] Jewish Orthodoxy inherited the concepts of uniqueness, and tried to block assimilation trends into the European culture. As such, the Jewish ghetto was reassembled on a voluntary basis, as a subsociety that opposes the democratic order.

The Satmar Rebbe sharply confronts nature and uniqueness. According to him, democracy can be a good political system for the Gentiles but it is not necessarily good for the Jews. Only the laws of the Torah, interpreted by the right religious authorities, are meant for, or worthy of, the Chosen People.[92] The rabbi correctly understood that the

---

[87] *Ibid.*, 149. Kadosh, *Extremist*, pp. 88–95. [88] Lamm, "The Ideology," pp. 15
[89] Teitelbaum, *Sefer*, pp. 51. [90] *Ibid.*, pp. 51–3.
[91] Sorotzkin, *Orthodoxy*, pp. 133–200.
[92] Lamm, "The Ideology," pp. 46; Teitelbaum, *Sefer*, pp. 164.

Zionist movement is secular and indifferent, even sometimes hostile, to religious laws. The state doesn't always consider the rabbis' opinions, and the Knesset, Israeli parliament, replaces the authority of the rabbis. His conclusion is that there can be no way to have a democratic system that can be subjected to the Divine law. However, Jews are not Gentiles, and based on the concept of uniqueness, there is no way to "normalize" them, as Zionists attempt. The Rebbe labeled Zionism as heresy and opposed any contacts with it.[93] He claimed that the acceptance of the state and the faith in the Torah are two oppositions that cannot be reconciled inside one man.[94]

The rabbi also attacked the Haredi parties that participate in the Israeli political system. Teitelbaum argued that the Haredi participation in politics legitimizes Zionism. He prohibited his followers to take part in the parliament, where anti-Torah laws are being enforced. He stated that it is better to give your life and not to take part in a system that he describes as heresy and idolatry. Furthermore, Knesset member have to take an oath before they assume office. For him, this oath is tandem to establishing the kingdom of heaven on earth before its time.[95] The prohibitions that fall on the elected to the parliament, he argues, are true also for the voters. Therefore he called on his supporters to boycott the elections and to reject any financial support from the government.[96]

The principle of Ahavat Yisrael ("love of Israel") is one of the most important tenets of Hasidism. Love for every member of the Jewish people was one of the key demands of the founding fathers of the Hasidic movement, who emphasized that this love was unconditional and extended to every Jew, including sinners and the wicked. However, the Satmar Rebbe reinterpreted the concept of Ahavat Yisrael in keeping with his dualistic approach. The scholar Refael Kadosh suggests that the main innovation of the Satmar Rebbe was to confine the concept of Ahavat Yisrael to his immediate community; regarding all other Jews, an obligation was imposed to distance oneself from their wickedness. Accordingly, boundless love for one's own is mirrored by hatred for everyone else. Moreover, insularity and internal cohesion were intended as a firm barrier against the *erev rav*. In other words, in order to observe

---

[93] *Ibid.*, pp. 164.   [94] *Ibid.*, p. 8. See also Nadler, "Piety," pp. 138–41.

[95] Teitelbaum, *Sefer*, pp. 219.

[96] Menachem Friedman, "Neturei Karta and the Sabbath Demonstrations in Jerusalem, 1948–1950." In: Avi Bareli (ed.), *Divided Jerusalem, 1948–1967: Sources, Summaries, Selected Incidents, and Ancillary Material*. Jerusalem: Ben Zvi Institute, 1994, pp. 224–40 (in Hebrew).

the commandment of Ahavat Yisrael properly, the Satmar Hasidim must distance those not worthy of this love. According to the Rebbe's approach there can be no compromise or flexibility permitting association with the wicked. The task of every Jew is to maintain his purity and to steer clear of even the slightest impurity and evil.[97]

Why does God allow evil powers to get stronger? Why do the majority of the Jewish people support such trends? The rabbi's response is that this is a test of faith. God is putting his people into test after test, and so far the results are grave. Heretical Zionism was able to ensnare even righteous and honest Jews. According to him, the consequence of the deception is serious: the heretical system found fertile soil even among Torah-observant Jews. Only massive repentance can allow king messiah to come for the final redemption. The rabbi's role is to protest against these great sins.

CONCLUSION

A detached observer might conclude that the motivating force behind the radical stream of Hasidic ultra-Orthodoxy was anti-Zionism. However, a more careful examination shows that the essential approach was one of antimodernism; the negation of Zionism was merely one component of this broader worldview.

This Haredi approach rejects innovation and the adaptation of Jewish lifestyle to the modern era, and includes several components. Firstly, it tends to be strictly conservative and to reject any form of innovation. The optimistic assumption of early Hasidism that the world could be repaired and the Divine sparks lit within mundane shells, and the accompanying belief in outreach to those far removed from the faith (such as secular Jews) was replaced by pessimism.[98] The clearest manifestation of this pessimistic approach was the demand to establish isolated and segregated communities. The trend to insularity also entailed the utter rejection of changes in external appearance, such as clothes and hairstyle. Margaliot and others who shared this approach found Halakhic and Kabbalistic support for their insistence on maintaining external appearance as an integral part of religious identity; the slightest deviation from this approach was seen as tantamount to the destruction of the entire religion.

---

[97] Kadosh, *Extremist*, pp. 134–60.
[98] Allan Nadler, "The War on Modernity of R. Hayyim Elazar Shapira of Munkacz," *Modern Judaism* 14(3) (1994), 254–5.

Teitelbaum worked diligently to reintroduce Hasidic dress and even to impose stricter standards than in the past. Although Teitelbaum took the traditional European shtetl as his model, he made various changes, such as introducing the obligation to wear a Stueimel on the Sabbath, despite the fact that this had not been customary in prewar Hungary. His objective was to create additional external barriers separating Hasidic Jews from other people. Opposition to reform in education was a further hallmark of this worldview.

Another aspect of the radical ultra-Orthodox approach is principled opposition to participation in modern Jewish politics. Although the modern era enabled the Haredim to enjoy political representation, radical ultra-Orthodoxy opposed this as a form of integration in modern life. This contrasts with the approach of Agudat Yisrael, which did not reject participation in the political game in Poland and later in Israel. Opposition to political involvement also seems to have weakened over the years in the United States and Satmar Hasidim have exploited their political strength on federal and local issues. The objections were fiercer in the case of Israeli politics, however, and this position even acquired a theological dimension over the years. It should be noted, however, that Yoel Teitelbaum was not opposed to his followers participating in municipal elections in Jerusalem and Bnei Brak, as opposed to the elections to the Knesset, where he demanded a total boycott.

The antimodernist approach of these circles was reflected clearly in their attitude toward women. An inherent component of the rejection of modernism was the refusal to accept the principle of gender equality. Countless restrictions and safeguards were imposed in order to prevent any possibility of relaxation in the rules of dress for women. "Modesty patrols" were even formed in order to enforce strict dress codes. As we saw, however, women in Satmar rebelled against the prohibition against wearing wigs, and Teitelbaum was forced to permit this practice against his own beliefs and contrary to the approach of the Hungarian Hasidic rabbis. In Jerusalem, the Hasidim managed to overcome protests from women and impose the ban on wigs.

These circles also opposed lenient trends in the field of girls' education. However, reality proved stronger than ideology in this respect. In Israel and in the United States, women came to play a key role in earning a livelihood in the Hasidic family. The strict laws against women's education emerged as unrealistic. Providing women with a technological and scientific education became desirable in order to enable them to find work and compete in the job market. The Satmar Rebbe even established an educational network for girls that competed with the network founded by Agudat Yisrael and emphasized a modern and technological education. Women now form the backbone of Haredi society as its main breadwinners. Their progress has been unstoppable and brings both advantages and challenges. The strict modesty rules seem designed to curtail their rising status and power.

The principled opposition in these circles to any change in the religious way of life has an eschatological foundation. According to this approach, the End Times are imminent and the signs suggest the impending arrival of messiah. The rabbis base their position on passages in the Babylonian Talmud describing the period before the arrival of messiah. They compare their own time to that described in the sources and reach the conclusion that this is precisely the period alluded to. The messianic model they present includes a period of such severe deterioration that only the messiah can bring salvation. Rabbi Chaim Elazar Shapira went further still, spending major parts of his life in a state of acute eschatological expectation and even engaging in magic acts intended to expedite the End. According to the radicals, all the signs suggest that the period of deterioration has reached its nadir, so that God now has no alternative but to send the messiah. The catastrophic messianic strand of theology argues that religious Judaism has reached the brink of spiritual and physical annihilation; the faithful need only cling to the ancestral ways without any change for a little longer. Many of those who adhered to this view claimed that the numerous difficulties encountered by those who maintain this way of life, which effectively entailed abject poverty, were actually a test of faith.

The eschatological approach also included a strong component of dualism and demonology. The believers argued that their small group represented faithful Jews who would enjoy complete redemption and all the blessings of paradise.[99] They stood against the assorted sinners and transgressors known as the *erev rav* – the wicked disguised as Jews, descendants of Egyptians who joined the Israelites as they left Egypt. For the radical ultra-Orthodox leaders, the identification of their adversaries as the *erev rav* and the increasing number of sinners among the Jews

---

[99] Aharon Roth (1894–1947), another important rabbi in these circles whom I didn't discuss in this book, offered a detailed account of the wonderful privileges that awaited the righteous in paradise, as well as the grave punishments that would be meted out in hell to the wicked. See Aharon Roth, *Shomrei Emunim* 2, Jerusalem: unspecified publisher, 5719 – 1959 (in Hebrew).

provided proof that these were indeed the final days, since the messianic period entailed an absolute distinction between the righteous and the impure. Accordingly, they argued, the sinners were removing themselves from the Jewish people as part of the End Times events.

For radical ultra-Orthodoxy, the identification of the sinners as the reincarnations of Gentiles who now reveal their true identity, and who accordingly are to be seen as outside the confines of the Jewish people, solves a significant problem. As we have seen, Talmudic verses preached tolerance of Jewish sinners and an insistence that they remained part of the Jewish people. The zealots circumvented this problem by arguing that the sinners were not, in fact, Jewish and accordingly not deserving of leniency.

It is important to emphasize that the dichotomy was not merely between radical ultra-Orthodox Jews, on the one hand, and Zionists or Reform Jews, on the other. Anyone who failed to follow their approach was characterized as a sinner. These groups disassociate themselves not only from the non-Orthodox society, but also from mainstream Orthodoxy.[100] Margaliot differentiated between the Religious Zionist and Agudat Yisrael in terms of the severity of his criticism, but Chaim Elazar Shapira was equally condemning of them all (as well as other Hasidic movements). The radicals' campaign against religious deviation was first and foremost aimed internally at the Orthodox Jewish world, opposing any modicum of moderation and compromise.

On the issue of messianism, it is worth recalling the legend of the Three Oaths and the question of expediting the End. This research shows that Amram Blau was the first authority to employ the legend about the Divine prohibition against expediting the End while blaming the Holocaust on the Zionist rebellion against God's dominion. He made these comments in 1947, well before Teitelbaum adopted the same approach in *VaYoel Moshe*, published in 1956 (published in full in 1961). Teitelbaum opposed any active steps to expedite the End, since the sources suggested that God would react harshly to such a rebellion against His authority. He saw the murder of millions of Jews in the Holocaust as a collective punishment imposed on the chosen people due to the Zionist rebellion. However, our present study has shown that other methods may be used to expedite the End in addition to the Zionist path. Thus, for example, Rabbi Chaim Elazar Shapira employed Kabbalistic magic in an attempt

---

[100] Keren-Kratz, "Marmaros."

to cause the messiah to arrive. Teitelbaum's criticism must therefore be interpreted as applying not only to the Zionist, but also to mystics such as Shapira.

In my opinion, there is a logical flaw in the position that both blames the Zionists for the Holocaust and claims that they belong to the *erev rav*. The latter claim implies that the Zionists are the descendents of Egyptian sorcerers and are not even Jewish. If this is the case, how can it be claimed that they bear an obligation of mutual responsibility with the Hasidim? How can it be argued that their sins led to the death of pure members of the Hasidic fold? If they are the descendents of the *erev rav*, there is no common fate bonding them to the faithful. If their sins indeed led to the Holocaust, such a common fate exists. Thus this claim inherently refutes the entire demonological theory developed by these circles.

The model presented by the circles discussed in this study does not extend to a call to violence. Although Haredi radicals draw on a Biblical narrative that includes the use of extreme violence against sinners, they explicitly stress that their approach does not include the use of force. The zealotry they seek to apply is one of protest and reproach, insularity and demonstration.

The question of the approach to the Land of Israel among these circles is an interesting one. Here, too, their response seems to be the result of their efforts to confront the tremendous enthusiasm created by the Zionist movement. The arguments raised by Yoel Teitelbaum, Chaim Elazar Shapira and Yeshayah Asher Zelig Margaliot against Jewish emigration to the Land of Israel included the claim that the importance of actions is amplified in the Land, so that sins committed there are particularly grave. All three rabbis rejected the claim that there is a Halakhic imperative to emigrate to the Land of Israel, and Teitelbaum even argued that there is a Halakhic prohibition against doing so before messiah arrives.[101] Thus they appear to regard the Land of Israel as a dangerous place that is to be avoided.

In the next chapter I will look in greater depth at the nature of religious zealotry in Jewish history in comparative perspective.

---

[101] For further discussion, see: Sorotzkin, *Orthodoxy*, pp. 400–9.

7

Jewish zealotry – past and present

In this chapter I seek to describe the phenomenon of religious zealotry in Jewish history in general terms. To this end, I compare three instances: radial ultra-Orthodoxy (the subject of this book); messianic Religious Zionism, which I have previously examined in depth;[1] and the Jewish zealots of the Second Temple period who led the revolt against Rome in 66–70 CE. Although my historical comparison will focus mainly on the Second Temple rebels, I will also discuss other movements of the same period, such as the Qumran sect and early Christianity, and will show the influence of the Maccabean Revolt on the Great Revolt against Rome.

To date, the number of studies comparing ancient and modern times in this field has been relatively limited, though other scholars have noted similarities and lines of development between the different periods. Yehuda Liebes compared the thought of Yeshayah Asher Zelig Margaliot with the philosophy of the Judean Desert sect,[2] a religious group of late Second Temple Period, one of the "parties" mentioned by Josephus. Joel Marcus compared patterns of apocalyptic messianism in the various periods. Marcus noted that scholars of the ancient period could gain useful insight into their period of study by addressing the comparative dimension.[3] Radical ultra-Orthodoxy and messianic

---

[1] Motti Inbari, *Messianic Religious Zionism Confronts Israeli Territorial Compromises.* New York: Cambridge University Press, 2012; *idem, Jewish Fundamentalism and the Temple Mount – Who Will Build the Third Temple?* Albany: SUNY, 2009.

[2] Yehuda Liebes, "HaEdah HaHaredit in Jerusalem and the Judean Desert Sect," *Jerusalem Research in Judaic Studies* 3 (1981), 135–52 (in Hebrew).

[3] Joel Marcus, "Modern and Ancient Jewish Apocalypticism," *Journal of Religion* 76(1) 1996, 1–27.

Religious Zionism are modern phenomena. In this chapter, I will examine the extent to which they replicate patterns of Jewish radicalism from ancient times.

Scholars of religious fundamentalism emphasize the modern character of the phenomenon as a counterreaction to secular culture.[4] My decision to enter into a comparison of this phenomenon with ancient times was informed by my assessment that undeniable similarities can be found between the three movements I examine here. Radical ultra-Orthodoxy and the rebels of the Second Temple period overtly referred to themselves as "zealots" and claimed Biblical support for the practice religious radicalism. The adherents of messianic Religious Zionism are not self-defined as "zealots," but a closer examination of their thought and actions also reveals patterns of religious radicalism that, to an extent, replicate those of ancient times. In this chapter I will offer a preliminary comparison.

Due to the significance of the textual precedent justifying religious militancy, I will begin by considering the issue of zealotry as a religious category as presented in the Bible and the rabbinical literature. I will then present the three movements I have chosen to examine, and compare them on the basis of several parameters: messianic expectation, the attitude to violence, the attitude to Jewish nationhood in the Land of Israel, and the attitude to the Halakhah (Jewish religious law).

ZEALOTRY

In the Bible, Yahweh's zeal is probably best understood as an expression of his holiness. Zealotry can be divided between zeal to God Himself and zeal to His laws.[5] The term "zealotry" is taken from the Biblical story of Pinchas, which is told in Numbers 25 and focuses on the following drama: The People of Israel, camped at Hittin on their way to the Land of Israel, met Moabite women and men began to pursue them. The sexual act this involves constituted part of the Baalite ritual of the Moabites. God was furious with the Children of Israel and imposed a plague that left 24,000 dead. Moses summoned the leaders of the people and demanded

---

[4] Gabriel A. Almond, R. Scott Appleby, and Emanuel Sivan, *Strong Religion – The Rise of Fundamentalism around the World*. Chicago: University of Chicago Press, 2003, p. 17; Shmuel N. Eisenstadt, *Fundamentalism, Sectarianism and Revolution – The Jacobin Dimension of Modernity*. Cambridge: Cambridge University Press, 1999, pp. 1–3.

[5] Martin Hengel, *The Zealots: Investigations into the Jewish Freedom Movement in the Period from Herod I until 70*. Edinburgh: T. & T. Clark, 1989 [German origin 1976], p. 146.

that they stop their evil acts. While they were discussing the matter, Zimri son of Salu, prince of the tribe of Shimon, appeared together with a Midianite woman, Kozvi daughter of Zur. The Bible does not tell us clearly what happened next, but it was enough to cause great weeping among all those gathered at the scene.

Zimri's appearance was clearly a challenge to Moses. Just as he was demanding that the men stop fraternizing with Moabite women, one of the leading members of the tribe of Shimon appeared together with a Gentile woman. Although the text is ambiguous, it seems that in the tent an act of sexual intercourse was observed by the entire people, as part of the Baalite ritual. Pinchas, who saw this act, seized his spear and stabbed both Zimri and Kozvi. At this precise moment the plague ended. Moreover, God spoke to Moses:

> Pinchas, the son of Eleazar, the son of Aaron the priest, has turned My wrath away from the children of Israel, in that he was very zealous for My sake among them, so that I consumed not the children of Israel in My zeal. Wherefore say: Behold, I give unto him My covenant of peace; and it shall be unto him, and to his seed after him, the covenant of an everlasting priesthood; because he was zealous for his God, and made atonement for the children of Israel. (Numbers 25:11–13)

Thus we see that not only does Pinchas kill two people without any trial and he is not punished for this act. On the contrary, his descendents are awarded an everlasting priesthood. It is also notable that it is not Moses or the tribal elders who act as zealots; Pinchas operates on his own, with no need for court or law. He feels that he knows what is zealotry to God and what is God's will, and he acts at that precise moment in accordance with the command of his conscience. Thus we see that the zealotry for God was a spontaneous act that required the use of violence for the sake of God.

The scholar Louis Feldman argues that the rabbis supported the zealotry of Pinchas as described in the Bible because his actions enjoyed divine blessing.[6] Moreover, the Midrash identified Pinchas and the Prophet Elijah as a single character (i.e., the latter was perceived as a reincarnation of the former), and hence as the bearer of messianic qualities. Abram Spiro argues that this opinion has its origins in the religious debates between Jews and Samaritans.[7] However, the Talmud also

---

[6] Louis Feldman, *"Remember Amalek!" Vengeance, Zealotry, and Group Destruction in the Bible according to Philo, Pseudo-Philo, and Josephus*. Cincinnati: HUC Press, 2004, pp. 193–216.

[7] Abram Spiro, "The Ascension of Phinehas," *Proceedings of the American Academy for Jewish Research* 22 (1953), 91–114.

includes criticism of Pinchas, and the rabbis were concerned by his evasion of the judicial process and his choice to act without authorization. Feldman quotes the Babylonian Talmud (*Sanhedrin* 82a), which states that Zimri received special permission to marry a Midianite woman, and adds that Rabba bar bar Hannah and Rabbi Hisda declared that if a zealot asked them whether he should take the law into his own hands, they would advise him not to do so, despite the Biblical precedent. The Babylonian Talmud also states that had Zimri instead turned round and killed Pinchas, he would have been found innocent, since Pinchas had the status of a "pursuer."[8] Rabbi Judah ben Simeon ben Pazzi (Jerusalem Talmud, *Sanhedrin* 9:6 27b) goes so far as to state explicitly that Pinchas transgressed against the will of the Sages.[9] Eliezer Segal argues that the rabbis of the Babylonian Talmud viewed Pinchas's attacks as justified in special constellation or circumstances that were valid only to the Second Temple period. They wished to diminish the impact of Biblical validation to uncontrolled violence.[10]

The zeal of Pinchas is also mentioned with great approval at the books of Maccabees. Matitiyahu (died ca. 166 BCE) is said to have refused to offer a pagan sacrifice in Modein and thereby to have initiated a revolt against the decree of Antiochus IV Epiphanes that forbade under the threat of death the observance of Jewish Law (1 Macc. 2:1–28). Matitiyahu killed a Jew who was offering a sacrifice on a pagan alter, he also killed the king's officer who was forcing them to sacrifice, and he tore down the altar. His actions were described as following: "Thus he burned with zeal for the law, just as Pinchas did against Zimri son of Salu. Then Matitiyahu cried out in the town with a loud voice, saying: 'Let everyone who is zealous for the law and supports the covenant come out with me!'" (1 Macc. 2:26–7) (RSV).[11]

To summarize the findings thus far: religious zealotry has its origins in a Biblical precedent and embodies support for violence in order to glorify

[8] Michal Wolf, "The Halakhic Attitude to Din Rodef and Din Moser." In: Moshe Arad and Yuval Wolf (eds.), *Delinquency and Social Deviation: Theory and Practice*. Ramat Gan: Bar Ilan University Press, 2002, pp. 215–49 (in Hebrew).

[9] Feldman, *Remember*, pp. 214.

[10] Eliezer Segal, "Disarming Phineas: Rabbinic Confrontations with Biblical Militancy." In: David J. Hawkin (ed.), *The Twenty-first Century Confronts Its Gods: Globalization, Technology, and War*. Albany: SUNY, 2004, pp. 141–56.

[11] Joseph Sievers, "Hasmoneans." In: John J. Collins and Daniel C. Harlow (eds.), *The Eerdmans Dictionary of Early Judaism*, Grand Rapids, Mich.: William B. Eerdmans, 2010, pp. 705–9.

God's name. This phenomenon involves an unstoppable sense of mission that circumvents conventional Halakhic procedures, such as the principle of a judicial hearing prior to determining an offender's guilt. Zealotry includes an anarchistic dimension, since the zealot himself is judged only after his actions. Pinchas and the Prophet Elijah are perceived as two characters who acted in accordance with the approach of religious violence, and accordingly some scholars saw them as a single individual imbued with messianic potential. However, the rabbinical literature was reluctant to condone violence and restrictions were imposed on its application.

A DESCRIPTION OF THE MOVEMENTS TO BE COMPARED

Radical ultra-Orthodoxy as an ideological and sociological phenomenon has its origins in the mid-nineteenth century, when the Hungarian congregations seceded from the general Jewish community. Its essence lies in the negation of the modernization of the Jewish people and the adoption of an opposite ideological model sanctifying the customs of the past. This is an extreme stream motivated by eschatological expectations and, accordingly, it tends to dualism and to the demonization of all those Jews who are willing to submit to modernism. For radical ultra-Orthodoxy, any deviation from the ways of the past, even if tactical, is explained as the strengthening of Satanic forces whose influence must be avoided.

The exponents of this approach accept the assumption that Jewish history has reached its end and that the messianic age is imminent. They find proof for this assertion in an examination of the material and spiritual condition of the Jewish people, which has deteriorated to such a point that the messiah offers the only possible hope of salvation. They argue that Jewish history shows a regressive pattern, so that present-day reality marks its nadir. This approach is based on several statements from the Babylonian Talmud and on Hasidic traditions. The only reason why the messiah has not yet arrived, they assert, is that this is being delayed by the people's sins.

Radical ultra-Orthodoxy later developed into an anti-Zionist movement that viewed patterns of Jewish nationhood as further evidence of the strengthening of Satanic forces and as part of the preparations for the ultimate battle between good and evil. According to proponents of this approach such as Yoel Teitelbaum, head of the Satmar Hasidim, and Amram Blau, founder of Neturei Karta, whom I discussed earlier, the Holocaust was a divine punishment for the Jewish people's support of

Zionism. Such exponents were also fiercely critical of other streams within Orthodox Judaism that were willing to compromise with Zionism and claimed justification for cooperating with the movement.

The spokesmen for this approach employ aggressive and violent rhetoric and even refer to themselves as "zealots." However, their violence is mostly verbal and they tend not to use of hard physical violence. Their efforts concentrated on separating themselves from the remainder of the Jewish and non-Jewish population by creating enclaves and imposing physical barriers of appearance, dress, and language.

Messianic Religious Zionism is an ideological and political stream that blends Orthodox religiousity with nationalism. Very soon after its emergence, Religious Zionism undertook a process aiming to understand how the development of the secular Zionist movement actually represented a stage in an unfolding messianic process. These approaches are identified, in particular, with the religious philosophy of Rabbi Avraham Yitzhak Hacohen Kook (1865–1935). While ostensibly adopting the general Zionist definition of the movement's purpose, this approach also imbued it with specific religious meaning: The Rabbi argued that while Zionist activity calls for action in the material realm, simultaneously its innermost core aspires to eternal spiritual life – and this constituted the "real" foundation for the Zionist movement's operations and aims, even if the movement itself was not aware of this.[12] The argument contended that the long-awaited messianic era was about to arrive, and would be realized once secular Zionism chose the true path: the complete worship of God.[13]

This ideology turned into a political movement after the Yom Kippur War (1973). The Gush Emunim ("Block of the Faithful") movement was founded in February 1974. Led by young Religious Zionist activists, Gush Emunim was supported by both Orthodox bourgeois urban circles and secular supporters of the Whole Land of Israel movement.[14] Gush Emunim sought to prevent territorial concessions and to push for the application of Israeli sovereignty to Judea, Samaria, and the Gaza Strip – territories conqurerd during the Six Days War (1967). It attempted to actualize its objectives by settling Jewish communities in the occupied territories.

---

[12] Dov Schwartz, *Faith at a Crossroads – A Theological Profile of Religious Zionism.* Leiden, Boston, and Koln: Brill, 2002, pp. 156–92.

[13] Motti Inbari, "Religious Zionism and the Temple Mount Dilemma: Key Trends," *Israel Studies* 12(2) (2007), 29–47.

[14] Dov Schwartz, *Religious Zionism: History and Ideology.* Boston: Academic Press, 2009.

Immediately following its inception, a group of graduates of Mercaz Harav Yeshivah joined Gush Emunim. The group's spiritual leader was Rabbi Zvi Yehuda Hacohen Kook (son of Rabbi Avraham Itzhak Kook), who soon assumed a leadership role in the young movement. The members of this group believed that the return of the Jews to the Land of Israel under the auspices of the secular Zionist movement reflected the first stage in God's will to redeem His people. Accordingly, the spectacular Israeli victory in the Six Day War of 1967 was perceived as a manifestation of the Divine plan, and as a preliminary stage in the process of redemption.[15] For them, the holiness of the land of Israel and the holiness of the State of Israel are blended. According to the junior Kook, the Land of Israel – comprised of land within the 1948 borders, the territories acquired in 1967, and even Transjordan – is one unit, a complete organic entity imbued with its own will and holiness. This entity is connected and united with the entire Jewish people – present, past, and future – so that the people and the land are in a complete oneness. Therefore, no one has a right to give away part of the land.[16] Since the unity of the Whole Land came as a result of the actions of the Zionist movement, it could, therefore, be understood as a tool that was and could be further implemented to actualize God's will. As such, the Israeli state, though secular, should be sanctified as it is part of the messianic process.[17]

Having described the two modern streams, I will now turn to the zealots of the Second Temple period. Our knowledge of the great Jewish revolt against the Romans (66–70 CE) comes mainly from the writings of the Jewish historian Josephus Flavius. His descriptions are scattered over several different essays in which he revealed varying attitudes toward the rebels. His comments are marred by inconsistencies, and his overall tone toward the rebels is unsympathetic.[18]

Josephus regarded all the rebel groups as a distinct stream, a "fourth philosophy," alongside the other streams in Jewish society at the time – the Pharisees, Sadducees, and Essenes. Most scholars of the revolt, however, identify two separate rebel groups – the zealots and the Sicarii,

---

[15] Moshe Hellinger, "Political Theology in the Thought of 'Merkaz HaRav' Yeshiva and its Profound Influence on Israeli Politics and Society since 1967," *Totalitarian Movements and Political Religions* 9(4) (2008), 533–50.

[16] Aviever Ravitzky, *Messianism, Zionism, and Jewish Religious Radicalism.* Chicago and London: University of Chicago Press, 1993, pp. 122–44.

[17] *Ibid.*, pp. 136–41.

[18] Mark A. Brighton, *The Sicarii in Josephus's Judean War: Rhetorical Analysis and Historical Observations.* Atlanta: Society of Biblical Literature, 2009.

which were accompanied by other unorganized groupings referred to by Josephus as bandits or brigands. Scholars of the period disagree sharply on the question as to whether these groups shared a uniform ideology. Martin Hengel argued that all the rebels should be regarded as sharing a common approach rooted in the "fourth philosophy" stream founded by Judas of Galilee in 6 CE. Richard Horsley, by contrast, claims that the Zealots – as distinct from the Sicarii – were a social group rather than a philosophical or religious stream. He suggests that the Zealots were the product of a refugee experience created by the scorched earth policy adopted by the Romans as they suppressed the revolt, so that fleeing peasants had no alternative but to fight back. He presents the Zealots' revolt as a class conflict against Rome and against the Jewish aristocracy in Jerusalem, which supported Rome, rather than as a movement with religious characteristics.[19] Horsley and Hanson had shown that from the death of Herod (4 CE) until the beginning of the Great Revolt (66 CE), the social unrest produced several different and separated messianic and prophetic movements, who didn't follow a single ideology, hence refuting Hengel's theory.[20] For the purposes of our discussion, I will adopt the position of Yisrael Ben Shalom, who sees zeal (not to be mistaken by the Zealot Party) as an ideological force, rather than a single, orderly movement.[21]

The reasons for the eruption of the Great Revolt were varied and included socioeconomic factors, Roman misrule, tension between Jews and non-Jews due to questions of ritual purity, hatred of the pro-Roman Jewish aristocracy, and nationalist sentiments. The revolutionaries consisted of diverse groups. Some hailed from the countryside, others from the city of Jerusalem. Some were priests, others were lay. Some were wealthy, others poor. Some had utopian goals and spent most of their energy attacking the rich and the hereditary aristocracy. Some fought for power, some fought out of hatred to Rome. According to Shaye Cohen, many of the revolutionaries believed that the Messiah would soon come to redeem Israel and all the Jews have to do was to get the ball rolling; God and the angelic hosts would do the rest. One of the major reasons the

---

[19] Richard Horsley, "The Zealots: Their Origin, Relationships and Importance in the Jewish Revolt," *Novum Testamentum* 28(2) (1986), 159–92.

[20] Richard Horesly and John Hanson, *Bandits, Prophets, and Messiahs: Poular Movements at the Time of Jesus.* Minneapolis: Winston Press, 1985.

[21] Yisrael Ben Shalom, *The House of Shammai and the Zealots' Struggle against Rome.* Jerusalem: Yitzhak Ben Zvi Institute and Ben Gurion University Publishers, 1993, p. xi (in Hebrew).

Jews lost the war is that they were unable to mount a united front against the Romans. They spent much of their time killing each other.[22]

Doron Mendels argues that as long as the Jews were able to cling to a national emblem, they did not revolt. The schism between religious Jews and Hellenists began to emerge in the Herodian period. Following the death of Agrippa I in 44 CE, the government of the country was concentrated exclusively in Roman hands. No single individual emerged who was able to unite the Jews around a national emblem. Following the abolition of the monarchy, the army disbanded and the Temple was managed by detested priests identified with the Roman occupiers. The tension between the different groups became untenable and the threads unifying the Jewish people dissolved.[23]

The rebellion erupted in May 66 CE following a local incident in Caesarea, a city founded by Herod that had a strongly Hellenistic character. The procurator Florus sided with the Hellenists and created a provocation in Jerusalem by seizing treasure from the Temple. The protests by residents of Jerusalem fueled the revolt and stopped collecting funds for the emperor in the Temple. The Romans sent the 12th Legion to suppress the revolt, but to no avail. A new leadership of a nonradical character emerged in Jerusalem, but enjoyed independence for only a brief period before Vespasian landed in Palestine in 67 CE with an enormous army in order to suppress the revolt. Vespasian conquered various parts of the country and used extreme force. In 68 CE the Emperor Nero committed suicide. Vespasian called back to Rome and later he was declared his successor. His son Titus was charged with continuing the campaign against the revolt. Titus besieged Jerusalem, but he only broke through into the city two years later. Large numbers of refugees found a safe haven in Jerusalem, but instead of preparing for battle they devoted most of their energies to an internal struggle between the proponents and opponents of compromise with the Romans. It was only during this period that the zealots became a significant force. In 70 CE, Titus broke into Jerusalem, crushed the Jewish resistance and burned the Temple. In 73 CE, Masada – the Sicarii fortress that was the last stronghold of opposition to Rome – fell.[24]

[22] Shaye Cohen, *From the Maccabees to the Mishna*. Philadelphia: Westminster Press, 1987, pp. 31–2.
[23] Doron Mendels, *The Rise and Fall of Jewish Nationalism*. New York: Doubleday, 1992, pp. 356–8.
[24] *Ibid.*

A PROFILE OF ZEALOTRY

In this section I will present some of the key ideological hallmarks of zealotry as manifested in the Second Temple period and consider the extent to which these traits may also be identified in the modern Jewish movements.

Mundane dominion versus divine dominion

I will base my discussion of the characteristics of Second Temple zealotry in this section primarily on Martin Hengel's important study. Although Hengel's research has been the subject of considerable criticism, its essence lies in the question as to whether the zealotry of the time constituted a single stream, as Hengel argued, or distinct streams with divergent motives. The criticism of his study does not fundamentally challenge his conclusions that I use for this research.[25]

Martin Hengel argued that the ideology of the zealots who led the revolt against Rome had its origins in the teachings of Judas of Galilee, which were consolidated around 6 CE. Josephus refers to Judas as the leader of the fourth philosophical stream.[26] According to Judas of Galilee, there is an inherent tension between the rule of God and human rule. The rule of God is perceived in eschatological terms, as something that may be imposed in the future. In this eschatological vision, God's dominion will be direct and all human forces will be exhausted. Judas argues that the eschatological era can be brought imminently. Accordingly, he rejected passive anticipation of God's dominion and demanded that his followers withdraw their loyalty from the Roman emperor. His perception of divine rule required the immediate cessation of obedience to mundane rule; his followers were expected to rely on God not to abandon them in their struggle against the Roman Empire. Judas's analysis of the achievements of Jewish history during the Hasmonean period (140–37 BCE) informed his solution to the problem of oppressive

[25] Morton Smith, "Zealots and Sicarii, Their Origins and Relation," *Harvard Theological Review* 64(1) 1971, 1–19; Horsley, "The Zealots."

[26] Yisrael Ben Shalom rejects this theory and argues that the zealous ideal has its origins in the period of the Hasmonean revolt. Ben Shalom, *House of Shammai*, p. 157. On the connection between the philosophical motives of the Great Revolt and those of the Maccabean revolt, see Willliam Farmer, *Maccabees, Zealots and Josephus: An Inquiry into Jewish Nationalism in the Greco-Roman Period*. New York: Columbia University Press, 1956.

rule. He argued that Jews should confine themselves to their own binding laws, without recourse to Gentile ways.[27]

The deification of the emperor arrived in Palestine as the result of Roman hegemony. Herod (37–4 BCE) built several temples in his own honor and introduced aspects of Hellenistic culture, such as games and theaters. Judas of Galilee demanded that Jews choose between God and the emperor. Support and loyalty for the emperor was perceived as idolatry. Since the emperor demanded that he be honored as a god, his worship was perceived as the violation of the First Commandment.[28]

According to the leaders of the zealots, Judas and Saddok, the messianic course of history is determined not only by God but also by the actions of the people. Progress along this path may be rapid or slow, and it may even halt completely. If the Jews fail to obey God, the promised redemption may be transformed into divine judgment. Thus redemption will not come automatically; the faithful Jew has a role in the messianic drama by disconnecting himself from Roman rule, which is the antithesis to divine rule.[29] Accordingly, the revolt against Roman rule and its agents is perceived as an essential stage in the establishment of the rule of God, which will bring with it the realization of the eschatological End.

These rebellious tendencies were manifested in the boycott of the census held by the emperor, which was widely regarded as a tool for usurping property and raising taxes. Opposition to the payment of taxes now acquired a theological dimension: the payment of tax was interpreted as the violation of the prohibition against idol worship, since the revenue was used to serve an illegitimate imperial regime. The difficulties and suffering caused by the revolt were regarded as a test of faith; only those who met the test would be considered eligible for the imminent redemption. The zealots saw themselves as loyal to the sole rule of God and refused to refer to any human as "lord." The demands to accept the emperor as ruler and lord were rejected, and the tax revolt erupted.

The goal of the rebel movement was to secure political liberty as a precursor to messianic redemption. Coins from the period show that the expectation of messianic redemption and political liberty were inexorably intertwined. The liberation of the Temple formed the heart of the zealot's messianic expectations.[30] The assertion that the messianic dominion of God had already begun led to the rejection of the emperor's mundane rule and was regarded as the first step toward eschatological liberty.

---

[27] Hengel, *Zealots*, pp. 90–93.   [28] *Ibid.*   [29] *Ibid.*, p. 122.   [30] *Ibid.*, p. 110.

Accordingly, the movement was based on an ideological and religious basis and rejected political pragmatism or power-based calculations. The assumption was that God would intervene to help the faithful and lead them to victory.[31]

Modern movements

The rejection of the legitimacy of the ruling powers, refusal to collaborate with them in any form (to the point of a political rejection of the ruler), boycotts of censuses and refusal to pay taxes are all hallmarks of Neturei Karta in Israel. This is a rejection of any type of Jewish government prior to the coming of the messiah. The Satmar Hasidim in the United States believe in the imminence of a messianic era as the final stage before the arrival of the true messiah. Accordingly, they perceive the suffering of the faithful as a test of faith and the final selection of those worthy of redemption. The rebellious nature of the movement against Jewish dominion and its rejection of innovation and compromise in the name of modernism are also perceived as actions that expedite the End. Here, too, divine rule is seen as incompatible with human Jewish rule, and this forms the basis for Satmar's opposition to Zionism. This approach does not reject Gentile governance per se, but rather Jewish political activism. Exile is accepted as an essential condition for the messianic age, and political passivity is sanctified as a value that expedites the End.

Radical ultra-Orthodoxy and the Second Temple zealots associate political liberty with messianic liberty. The difference between them lies in their attitude toward political activism. While the Second Temple zealots believed that their actions could secure the desired liberty, radical ultra-Orthodoxy had lost faith in the ability of Jews to change their fate through political action and therefore demands passivity. Both movements are fueled by an apocalyptic and catastrophic worldview that sees contemporary reality as a prelude to the messianic era. However, the conclusions they draw from this analysis are diametrically opposed. The Second Temple zealots saw the nearing of the End Times as demanding political action and rebellion, while for the ultra-Orthodoxy it led to passivity. It should be noted, however, that this passivity does not mean a complete avoidance of any political action, but rather opposition to Jewish dominion; accordingly, their approach left room for activism in the form of demonstrations, the publication of posters, and propaganda.

---

[31] *Ibid.*, pp. 131–40.

Messianic Religious Zionism also shares several hallmarks of Second Temple zealotry. In particular, it sees messianic redemption as a phenomenon that is occurring in the immediate present, and that depends on human actions. Exponents of messianic Religious Zionism also see an indelible connection between liberty and messianic redemption. However, the case of Religious Zionism differs from that of the Second Temple since the establishment of the State of Israel means that Jews have already won political liberty. Accordingly, a multistaged theology developed in these circles, based on the claim that the State of Israel marks no more than the beginning of a messianic process that will ultimately lead to full redemption and the eschatological End. Since there is no inherent conflict here with human rule, this approach avoids the dichotomic perception of secular government as a sacrilege and favors a compromise whereby secular Jewish government is regarded as the first stage toward the establishment of the Kingdom of God. The formula evolved by Gush Emunim allowed for political pragmatism alongside a strong messianic orientation. Some of the settler rabbis have developed a complex interpretation of reality that does not view redemption as automatic, but argues that it depends on human action and may include instances of regression as well as moments of progress.[32]

Zealotry and violence

William Farmer argues that Jewish nationalism in the Hellenistic period was interpreted as zealous adherence to the covenant and to the concept of the Jews as the Chosen People. This explains the radical rejection of idol worship. The principle of God's covenant with the Jews combined two elements: the Jews were required to observe strictly the religious law as recorded in the Books of the Law; in return, they would receive God's protection and enjoy Jewish sovereignty in the Land of Israel. Observance of the law and the realization of the covenant were two sides of the same coin. Thus the Maccabean Revolt (167–4 BCE) erupted in protest at the willingness of some Jewish people – God's Chosen People – to adopt the cultural and economic norms of the Hellenistic world, with its cosmopolitan and polytheistic tendencies. Actually, some Jews in Jerusalem seem to welcome Antiochus' entrance into Jewish affairs (1 Macc. 1:11–5). Hellenism gain dominance not only through coercion but also through a

---

[32] Zvi Tau, *On the Faith of Our Times – Guidelines for Understanding the Period*, 1. Jerusalem: Hosen Yeshuot, 5754 – 1994 (in Hebrew); Inbari, *Messianic*, pp. 59–71.

process of assimilation.[33] By 167 BCE Antiochus IV abolished the traditional Jewish law as the law of Judah, and established a new order of worship. Zeal for religious law fueled the Maccabean Revolt by way of a counterreaction to assimilation and coercion.[34]

Hengel quotes several instances from the Books of the Maccabees in which Matitiyahu, the leader of the Maccabean Revolt, advocated the zealous observance of religious law and the waging of a holy war against the political oppression of the Seleucid regime. Since the Biblical narrative emphasizes that the Land of Israel is reserved for the Jewish people, the expulsion of a foreign conqueror from its territory is perceived as the manifestation of God's will and the observance of the covenant. However, zealotry also has an additional dimension – zealous observance of the laws of the Torah, in return for political liberty in the Land of Israel.[35]

Since the time of Matitiyahu, zealotry has been a normative religious category. Accordingly, the Maccabees and the zealots share similar characteristics. Just as Pinchas, in a moment of distress, murdered a transgressor and acted as the representative of God to free Israel of punishment, so Matitiyahu and his sons punished those who violated religious law and collaborated with the alien enemy. Zealotry to religious law demands devotion and is regarded as a sacred and obligatory war. The motivation for the struggle was essentially religious and the Maccabees, like the later zealots, saw the presence of an imperial force in the Land of Israel as sacrilege.[36]

The Second Temple zealots drew on the tradition of Pinchas to reinforce their stance and secure theological justification for their struggle. The zealots viewed themselves as an instrument through which God could demand zealous rage and wreak justice on those who violated religious law. The spontaneous character of the zealous tradition provided justification to act even if it is against the positions of the rabbinical leadership and the Sanhedrin, just as Pinchas acted without the support of Moses and the elders. Accordingly, the zealots took up arms and believed that through violence they could deflect God's rage and proceed toward redemption.[37]

---

[33] Daniel Harrington, "Maccabean Revolt." In: John J. Collins and Daniel C. Harlow (eds.), *The Eerdmans Dictionary of Early Judaism*. Grand Rapids, MI: William B. Eerdmans, 2010, pp. 900–2.
[34] Farmer, *Maccabees*, p. 154.   [35] Hengel, *Zealots*, p. 154.   [36] *Ibid.*, pp. 171–3.
[37] *Ibid.*, p. 173.

During the Maccabean Revolt, zeal was understood as a passionate giving of oneself to God's cause that was associated with a readiness to avenge every form of sacrilege. Zeal had already become an influential religious attitude in Palestinian Judaism during the Maccabean period. It shows clearly that zeal for God and his laws were established as a distinct form of piety in that tradition.

The zealots repeatedly showed the same readiness to take the law into their own hands and even to use violent means to preserve the integrity of God's law and his sanctuary, often sacrificing their own lives in the process. Whenever the people had the impression that the laws of their God or His Temple were threatened by the Roman rulers, they rose up and protested for their religious rights. They did not even shrink from open revolt.[38]

Zealotry was implemented through violence since God's fury is manifested in violence. Thus the zealots employed violent means in order to impose the law or to defend the Tabernacle against defilement. Whenever the divine blessing of Israel was jeopardized, whether due to internal factors (assimilation) or external (occupation), the use of violence was viewed as a religious obligation.[39]

Modern movements

Messianic Religious Zionism does not see itself as a zealot movement and has not adopted an ethos that glorifies violence. However, a deeper analysis of the thought and practice of this movement shows that the founding principle behind its actions is the conquest of the Land of Israel, which may be achieved by violent means. This movement associates Jewish rule over the entire Land of Israel with messianic redemption, and in this respect its ideology has similarities with historical zealotry. Messianic Religious Zionism adopted the principle of conquering the Land as a basic tenet, as indeed did secular Zionism. It also sees the control of the territory of Biblical Israel as a manifestation of the covenant between Israel and God as part of the path leading to messianic redemption. The principle of political passivity that characterized rabbinical Judaism in the Diaspora was rejected in favor of nationalism. Messianic Religious Zionism does not reject the use of force in the name of liberty. This stream attributes considerable weight to militarism, as evidenced by the large number of soldiers and officers from these circles in the Israel

[38] *Ibid.*, pp. 177–183.   [39] *Ibid.*, pp. 224.

Defense Force. The conquest of the Land and the defense of its borders are perceived as an end that justifies the means.[40] Even the more militant circles within this group have a self-definition that verges on Fascist nationalism.[41]

However, Second Temple zealotry emerged as a movement against the alien occupation of the country, and its violent character reflected its aspiration to free itself of the occupiers. Messianic Religious Zionism, by contrast, developed as the result of the expansion of Israel's borders following the Six Day War. The conquest and holding of these parts of the Land were undertaken by the State of Israel, and messianic Religious Zionism forms part of the overall fabric of national society.

Messianic Religious Zionist circles perceive the struggle for the Whole Land of Israel as a supreme value, and the movement focuses its efforts on strengthening the Jewish presence in the territories conquered in the Six Day War. Its activists feature prominently among the most hawkish circles of contemporary Israeli politics, and for the most part they reject any possibility of territorial compromise. Rabbi Zvi Yehuda Kook even threatened civil war if any territory belonging to the State of Israel were handed over in return for peace.[42] However, it is important to emphasize that his successors have rarely adopted such an extreme position; to date, the struggle against the evacuation of territory as was done after Israel-Egypt peace accords (1982), the Oslo Accords (1992–1995) and the Disengagement (2005) has been waged mainly through passive resistance. Nevertheless, more militant attitudes can be found in some sections of this public concerning violence against Palestinians. This position seems to be gaining prominence among the younger members of the movement, who have sometimes been identified with the "Youth of the Hills" and with the so-called "price tag" attacks.

---

[40] Eliezer Don Yehiya, "The Book and the Sword: The Nationalist Yeshivot and Political Radicalism in Israel." In: Martin E. Marty and Scott Appleby (eds.), *Accounting for Fundamentalisms*, Chicago: University of Chicago Press, 1996, pp. 264–302; Ami Pedhazur, *The Triumph of Israel's Radical Right*. New York: Oxford University Press, 2012.

[41] Inbari, *Jewish Fundamentalism*, pp. 51–78, 131–60.

[42] Kook said in 1974: "When it comes to Judea and Samaria, the Golan Heights – it [territorial compromises] will not happen without a war! Someone asked me whether I want to wage a 'civil war.' I will not enter here into matters of terminology and I will not use names as to how this will happen, but the fact is that it will not happen without a war!" Zvi Yehuda Kook, "The Nation of Israel Stand Up and Live." In: Zalman Melamed (ed.), *Eretz Hatsvi – Our Rabbi in the Battle over Our Entire Land*. Bet El: Netivei Or, 1994, p. 25 (in Hebrew).

Since the use of force in order to conquer the Whole Land of Israel and to maintain Israeli dominance in the conquered areas is undertaken by the nation state as a whole, messianic Religious Zionism has not needed to develop an ethos of violence as an ideological principle. As noted, however, it is impossible to ignore the militaristic tendencies of the movement.

Radicalization in terms of the attitude to the Halakhah has also emerged as a hallmark of messianic Religious Zionism. This includes the emergence of a tendency known as "Hardal," a Hebrew acronym for National Religious Haredi. This approach is characterized by a particularly strict observance of the religious law, the devotion of long hours to Torah study at the expense of secular learning, a strict approach to modesty (a key feature of the Haredi community), and fierce nationalism.[43]

Radical ultra-Orthodoxy has also adopted most of the characteristics of zealotry: It is zealous of the Land of Israel, and it is zealous of the Halakhah and applies rigid standards to its interpretation.

Zeal for the Land of Israel is manifested in opposition to Zionism. As explained in this book, this stream has forcefully rejected any form of Jewish nationhood in the Land of Israel prior to the coming of messiah, and therefore utterly opposed Zionism as a political movement. The success of the Zionist enterprise was interpreted as a sign of the growing strength of Satan and Zionist leaders were perceived as Satanic agents. The fierce rejection of Zionism was described in terms of zealous concern for God's honor and for the covenant between the Jewish people and its God – a covenant that must be realized in a miraculous and passive form, and under no circumstances through physical endeavor.

In terms of the attitude to violence, however, a process of development can be seen in radical ultra-Orthodoxy. This stream does not advocate extreme violence, and in this respect it reflects the changes that occurred in rabbinical Judaism following the failure of the revolt against the Romans. Following the major revolts, which also included the revolt of Bar Kochva (132–136 CE), the rabbinical literature adopted an approach that advocated nonviolence. The rhetoric used to support passivity proposed that the destruction of the Temple was the result of the people's sins, and the way to secure the renewal of Jewish nationhood was through repentance. Once this process was complete, God

---

[43] Gideon Aran, *Kookism – The roots of Gush Emunim, Jewish Settlers' Sub-Culture, Zionist Theology, Contemporary Messianism.* Jerusalem: Carmel, 2013, pp. 29–110 (in Hebrew).

would send the messiah to renew Jewish nationhood and build the Temple. In the meantime, however, only repentance could help rebuild the nation and maintain its connection with God. According to rabbinical tradition, the failure of the war against Rome was due to the presence of the evil impulse within the Jewish heart. The subsequent messianic tradition argued that ultimate redemption cannot be the product of human action, and the only way to expedite its arrival is through religious conduct. The rabbis emphasized observance of religious law and opposed any form of messianic speculation. As we have discussed, one of the prominent examples of this is the legend of the Three Oaths imposed on the People of Israel by God, which negated messianic activism prior to the arrival of the messiah.[44]

Radical ultra-Orthodoxy sees itself as a zealous stream and employs zealous rhetoric. It perceives its struggle against modern culture in general, and Zionism in particular, as demanding devotion and a willingness to prepare for war. However, this war is understood in rhetorical rather than physical terms. In this respect this stream represents a synthesis of the nonviolent approach of rabbinical literature and the value of zealotry. The violent aspect of Second Temple zealotry was moderated and transformed into rhetoric. As David Myers noted, Satmar Hasidim employs a "pervasive language of war that emerged out of a sense of the grave perils posed by modernity."[45] Verbal militarism includes insults, curses, and sometimes even prayers for the death of what they would consider a wicked individual. When physical violence is used, it is directed internally within the movement in order to impose conformity on such issues as modesty. I would qualify Myer's depiction somewhat: it should be noted that violence is sometimes used in the form of harassment, the blocking of roads, curses, and even stone throwing. However, radical ultra-Orthodoxy has not developed an ideological affinity to violence.

As Daniel Boyarin has shown, the Talmud formed the feminine man, whose main quality was not aggressiveness, strength or power, but self retreatment in situations of conformation. Instead of expressions of heroism in battle, heroism was redefined as an expression of the study

---

[44] Robert Eisen, *The Peace and Violence of Judaism: From the Bible to Modern Zionism*. New York: Oxford University Press, 2012, pp. 82–6; Reuven Firestone, "Holy War in Modern Judaism? 'Mitzva War' and the Problem of the 'Three Vows,'" *Journal of the American Academy of Religion* 74(4) (2006), 954–82.

[45] David Myers, "'Commanded War:' Three Chapters in the 'Military' History of Satmar Hasidim," *Journal of the American Academy of Religion*, 81(2) (2013), 1–46.

of the Torah. Haredi society continues this trend, and is unwilling to use force in its public struggles.[46]

Martyrdom

A further characteristic of Second Temple zealotry was the emergence of a phenomenon of martyrdom. The martyr was a person who preferred a violent death to compliance with an oppressive demand of hostile authorities. The Maccabean martyrs decided to sacrifice their lives in order to remain faithful to their Jewish practices. The Martyrs are presented as model figures and indicate a proper way of life for other Jews (2 Macc. 6:28, 31). In the eyes of the martyrs, their action is viewed as restoration of the covenant relation between God and the Jewish people that was violated by the transgression of God's laws by godless Jewish leaders. Their intercessory prayer just before dying invoked God's mercy for the people as well as punishment for the foreign king.[47] A famous example of this is Hannah and her seven sons, who according to 2 Maccabees, Chapter 7, were seized along with their mother by Antiochus IV Epiphanes, presumably shortly after the beginning of the religious persecutions in 167/166 BCE and ordered to prove their obedience to the king by partaking of swine's flesh. The brothers defiantly refused to do so. Encouraged in their resolve by their mother, they were executed after suffering unspeakable tortures. When the mother was appealed to by the king to spare the youngest child's life by prevailing upon him to comply, she urged the child instead to follow in the path of his brothers, and she herself died shortly thereafter. Another example are the fighters at Masada, whom Josephus claims engaged in an act of mass suicide, though some modern scholars challenge his version of events: only a small number of bones have been found at the site, despite the fact that he claimed that the number of dead was as high as 960.[48]

By contrast, messianic Religious Zionism has not developed a distinct ethos of martyrdom beyond that which developed as part of the Zionist movement as a whole. In 1920, Yosef Trumpeldor fell while defending the settlement of Tel Chai, and he has since been "sanctified" as a secular

---

[46] Daniel Boyarin, *Unheroic Conduct: The Rise of Heterosexuality and the Invention of the Jewish Man.* Berkeley, CA: University of California Press, 2007, pp. 1–29.

[47] Jan Willem Van Henten, "Martyrdom." In: John J. Collins and Daniel C. Harlow (eds.), *The Eerdmans Dictionary of Early Judaism.* Grand Rapids, MI: William B. Eerdmans, 2010, pp. 917–9.

[48] See: Brighton, *Sicarii,* pp. 106–10.

Zionist martyr who is alleged to have declared: "It is good to die for our Land." In the margins of messianic Religious Zionism there have been some isolated instances of martyrdom. One example of this is Baruch Goldstein, who murdered twenty-nine Muslim worshippers at the Cave of the Patriarchs in Hebron in 1994 and who was himself killed in his attack. Another is Natan Eden Zadeh, who murdered four Arab passengers on a bus in 2005 and was also killed. These figures have not been perceived as role models and their death has not been glorified by the central stream of messianic Religious Zionism. Both can be regarded as acts of zealotry rather than martyrdom, since their death was an unintended by-product of their actions.[49]

Radicalization of religious law

Hengel argues that an important aspect of zealotry that can be seen both in the case of the Essenes and in Jesus' sermons is the demand for full obedience to the laws of the Torah. Hostility to the graven image of the emperor, even on coins; the demand that pagans undergo circumcision, even by force (as occurred during the period of Maccabean rule); and the radical prohibitions against intermarriage and sexual relations with Gentiles can all be seen as examples of an extremist interpretation of the Torah constitution and the heightened use of the death penalty in order to achieve purity as required by the Torah. This was a militant doctrine of action as the expression of zealous confession. The tendency to radicalization of religious law can also be seen in the case of the Essene community and in Jesus' polemics, for example, in his anticipation of the imminent eschaton. Thus the anticipation of apocalypse encouraged religious extremism. The demand for the exclusive dominion of God and the attempt to achieve total purity are intended by way of preparation for the eschatological End. The zealots did not see themselves as engaged in changing or reforming the laws of the Torah, but rather in strengthening its hold. Josephus, however, frequently criticized them for amending the laws of old.[50]

Yisrael Ben Shalom identifies the philosophy of the Second Temple zealots with the House of Shammai. He describes the tendency to conservatism and ridigity that characterized the House of Shammai as the ancient Halakhah that evolved during the period of the Hasmonean

[49] Inbari, *Messianic*, pp. 143–5.   [50] Hengel, *Zealots*, pp. 227–8.

Revolt, and demanded an admirable level of personal piety. The House of Shammai believed that collective repentance and an active struggle against Rome could expedite the end of the dominion of evil and prepare the way for the messianic age, ultimately leading to the longed-for kingdom of heaven. By contrast, the House of Hillel advocated a pragmatic approach that favored compromise and accordingly sought to avoid confrontation with Rome.

The sages of Shammai laid the groundwork for the trend to zealotry, and it was from their ranks that groups of warriors equipped with an uncompromising ideology and a high moral standard would later emerge. As the revolt erupts, we hear explicit reports that elders from the House of Shammai are involved in a bloody confrontation with the House of Hillel. The ancient Halakhah and the connection between Shammai and the Hasmonean kingdom positioned the House of Shammai at the head of the struggle against Rome and against the Jewish collaborators. After the revolt, the House of Shammai ceased to exist.[51]

Modern movements

Increasing extremism as a religious norm is a feature of all the Orthodox streams,[52] but radical ultra-Orthodoxy appears to lead the field in this respect. My study has identified the manner in which ultra-Orthodoxy emerged as a counterreaction to the phenomena of secularization and religious reform, and highlights its closed and isolationist character. The movement views itself as the last pure remnant and struggles to protect its way of life. This movement also believes that repentance and an active struggle against Zionism can pave the way for messianic redemption.

Researchers of Jewish Orthodoxy have shown that its characteristic radical interpretation of religious law is the product of confusion in an era of profound change in Jewish history. Its purpose is to prevent religious error, according to the logic that "the more (observance) the better." According to Charles Liebman, the expansion of the religious law was to include the public as well as the private realm, and to put greater restrictions and hardship on implementing the law. He argued that the rise of extremism in the Jewish world is due to the breakdown of the Jewish community and the breaking of the institutions that were able to restrain the radicals. In addition, the search for a harsher interpretation of

---

[51] Ben Shalom, *House of Shammai*, pp. 229–30.
[52] Samuel C. Heilman, *Sliding to the Right: The Contest for the Future of American Jewish Orthodoxy*. Berkeley: University of California Press, 2006.

the law consistent with the desire to assure one's self and others that one is indeed living accordance with what is commanded to do by the law.[53]

An unwillingness to compromise over the Land of Israel for the sake of peace is one of the hallmarks of messianic Religious Zionism. The sanctification of the Land as a supreme value overrides any other value, such as the commandment to avoid bloodshed or the imperative to pursue peace. This order of priorities can be seen as the adoption of an increasingly extreme approach to the laws of the Torah. Very few members of this stream have ever supported territorial compromise and the movement as a whole has vehemently opposed any withdrawal from areas of the entire Land of Israel. Individuals who have adopted a more moderate position on these issues, such as Rabbi Yehuda Amital, have found themselves marginalized within Religious Zionist circles.[54]

Eschatology and the pangs of messiah

As we have already noted, the Jewish revolt against Rome was accompanied by messianic expectations that the age of redemption had already arrived, and that active efforts were needed to complete its realization. Hengel quotes Josephus, who claimed that the outbreak of the revolt was accompanied by a prophecy concerning the imminent appearance of "one like the son of man" as described in the Book of Daniel (7:13). Thus Judaism in Palestine at the time was influenced by the expectation of a personal messiah. A further prophecy, in Numbers 24:7, regarding the appearance of the Star of Jacob was also known. The eschatological expectation was for the restoration of Israel for an idealized form of its former state. The restored state would be led by a messiah, that is to say, a legitimate king from a Davidic line who would restore the monarchy.[55] Horsley and Hanson claim that the writings of Josephus tell us that from the death of Herod until the outbreak of the revolt there were several

---

[53] Charles Liebman, "Extremism as a Religious Norm," *Journal of the Scientific Study of Religion* 22(1) (1983), 75–86. Albert Baumgarten qualified Liebman's theory, arguing that extremism is not a general norm, but each case has to be studied according to itself. Albert Baumgarten, "The Nature of Religious Extremism." In: Meir Litbak and Ora Limor (eds.), *Religious Zealotry*. Jerusalem: Zalman Shazar Center for Jewish History, 2007, pp. 43–56 (in Hebrew).

[54] Inbari, *Messianic*, pp. 72–80.

[55] John Collins, "Eschatology." In: John J. Collins and Daniel C. Harlow (eds.), *The Eerdmans Dictionary of Early Judaism*. Grand Rapids, MI: William B. Eerdmans, 2010, pp. 594–7.

messianic movements active among the peasants, where followers gathered around charismatic leaders. These leaders, anointed as kings, asserted their independence in armed rebellion. There were also parallel prophetic movements. Prophets inspired large groups of their followers to join in divinely led new actions of liberation from alien rule. These prophetic movements were inspired by some vision of eschatological act of deliverance.[56] Josephus talks about villains with purer hands but more impious intentions than the revolutionaries, who stirred up the people with supposed prophecies (JW 2.259–60). As John Collins had shown, although these "villains," meaning popular prophets, were not advocating violence, as apocalyptic ideology can be in many cases nonviolent, the way these prophecies were perceived by the masses promoted rebellion. Apocalypticism, argues Collins, more often than not, is quietistic. But nonetheless it fosters attitudes that are conducive to violence by polarization.[57]

The zealots anticipated that redemption would come on the ninth of the Hebrew month of Av – the traditional anniversary of the destruction of the First Temple. It is possible that Titus chose to break into the Temple on this same date in order to prove to the Jews that their prophecy had failed and to depict his action as a form of divine punishment.

During the siege of Jerusalem the belief that suffering was an essential component of the path to redemption was adopted more widely. The rebels believed that their suffering was the "pangs of messiah" due to its unprecedented severity. Accordingly, Hengel concludes that the rebels identified Rome with the fourth beast in Daniel 7, and the threat to the Tabernacle was perceived as part of the pangs of messiah. The decision to avoid all contact with Rome, which caused considerable hardship, was now seen as part of the process of purification and as a manifestation of a test of faith that distinguishes the remnant that would be saved. Even after the fall of Jerusalem the zealots continued their revolt, confident that the greater their distress, the greater the chance of redemption.[58]

Modern movements

A similar principle can be identified within radical ultra-Orthodoxy. The regressive concept of the decline of the generations, and the assertion that

[56] Horsley and Hanson, *Bandits*, pp. 244–54.
[57] John Collins, "Radical Religion and Ethical Dilemmas of Apocalyptic Millenarism." In: Zoe Bennett and David Gowler (eds.), *Radical Christian Voices and Practices*. New York: Oxford University Press, 2011, pp. 87–102.
[58] Hengel, *Zealots*, pp. 242–5.

current generation is the last before the coming of messiah, form a central strand in the theology of this stream. The sufferings of the Jews in modern times, and particularly during the Holocaust, and the collapse of the world of Torah due to secularization are perceived as conclusive evidence of the pangs of messiah. The expectation of imminent apocalyptic redemption adds a dimension of urgency to their persistent struggle against Zionism in the name of purity. The perception of suffering as a test of faith can also be seen in this movement. Eschatological calculations and expectations of a personal messiah can also be seen in the work of Rabbi Chaim Elazar Shapira of Munkacs, as discussed at length in Chapter 4.

By contrast, messianic Religious Zionism adopted an approach of progressive redemption. This has an essentially optimistic character and relies on human action. Accordingly, this stream did not adopt the expectation of devastation as a precursor to the coming of messiah. It is true that Rabbi Zvi Yehuda Kook also interpreted the Holocaust as a manifestation of a divine plan that would ultimately lead to redemption. According to his version, however, God eliminated the Jewish Exile in order to bring about the establishment of the State of Israel and national revival as part of the course to ultimate redemption.[59] The difficulties his students faced in the realization of these expectations due to actions by the State of Israel with territorial compromises that are inconsistent with their eschatological beliefs were also portrayed as a test of faith and determination.[60]

Holy war

As mentioned, there was no coherent ideology behind the Great Revolt. However, those who went to battle perceived their struggle as a holy war, and therefore as one in which God was also a partner. Accordingly, participation in the war was a religious obligation that overruled all other opinions and demanded the rejection of any pragmatic considerations or calculations based on the balance of power. The war against Rome was regarded in eschatological terms, and the expectation was that God would intervene on behalf of His soldiers. Eschatological expectations led to the perception of the Roman emperor as an apocalyptic enemy who was persecuting and crucifying the righteous; only his elimination could

[59] Ravitzky, *Messianism*, p. 109.   [60] Inbari, *Messianic*, pp. 59–71.

enable the establishment of a theocracy as the manifestation of God's rule.[61] The messianic passivity created by the failure of the revolt claimed that an individual messiah who would arrive from heaven would bring the end of history; accordingly, humans were forbidden to rebel against the will of the nations.[62]

Modern movements

The perception of war as an eschatological holy war can also be found in the two modern movements. Messianic Religious Zionism saw the Israeli victory in 1967 as evidence of divine and miraculous intervention. Accordingly, the establishment of the settlements and the continued holding of the Land of Israel within its Biblical borders are interpreted as human participation in the divine plan for Israel's redemption. Settling all sections of the Land of Israel demands special devotion. In effect, all the energies of this movement have been devoted to reinforcing the Jewish presence in the Territories, and they perceive their efforts as a struggle to draw the messianic End closer.[63] In the case of radical ultra-Orthodoxy, the struggle against Zionism is also perceived in eschatological terms, and therefore as a religious obligation. Here, too, the Hasidim are required to show special commitment and devotion to the struggle, even if this entails social isolation. Both the modern movements see the establishment of a theocracy in the End Times as the manifestation of God's dominion and as the ideal governmental model. However, of the two streams only radical ultra-Orthodoxy argues that such a reality can emerge only after the fall of Zionism by way of the apocalyptical enemy.

Enclave, modesty, and education

An additional nexus of concepts evident in the Second Temple period, and for which surprising analogies can be found in radical ultra-Orthodoxy, relates to the attitude toward religious enclaves. The Books of the Maccabees reports that the zealotry of Matitiyahu, the leader of the Hasmonean Revolt, led him to head for the desert along with all those who treasured truth. Zeal for religious law did not only lead to this self-imposed exile in the desert but also entailed the abandonment of property and the pursuit of a life of hardship. The escape to the desert embodied a

---

[61] Hengel, *Zealots*, pp. 303–12.   [62] *Ibid.*, pp. 280–87.   [63] Aran, *Kookism*.

spiritual endeavor to distance oneself from evil[64] and anticipation of Yahweh's acts of liberation – approaches evident among the Qumran community that can also be seen in the early Christian understanding of the role of John the Baptist. This belief was centered on Second Isaiah prophecy (40:3): "In the Wilderness prepare the way for Yahweh."[65]

The Qumran community also nurtured an apocalyptic worldview that led it to detach itself from Jewish society and go into exile in the desert by the Dead Sea. The members of the sect saw themselves as the Sons of Light and the majority of the Jewish people as the Sons of Darkness who would be eliminated following the eschatological war, together with God's other enemies. The Qumran sect anticipated the destruction and annihilation of the Pharisaical Jews who controlled Jerusalem and the Sadducee Jews who controlled the Temple, while they themselves would enjoy an eternal and plentiful life. The crucial divide was thus no longer between Jews and Gentiles, but between the faithful members of Qumran and outsiders, be they Jews or Gentiles.[66]

Modern movements

This description is reminiscent of the modern-day Haredi enclave – a place of refuge in which ultra-Orthodox Jews can avoid the influences of modern society. The religious enclave is also the place where the faithful can prepare themselves for their struggle against modern culture. The reliance on religious enclaves is one of the cornerstones of radical ultra-Orthodoxy,[67] which identifies its enemies less as the surrounding Gentiles and more as those Jews who have abandoned the ways of their ancestors. The latter are no other than the descendants of the *erev rav* (the "mixed multitude"), a Satanic force that can be expected to grow in strength before eventually being annihilated following the apocalyptic war. For radical ultra-Orthodoxy, the fact that the world of Torah is persecuted constitutes further evidence of the impending End.[68] Similarities can be seen between modern Haredi society and the Jews of Qumran:

---

[64] Hengel, *Zealots*, p. 249.   [65] Horsley and Hanson, *Bandits*, pp. 150–1.

[66] Marcus, "Modern."

[67] On the Haredi enclave's culture see: Yohai Hakak, *Young Men in Israeli Haredi Yeshiva Education – The Scholars' Enclave in Unrest*. Leiden and Boston: Brill, 2012.

[68] Rabbi Yeshayah Asher Zelig Margaliot authored a book that identified the Zionist followers as the reincarnation of the mixed multitude. He based his arguments on Kabbalistic literature, and his approach became central in radical ultra-Orthodox circles. Yeshayah Asher Zelig Margaliot, *Ashrei Ha'ish*. Jerusalem: Breslav Press, 5681–1921 (in Hebrew).

both may seem to be centered with the minutiae of religious law and both tend to be violent in their rhetoric, but apparently not in their actions.

One of the characteristics of the zealots of the Second Temple period was violent opposition to intermarriage and an insistence on maintaining ritual purity by penalizing those who had sexual relations with Gentile women. The testimonies suggest that from the Maccabean period onward, the zealots used violence in response to instances of sexual relations with Gentile women. An echo of this can be found in the Babylonian Talmud, which states: "He who takes the Aramean (i.e., alien) women is injured by the zealous" (*Mishnah Sanhedrin* 9,6). Separation from the Gentiles was enforced in various other fields, such as the prohibitions against the use of the Greek language, commercial ties with the Gentiles, and the study of philosophy.[69]

The Haredi enclaves are also characterized by segregation from the broader surroundings, including the development of clear mechanisms of distinction through external appearance and dress. The Haredi education system refrains as far as possible from teaching secular subjects, at least to male students. The modesty restrictions imposed in the Haredi enclave are also intended to protect sexual purity. The "modesty patrols" seek to protect the religious camp, and the methods used to impose standards of modesty have included violence and the shaming of those who deviate from the required path (as discussed in Chapter 3).

CONCLUSION

Zealotry is a religious category that has its origins in a Biblical model that, in extreme cases, supports the use of violence as a means for maintaining God's honor. Pinchas murdered the sinners and was rewarded with a blessing of eternal peace and priesthood. The identification of Pinchas with the Prophet Elijah, who is depicted in the Bible both as a violent character and as an individual of messianic dimensions, zealotry was perceived as a phenomenon that advanced eschatological goals.[70]

The principle of zealotry formed the basis for the Maccabean Revolt against the Seleucid kingdom (167–164 BCE). The rebellion was perceived as the realization of God's will by repelling an alien regime with Hellenistic and assimilative characteristics. The success of the revolt inspired the Great Revolt against the Romans (67–70 CE). In this case,

---

[69] Hengel, *Zealots*, p. 190. [70] Ben Shalom, *House of Shammai*, p. 161.

however, the zealous model identified with the approach of the House of Shammai proved unsuccessful. The zealots waged a hopeless and unbridled war that included not only a campaign against the external enemy in the form of the Roman empire, but also political assassinations of collaborators and attacks on Gentile women married to Jewish men.

In 1948 this nationhood was renewed with the establishment of the State of Israel, which was founded on a secular basis. Following the resurgence of Jewish nationalism in the early twentieth century, two movements with zealous characteristics emerged that are reminiscent of the character of the Great Revolt: messianic Religious Zionism and radical ultra-Orthodoxy.

Messianic Religious Zionism emerged as a stream in Israeli society following the dazzling Israeli victory in 1967 and saw the imposition of Israeli sovereignty in the Whole Land of Israel as the manifestation of God's will to redeem His people. Accordingly, this movement has struggled consistently to establish Jewish settlements in the areas conquered in the war and to oppose any tendency to compromise or to return territories for peace.

Radical ultra-Orthodoxy, meanwhile, is characterized by religious radicalism in preparation for the messianic age. This stream applies a regressive and pessimistic worldview, according to which the difficulties facing the observant public are evidence of the final period before the eschatological End. This movement sees itself as the faithful guardian of religious law and is vehemently opposed to any manifestation of Jewish nationhood in the Land of Israel before the coming of the messiah.

Some similarities can be seen between these three movements. Common themes include intolerance of other opinions; unswerving faith in its own way; an unshakeable faith in imminent messianic redemption (although the nature of this redemption is interpreted differently by each movement); and strict observance of the commandments.

Differences can be seen between both these modern movements and the ancient zealots, and both modern movements include moderating elements. Messianic Religious Zionism has not developed as an antiestablishment movement that rebels against an illegitimate regime. This movement forms part of the Israeli establishment, and has developed a theology that permits it to collaborate and even share values with the secular enterprise. Nevertheless, repeated confrontations with the state regarding the question of the retreat from the Entire Land of Israel for political compromise have led to the development of a more aggressive and antistatist tendency among some sections of the movement. The growing friction between the secular political institutions and this stream is weakening the mechanisms that have so far mitigated the confrontation between the two.[71]

Radical ultra-Orthodoxy is similar to the Second Temple zealots in its antiestablishment orientation and its identification of the State of Israel as an illegitimate power and as the representative of forces of evil. This stream has also nurtured a sense of discrimination and adopted a fiercely eschatological approach that anticipates an imminent apocalyptic war. At the same time, however, the movement has developed moderating tendencies. The exponents of this movement advocate a passive and non-violent struggle, thereby considerably mitigating the aggressive potential of this stream.

History has shown that when Jewish nationhood is described in religious and messianic terms it produces zealous tendencies. No single movement replicates in full the events or trends of the past that brought to the fall of the Second Commonwealth, and each zealous movement has its own nuances and emphases. Nevertheless, the modern-day zealots might have something to learn from history.

[71] Inbari, *Messianic*, pp. 107–32.

Epilogue

Contemporary trends in radical ultra-Orthodoxy

By way of an epilogue to the historical developments discussed in this book, I believe it will be illuminating to examine several contemporary issues relating to the Haredi world in general and the radical ultra-Orthodoxy in particular. At the time of writing, in September 2014, the Haredi world as a whole seems to be facing several significant challenges that threaten the cohesion and way of life of their communities. The first challenge is a financial one. The emergence of a society of scholars, particularly in Israel but also in the United States, in which the men engage in Torah study as their principal occupation has become an extremely significant financial burden. The situation in which Haredi families, many of which include a large number of children, are economically dependent on transfer payments since the men do not work, and the only income is that of the women, has led to widespread impoverishment. This situation is particularly prevalent in Israel, where the institution of the yeshivah has developed as a framework offering full-time Torah study for single and married men. This framework is designed, in part, to avoid the drafting of the men to the army. However, poverty statistics provided by the UJA-Federation of New York suggest that two-thirds of the Hasidic community in New York, which comprises some 50,000 households, are considered poor or "almost poor."[1]

Another crisis is facing the Haredi education system for men. The educational frameworks for youths and adults were intended to serve as a defensive shield against acculturation, but in practice they have become

---

[1] Jacob B. Ukeles, Steven M. Cohen, and Ron Miller, *Jewish Community Study of New York: 2011 Special Report on Poverty*. New York: UJA-Federation of New York, 2012.

institutions that encourage educational mediocrity in a premeditated attempt to prevent the students from acquiring vital professions in the job market. In Israel, as noted, these institutions also serve as a shield against military service. Many young Haredim drop out of these frameworks and live on the margins of Haredi society, changing its character. According to figures quoted by the researcher Yohai Hakak, between seven and eight percent of all Haredi students under the age of eighteen in Israel drop out of school every year. This is equivalent to some 20,000 youths in each year class.[2]

In addition to these two profound processes, a further potential crisis faces the Haredi community in Israel, although its ramifications remain unclear at this stage. I refer to the issue of military service. The Israeli Knesset passed a law in 2014 that will impose the draft on the majority of Haredi men each year, while 1,800 men defined as "geniuses" (*ilu'im*) will be permitted to continue the current arrangement providing an exemption from the draft for those whose "Torah study is their vocation." The law is supposed to be enforced from 2017; it remains to be seen whether it will actually be implemented. The forced and mass drafting of young Haredi men would constitute a turning point in the relations between the Haredi community and the State of Israel and could have dramatic repercussions.

The movements discussed in this book are not immune to the challenges I have outlined earlier. Military service by young Haredi men could lead to significant changes in the structure of the Haredi community. As noted, the "status quo" arrangements that emerged during the early years of the state allowed young Haredi men to defer military service in order to study Torah. Study has become an alternative to participation in the workforce and the state has permitted this sector to enjoy this special arrangement, provided the Torah students saw their studies as their vocation. This arrangement led to a practice whereby all the men of recruiting age (from eighteen through to their forties) were placed in institutions for Torah study that focus exclusively on religious studies. This led in turn to the trend that has caused the impoverishment of the Haredi community, whereby most of its male members do not work. This situation is reflected in the large number of educational institutions that in practice are willing to accept almost any male Haredi adult.

If the number of young Haredim drafted for military service increases, those involved will be able after their service to enter the job market and

---

[2] Yohai Hakak, *Young Men in Israeli Haredi Yeshiva Education: The Scholars' Enclave in Unrest*. Leiden: Brill, 2012, p. 16.

provide for their families. This will prevent the poverty that is prevalent in this society, while also obviating the need for educational frameworks that effectively serve as "babysitting" services for adults who are incapable of joining the job market.

Such a change could have a number of potential ramifications for Haredi society. On the one hand, this society might open itself up to Israeli society at large, bringing down the barriers that have protected the enclave. It it highly likely that fear of such a development explains much of the fierce opposition to the draft among the rabbinical leaders of the community. A further indirect consequence could be a greater sense of affinity and belonging with the State of Israel among large sections of the Haredi community due to the mediating impact of military service. It is also possible that religious standards could slip among those who join the army as young men experience their first opportunity to live outside the frameworks of the enclave.

However, the ramifications could also be the opposite of those I have just described. Many Haredim might develop a greater sense of resentment toward the state, perceiving that it is threatening to destroy the fabric of Haredi society. This could attract growing number of Haredim to the anti-Zionist streams, such as Neturei Karta and HaEdah HaHaredit. A violent response to the draft cannot be ruled out. Accordingly, while the draft may foster patterns of integration in Israeli society, I anticipate that anti-Zionist circles will also benefit from a counterreaction.

Another area that deserves attention is that of gender issues. Since 2011, there has been a trend toward increasingly strict modesty rules among women living in the Haredi enclaves in Jerusalem and several other areas. The "Taliban sect," as it has been dubbed by the Israeli media, is a group of Haredi women who seek to cover their bodies completely when in the public domain; their faces are covered by a veil. The epithet "Taliban" alludes to the similarity between their dress and the burka worn by Afghan women to cover their body and face.

Since Haredi zealots have always been at the vanguard of strict modesty campaigns, it might have been expected that they would welcome this development. In fact, however, the Beit Din Tzedek (supreme court) of HaEdah HaHaredit condemned this phenomenon in forceful terms.[3] The response of the Jerusalem zealots might seem puzzling, since they have never shown any inclination to oppose the adoption of stricter religious conduct.

---

[3] www.telegraph.co.uk/news/worldnews/middleeast/israel/7919501/Israeli–rabbis–clamp–down–on–burka.html (accessed September 1, 2013)

Women form the backbone of contemporary Haredi society since they are the main breadwinners. Their social advancement is inevitable and has ambivalent consequences. As I showed in Chapter 3, stricter modesty rules would appear to be designed to curb women's rising status.

Reports of the decision by the Beit Din Tzedek outlawing the "Taliban women" have overlooked an important point. The women's adoption of extreme dress norms actually manifested a high degree of empowerment of women, and possibly even an incipient revolt. It is possible that this aspect explains the court's forceful reaction.

As will be recalled, the Beit Din Tzedek has approved every possible stricture in public life. A casual observer of the Haredi public over recent years cannot fail to notice the clear trend to extremism. Gender segregation on buses and on the streets in Meah She'arim has spread to every corner of the public domain, including post offices and clinics.[4] It might seem that the action of the "Taliban women" in covering every inch of their body is merely the natural extension of this trend, but this is not the case.

The grounds given by the Beit Din Tzedek for condemning the women ostensibly related to the potential danger to human life (*pikuach nefesh*) due to complications in home childbirths as the result of their reluctance to give birth in hospital.

It would seem that the only way these women were able to protest against their social oppression and seize control of their own fate was by adopting the rules of the game in their community and inventing their own strictures. Through this process they became social leaders, and their distinct external appearance ironically emphasized their independence of masculine control. The ostensible message of sexual oppression conveyed by the women's "Taliban-style" dress was actually transformed into a tool for empowerment and autonomy.

It is possible that this was the reason for the angry response of HaEdah HaHaredit: the sight of women making their own decisions while the communal leaders were left powerless. After all, from the strict perspective of religious law there can be no specific objection to the women's dress.

This phenomenon is not confined to modest dress, but suggests the first signs of a feminine rebellion within Haredi circles. The same women refuse to send their children to school, decline sexual relations with their

---

[4] Ruth Carmi and Ricky Shapira-Rosenberg, *Excluded, For God's Sake: Gender Segregation and the Exclusion of Women in Public Space in Israel*. Jerusalem: Israel Religious Action Center, 2011.

husbands, and refuse to go to the Mikveh (ritual purification bath) – all in the name of modesty. The result is a weakening of male authority as women assume leadership functions.

The phenomenon of the "Taliban women" and the Haredi reactions to this development suggest the presence of a fault line under the surface of Haredi society in the context of gender relations. If women's voices become more audible, it is not impossible that this issue will gain greater prominence. Religious extremism and the constant addition of new strictures may create an internal mechanism that will eventually lead to rejection and rebellion. The "Taliban women" offer a model for such a rebellion, albeit in an unusual mirror-image way. A combination of a women's revolt and the high level of dropout of young Haredim from the community's educational frameworks could combine to cause profound shock to Haredi society in Israel.

Turning to the Hasidic community in New York, some interesting trends can also be discerned. There are no precise statistics regarding the number of Satmar Hasidim in New York. Accordingly, I would like to begin by explaining how I reached my assertion that the community numbers approximately 100,000 individuals. I will then discuss two demographic issues that may indicate future patterns of development in this community.

According to a survey conducted by the UJA-Federation of New York in 2011, there are some 50,000 households defined as "Hasidic" in New York. The total number of individuals in these households is estimated at 239,000.[5] Since not all the Hasidim belong to the Satmar sector, a more accurate breakdown is needed. The survey included questions about attitudes toward Israel among Jews. While Orthodox Jews in New York generally show a high level (seventy-five percent) of attachment to Israel, the figures in the Hasidic community are different. In general terms, fifty-six percent of those who defined themselves as Hasidic showed a level of attachment to Israel. This figure implies that forty-six percent of the Hasidic community is non-Zionist or anti-Zionist.[6] In numerical terms, this represents some 110,000 people affiliated to Satmar or to Hasidic courts with a similar ideological profile. If we look at the total Jewish population of New York – approximately 1,540,000 – the Satmar Hasidim thus account for some seven percent of the population.

---

[5] Steven M. Cohen, Jacob B. Ukeles, and Ron Miller, *Jewish Community Study of New York: 2011 Comprehensive*. New York: UJA–Federation of New York, 2012.
[6] *Ibid.*, pp. 223–4.

An examination of the demographic profile of Jewish children under the age of eighteen in New York yields a different picture. There are currently some 127,000 Hasidic children (thirty-seven percent of the total), and a similar number of children (131,000 or thirty-nine percent) from all the non-Orthodox streams. The number of children from the Modern Orthodox stream is 42,000 (twelve percent), while some 39,000 children come from the "Yeshivish" stream (i.e., non-Hasidic ultra-Orthodox circles – also approximately twelve percent).[7] These figures show that the weight of the Orthodox community as a whole within the total Jewish population will increase in the near future and will eventually account for the majority of New York Jews. Within the Orthodox sector, the dominant group will be the Hasidim. If we apply the aforementioned assumption that forty-six percent of Hasidim belong to anti-Zionist movements, this implies that approximately eighteen percent of the total Jewish population will be anti-Zionist. Barring any dramatic and unexpected developments in the profile of the community we can assume that these trends will characterize New York Jewry within one or two decades.

The figures presented above have several ramifications for the future. The first issue that deserves comment is that of support for Israel among New York Jews. The trends identified in the survey suggest that, in general, Israel will continue to enjoy widespread support among the New York community, which is the largest and most influential Jewish community in the United States. However, the anti-Zionist element within the community will grow significantly. Moreover, the study also identified a fall in support for Israel among non-Orthodox Jews. Only twenty-fve percent of those aged under fifty in this sector claimed that they feel "very attached" to Israel, as compared to sixty percent in the Orthodox community as a whole. Among non-Orthodox Jews over the age of fifty, the figure was forty-five percent.[8] We can therefore conclude that the level of support for Israel among New York Jews will fall, both because of the trend away from collective Jewish identity among young non-Orthodox Jews and because of the growing weight of the anti-Zionist Hasidim.

Poverty is a further issue that demands attention. The rapid growth of the Hasidic community in New York can be expected to lead to an increase in absolute terms in the number of poor Jews. As the survey commissioned by UJA-Federation of New York showed, there is a direct correlation between the level of poverty and the level of formal secular

---

[7] *Ibid.*, p. 216.　　[8] *Ibid.*, pp. 146–7.

education. It is possible that economic pressure will force the Hasidic community to introduce vocational training for men and enable greater participation in the workforce. If this is the case, this will undoubtedly influence the character of the community.

On June 9, 2013, a large demonstration was held in New York to protest the Israeli government's intention of drafting Haredi men. Some 30,000 people attended the demonstration, which was organized by the two wings of the Satmar movement, though other Haredi streams were also invited to participate. It is worth noting that this was the first time since the split in the movement in 2006 that the two Admors – Aharon Teitelbaum and Zalman Leib Teitelbaum – sat together on the same platform and cooperated in organizing the event.[9] The demonstration was the largest protest by anti-Zionist Hasidim since the 1980s, when rallies were held to object to the passage of buses through Haredi neighborhoods in Jerusalem bearing pictures of bikini-clad models.[10]

It is worth noting several aspects concerning the demonstration. Teitelbaum's death in 1979 led to a fierce war of inheritance between Moshe Teitelbaum, the official heir, and the widow Alta Feiga. The divisions in the movement led to the cessation of mass anti-Israel protests for over thirty years until the 2013 demonstration. One possible explanation for this hiatus is that the members of the movement were preoccupied with the internal divisions and had little time or energy for broader political issues. It is also worth noting that the UJA-Federation of New York regularly provides financial support for poor Hasidim. It is possible that the halt to the demonstrations reflected a pragmatic desire on the part of the leadership not to irritate the wider Jewish community by flaunting their anti-Israeli positions in order not to jeopardize this support. According to the article in the *Forward*, several figures in the Jewish community reacted angrily to the recent demonstration and threatened to halt budgets for the Satmar community.[11] Thus it would seem that the economic dependence of the Hasidic court on the broader Jewish community in New York has acted as a moderating factor. The potential growth of poverty in this community could increase this dependence still further, with all this implies in terms of the movement's public profile.

The survey raised another surprising finding: no fewer than thirty-one percent of Hasidim living in Williamsburg, New York – the center of the

[9] http://forward.com/articles/178568/did–satmars–bite–hand–that–feeds–them–with–anti–is/?p=all (accessed September 1, 2013).
[10] *Ibid.*   [11] *Ibid.*

Satmar sector – stated that they are "very attached" to the State of Israel.[12] It is difficult to explain this figure. It is possible that the respondents were less than serious in their replies, but it is also possible that the finding may reflect previously undetected trends. As I have shown, the Haredi community in Israel has seen the emergence of subversive trends led by women and youths against the rabbinical hegemony. It is not impossible that similar trends exist in the Hasidic enclave in New York. In attempting to interpret the finding of significant support for Israel among Satmar Hasidim, it is also important to take into account the tendency to fragmentation among Hasidic courts in general – a pattern that, as noted, has been seen in Satmar since 2006. The adoption of a more moderate ideological stance regarding Israel may reflect the need to sharpen the differences between the different factions. According to this analysis, the demonstration in June 2013 may be explained by reference to internal developments within the movement, in an attempt to unite its ranks and combat growing covert dissident tendencies.

The growth of radical ultra-Orthodoxy in the present generation is a remarkable phenomenon. This community faced enormous obstacles following its physical annihilation in Europe, and then faced the challenge of rehabilitation within hostile secular societies in Israel and the United States. Radical ultra-Orthodoxy continues to face significant challenges that may jeopardize its cohesion and resilience. However, history has shown that this community has a strong capacity to adapt and to overcome obstacles. Only time will tell what directions these trends will take and how they will shape the future of the movement.

I hope that this book has contributed to an understanding of this unique branch of contemporary Judaism.

---

[12] Cohen, Ukeles, and Miller, *Jewish Community Study*, p. 223.

Bibliography

Adler, Yitzhak. *The Order of the Last Year*. New York: Emet – Or Torah Munkacz, 5758 – 1997 (in Hebrew).

Almond, Gabriel, Scott Appleby, and Emmanuel Sivan. *Strong Religion – The Rise of Fundamentalism around the World*. Chicago: University of Chicago Press, 2003.

Alter, Avraham. *Collection of Letters from the Admor Shlita of Ger*. Augsburg: Self-publication, 5707 – 1947 (in Hebrew).

Altshuler, Mor. *The Messianic Secret of Hasidism*. Haifa: Haifa University Press, 2002 (in Hebrew).

Anonymous. "A Victim of the Sabbath Demonstrations Buried." *Davar*, September 3, 1956, 4 (in Hebrew).

"Anglican Bishop Attempts to Make Peace." *Davar*, February 22, 1948, 2 (in Hebrew).

"Avrahami Suggests Passage of 'Neturei Karta' or Their Dispersal in Israel." *Davar*, February 21, 1956, 2 (in Hebrew).

"Mazal Tov! Rabbi Amram Has Married His Convert." *Yediot Acharonot*, September 5, 1965, 21 (in Hebrew).

"Record This for a Memory in Writing." *HaHomah – Collection of Articles for Strengthening Religion* 24 (Ellul 5734 – 1974), 24–8 (in Hebrew).

"Three Separate Reports Published by the Commission to Investigate the Sabbath Demonstrations in Jerusalem." *Davar*, June 6, 1957, 4 (in Hebrew).

Aran, Gideon. *Kookism – The roots of Gush Emunim, Jewish Settlers' Sub-Culture, Zionist Theology, Contemporary Messianism*. Jerusalem: Carmel, 2013 (in Hebrew).

Ariel-Joël, David. "Messianism without Messiah: The Messiah Who Will Not Come." In: Ariel-Joël, David and others (eds.), *The War of Gog and Magog: Messianism and Apocalypse in Judaism, Past and Present*. Tel Aviv: Hemed Publishers, 2001, pp. 161–73 (in Hebrew).

Armstrong, Karen. *The Battle for God*. New York: Ballantine Books, 2001.

Avni, Haim. *Clients, Prostitutes and White Slavers in Argentina and in Israel.* Tel Aviv: Miskal, 2009 (in Hebrew).

Bacon, Gershon. "Birth Pangs of the Messiah: The Reflections of Two Polish Rabbis on Their Era." In: Frankel, Jonathan (ed.), *Studies in Contemporary Jewry 7: Jews and Messianism in the Modern Era: Metaphor and Meaning.* New York: Oxford University Press, 1991, pp. 86–99.

 The Politics of Tradition: Agudat Yisrael in Poland, 1916–1939. Jerusalem: Magnes Press, 1996.

Baer, Yitzhak. "The Historical Background of the Ra'aya Mehemena." *Zion* 5(1) (1940) 1–44 (in Hebrew).

Bauer, Yehuda. *Jews for Sale? Nazi-Jewish Negotiations, 1933–1945.* New Haven: Yale University Press, 1994.

Baumgarten, Albert. "The Nature of Religious Extremism." In: Litbak Meir and Ora Limor (eds.), *Religious Zealotry.* Jerusalem: The Zalman Shazar Center for Jewish History, 2007, pp. 43–56 (in Hebrew).

Bendorth, Margaret L. *Fundamentalism and Gender 1875 to Present.* New Haven: Yale University Press, 1993.

Bengis, Zelig Reuven. "Great Warning." *HaHomah* 59 (Tevet 5709 – 1949), 2 (in Hebrew).

Benor, Sarah Bunin. *Becoming Frum: How Newcomers Learn the Language and Culture of Orthodox Judaism.* New Brunswick, N.J: Rutgers University Press, 2012.

Ben Shalom, Yisrael. *The House of Shammai and the Zealots' Struggle against Rome.* Jerusalem: Ben Zvi Institute and Ben Gurion University Publishers, 1993 (in Hebrew).

Berkovitz, Michael. "Rejecting Zion, Embracing the Orient: The Life and Death of Jacob Israel De Haan." In: Kalmar, Evan D. and Derek Penslar (eds.), *Orientalism and the Jews.* Waltham: Brandeis University Press, 2005, pp. 109–24.

Blau, Amram. *Clarifying Matters.* Jerusalem: Horev, 5720 – 1959 (in Hebrew).

 The Claim of Amram Blau against the Court of HaEdah HaHaredit in Jerusalem. Jerusalem: self-publication, 5725 – 1964/5 (in Hebrew).

 The Judge in Your Days. Jerusalem: Horev, undated [probably published in Tishrei 5720 – October 1959] (in Hebrew).

Blau, Amram (ben Moshe). *Guardian of the Walls – Chapters in Memory of Moshe Blau.* Jerusalem: self-publication, 1976 (in Hebrew).

Blau, Ruth. *Guardians of the City.* Jerusalem: Idanim, 1979 (in Hebrew).

Boyarin, Daniel. *Unheroic Conduct: The Rise of Heterosexuality and the Invention of the Jewish Man.* Berkeley, CA: University of California Press, 1997.

Boyer, Paul. *When Time Shall Be No More.* Cambridge: Harvard University Press, 1992.

Brighton, Mark A. *The Sicarii in Josephus's Judean War: Rhetorical Analysis and Historical Observations.* Atlanta: Society of Biblical Literature, 2009.

Brown, Benjamin. "The Spectrum of Orthodox Responses: Ashkenazim and Sephardim." In: Ravitzky, Aviezer (ed.), *Shas: Cultural and Ideological Aspects.* Tel Aviv: Am Oved, 2006, pp. 41–96 (in Hebrew).

"The Two Faces of Religious Radicalism: Orthodox Zealotry and 'Holy Sinning' in Nineteenth-Century Hasidism in Hungary and Galicia." *Journal of Religion* 93(3) (2013), 341–74.

"'As Swords to the Earth's Body': The Opposition for East European Rabbis to the Idea of Congregational Schism." In: Goldstein, Yossi (ed.), *Yosef Daat*. Beer Sheva: Ben Gurion University Press, 5770 – 2010, pp. 215–44 (in Hebrew).

"The Eastern Sages and Religious Zealotry." *Akademot* 10 (5761 – 2001), 289–324 (in Hebrew).

Caplan, Kimmy, "'An Insolent, Dirty Convert Woman': Amram Blau and Ruth Ben David Marriage Affair." *Iyunim Bitkumat Israel*, 20 (2010), 300–35 (in Hebrew).

"The Development of Separation Circles among Haredi Zealots: The Case of Amram Blau." *Zion* 76(2) (2011), 179–218 (in Hebrew).

Carmi, Ruth and Ricky Shapira-Rosenberg. *Excluded, For God's Sake: Gender Segregation and the Exclusion of Women in Public Space in Israel*. Jerusalem: Israel Religious Action Center, 2011 (in Hebrew).

Carpenter, Joel. *Revive Us Again: The Reawakening of American Fundamentalism*. New York: Oxford University Press, 1997.

Cohen, Shaye. *From the Maccabees to the Mishna*. Philadelphia: Westminister Press, 1987.

Cohen, Steven M., Jacob B. Ukeles, and Ron Miller. *Jewish Community Study of New York: 2011 Comprehensive*. New York: UJA-Federation of New York, 2012.

Collins, John. "Eschatology." In: Collins, John J. and Daniel C. Harlow (eds.), *The Eerdmans Dictionary of Early Judaism*. Grand Rapids, MI: William B. Eerdmans, 2010, pp. 594–7.

"Radical Religion and Ethical Dilemmas of Apocalyptic Millenarism." In: Bennett, Zoe and David Gowler (eds.), *Radical Christian Voices and Practices*. New York: Oxford University Press, 2011, pp. 87–102.

Cooper, Levi Y. *The Munkacs Rebbe Chaim Elazar Shapira the Hasidic Ruler – Biography and Method*. Ramat Gan: PhD Dissertation, Bar Ilan University, 2011 (in Hebrew).

Darash, Menashe. *Neturei Karta of Meah She'arim*. Jerusalem: Atnahta Publishing House, 2010 (in Hebrew).

Dawson, Lorne. "Clearing the Underbush: Moving Beyond Festinger to a New Paradigm for the Study of Failed Prophecy." In: Tumminia, Diana and William Statos, Jr. (eds.), *How Prophecy Lives*. Leiden and Boston: Brill, 2011, pp. 69–98.

"When Prophecy Fails and Faith Persists: A Theoretical Overview." *Nova Religio* 3(1) (1999) 6–82.

Deitsch, Alexander. *Butzina Kadisha 1–2*. New York: Tiferes Publishing, 1998, 2000 (in Hebrew).

Don Yehiya, Eliezer. "The Book and the Sword: The Nationalist Yeshivot and Political Radicalism in Israel." In: Martin E. Marty and Scott Appleby (eds.), *Accounting for Fundamentalisms*. Chicago: University of Chicago Press, 1996, pp. 264–302.

Doshinsky, Yosef Zvi. "Pesak din." *HaHomah* 46 (21 Av 5708 – 1948), 1 (in Hebrew).

Douglas, Mary. *In the Wilderness: The Doctrine of Defilement in the Book of Numbers*. Sheffield: Sheffield Academic Press, 1993.

Purity and Danger: An Analysis of Concepts of Pollution and Taboo. New York and Washington, Psychology Press, 1966.

Eisen, Robert. *The Peace and Violence of Judaism: From the Bible to Modern Zionism*. New York: Oxford University Press, 2011.

Eisenstadt, Shmuel N. *Fundamentalism, Sectarianism and Revolution – The Jacobin Dimension of Modernity*. Cambridge: Cambridge University Press, 1999.

Elboim-Dror, Rachel. "The Ultimate Ghetto: A Subversive Ultra-Orthodox Utopia." *Jewish Studies Quarterly* 7(1), (2000), 65–95.

Elior, Rachel. *The Mystical Origins of Hasidism*. Oxford & Portland: Littman Library of Jewish Civilization, 2006.

Elitzur, Yuval. "Neturei Karta Declared Its Independence." *Ma'ariv*, August 24, 1979, 1 (in Hebrew).

Epstein, Gil S. and Ira N. Gang. "Understanding the Development of Fundamentalism." *Public Choice* 132(3/4) (2007) 257–71.

Falkozite, Chaim. *Holy Utterances*. Munkacs: Grafia Press, year of printing unclear (in Hebrew).

Farbstein, Esther. *Beseter Hamadregah: Orthodox Jewry in Hungary Facing the Holocaust*. Jerusalem: Mosad Harav Kook, 2013 (in Hebrew).

Farmer, Willliam. *Maccabees, Zealots, and Josephus: An Inquiry into Jewish Nationalism in the Greco-Roman Period*. New York: Columbia University Press, 1956.

Feiner, Shmuel. *The Origins of Jewish Secularization in 18th Century Europe*. Philadelphia: University of Pennsylvania Press, 2011.

Feldman, Louis. *"Remember Amalek!" Vengeance, Zealotry, and Group Destruction in the Bible according to Philo, Pseudo-Philo, and Josephus*. Cincinnati: HUC Press, 2004.

Ferons, James. "Israeli Sect Head to Wed a Convert; Orthodox Chief, 72, Leaves Holy City for Divorcee, 45." *New York Times*, August 2, 1965, 11.

Ferrari, Robert. "The 'Crime Passionnel' in French Courts." *California Law Review* 6(5), (1918), 331–41.

Ferziger, Adam. *Exclusion and Hierarchy: Orthodoxy, Nonobservance, and the Emergence of Modern Jewish Identity*. Philadelphia: University of Pennsylvania Press, 2005.

Festinger, Leon, Henry W. Reicken, and Stanley Schachter. *When Prophecy Fails: A Social and Psychological Study of A Modern Group That Predicted the Destruction of the World*. Minneapolis: University of Minnesota Press, 1956.

Firestone, Reuven. "Holy War in Modern Judaism? 'Mitzva War' and the Problem of the 'Three Vows.'" *Journal of the American Academy of Religion* 74(4), (2006), 954–82.

Frankel, Yuval. "Haredi and Religious Judaism in Jerusalem during the Siege." *HaTziyonut* 18, (1994), 247–289 (in Hebrew).

Friedman, Menachem. "Jewish Zealots: Conservative versus Innovative." In: Silberstein, Laurence J. (ed.), *Jewish Fundamentalism in Contemporary*

Perspective – Religion, Ideology, and the Crisis of Modernity. New York: NYU Press, 1993, pp. 148–63.

"Messiah and Messianism in Habad-Lubavitch Hasidism." In: Ariel-Joël, David [et al.] (ed.), *War of Gog and Magog: Messianism and Apocalypse in Judaism – Past and Present*. Tel Aviv: Yediot Ahronot Publishers, 2001, pp. 161–173 (in Hebrew).

"Neturei Karta and the Sabbath Demonstrations in Jerusalem, 1948–1950." In: Bareli, Avi (ed.), *Divided Jerusalem, 1948–1967: Sources, Summaries, Selected Incidents, and Ancillary Material*. Jerusalem: Ben Zvi Institute, 1994, pp. 224–40 (in Hebrew).

Haredi Society – Sources, Trends, and Processes. Jerusalem: Jerusalem Institute for Israel Studies, 1991 (in Hebrew).

Society and Religion – Non-Zionist Orthodoxy in the Land of Israel, 1918–1936. Jerusalem: Ben Zvi Institute, 5738 – 1978 (in Hebrew).

Fuchs, Avraham. *The Admor of Satmar*. Jerusalem: self-publication, 5740 – 1980 (in Hebrew).

Fund, Yosef. *Separation or Integration: Agudat Yisrael confronts Zionism and the State of Israel*. Jerusalem: Magnes Press, 1999 (in Hebrew).

Gelber, Yoav. *Palestine 1948: War, Escape and the Emergence of the Palestinian Refugee Problem*. London: Sussex Academic Press, 2006.

Gelbman, Shlomo Yaacov. *Moshian Shel Yisrael 1–9*. Kiryas Yoel: Ohel Torah Publishers, 1989–2008 (in Hebrew).

Goldstein, Moshe. *Jerusalem Travels*. New York: Emet – Or Torah Munkacz, 5764–2004 (in Hebrew).

Tikkun Olam. Mukacevo: Druck H. Guttmann, 5696 – 1936 (in Hebrew).

Gordon, Leonard D. "Toward a Gender-Inclusive Account of Halakhah." In: Rundavsky, Tamar (ed.), *Gender and Judaism – The Transformation of Tradition*. New York and London: NYU Press, 1995, pp. 3–12.

Green, Arthur. "Ger Hasidic Dynasty." *YIVO Encyclopedia of Jews in Eastern Europe*, www.yivoencyclopedia.org/article.aspx/Ger_Hasidic_ Dynasty (accessed on 24 February 2012).

Greenberg, Gershon. "Foundations for Orthodox Jewish Theological Response to the Holocaust: 1936–1939." In: Eckardt, Alice (ed.), *Burning Memory: Times of Testing and Reckoning*. Oxford: Pergamon Press 1993, pp. 71–94.

Haeri, Shahla. "Obedience versus Autonomy: Women and Fundamentalism in Iran and Pakistan." In: Marty, Martin and Scott Appleby (eds.), *Fundamentalisms and Society: Reclaiming the Sciences, the Family and Education*. Chicago: University of Chicago Press, 1993, pp. 181–213.

Hakak, Yohai. *Young Men in Israeli Haredi Yeshiva Education – The Scholars' Enclave in Unrest*. Leiden & Boston: Brill, 2012.

Halevy, David. *Murder in Jerusalem: The Affair of the Murder of Prof. De Haan*. Bnai Brak: Tefutza, 1987 (in Hebrew)

Hardacre, Helen. "The Impact of Fundamentalisms on Woman, the Family, and Interpersonal Relations." In: Marty, Martin and Scott Appleby (eds.), *Fundamentalism and Society: Reclaiming the Sciences, the Family, and Education*. Chicago: University of Chicago Press, 1993, pp. 129–50.

Harel, Isser. *The Yossele Campaign*. Tel Aviv: Yediot Acharonot, 1982 (in Hebrew).

Harel, Yaron. *Intrigue and Revolution: The Appointment and Dismissal of Chief Rabbis in the Communities of Baghdad, Damascus and Aleppo, 1744–1914*. Jerusalem: Ben Zvi Institute, 2007 (in Hebrew).

Harrington, Daniel. "Maccabean Revolt." In: Collins, John and Daniel C. Harlow (eds.), *The Eerdmans Dictionary of Early Judaism*. Grand Rapids, MI: William B. Eerdmans, 2010, pp. 900–2.

Harris, Jay M. "Fundamentalism: Objections from a Modern Jewish Historian." In: Hawley, John S. (ed.), *Fundamentalism and Gender*. New York: Oxford University Press, 1994, pp. 137–73.

Harris, Ruth. "Hysteria and Feminine Crimes of Passion in the Fin-de-Siècle." *History Workshop* 25 (1988) 31–63.

Heilman, Samuel. *Sliding to the Right: The Contest for the Future of American Jewish Orthodoxy*. Berkeley: University of California Press, 2006.

Heilman, Samuel and Menachem Friedman. "Religious Fundamentalism and Religious Jews: The Case of the Haredim." In: Marty, Martin E. and Scott Appleby (eds.), *Fundamentalism Observed*. Chicago: The University of Chicago Press, 1991, pp. 197–264.

The Rebbe: The Life and Afterlife of Menachem Mendel Schneerson. Princeton: Princeton University Press, 2010.

Hellinger, Moshe. "Political Theology in the Thought of 'Merkaz HaRav' Yeshiva and its Profound Influence on Israeli Politics and Society since 1967." *Totalitarian Movements & Political Religions* 9(4), (2008), 533–50.

Hengel, Martin. *The Zealots: Investigations into the Jewish Freedom Movement in the Period from Herod I until 70*. Edinburgh: T. & T. Clark, 1989 [German origin 1976].

Hershkowitz, Yitzhak. "Rabbi Chaim Yosef Sonnenfeld." In: Brown, Benjamin and Nissim Leon (eds.), *Hagdolim: The People Who Shaped Haredi Judaism in Israel: A Collection of Essays in Honor of Professor Menachem Friedman*. Jerusalem: Van Leer (forthcoming) (in Hebrew).

The Redemption Vision of Rabbi Yissachar Shlomo Teichtel, HY"D: Transitions in His Messianic Perception during the Holocaust. Ramat Gan: PhD Dissertation, Bar Ilan University, 2009 (in Hebrew).

Hildesheimer, Meir. "The Attitude of the Ḥatam Sofer toward Moses Mendelssohn." *Proceedings of the American Academy for Jewish Research* 60, (1994), 141–187.

Horsley, Richard. "The Zealots: Their Origin, Relationships and Importance in the Jewish Revolt." *Novum Testamentum* 28(2), (1986), 159–92.

Horesly, Richard and John Hanson. *Bandits, Prophets, and Messiahs: Popular Movements at the Time of Jesus*. Minneapolis: Winston Press, 1985.

forward.com/articles/178568/did-satmars-bite-hand-that-feeds-them-with-anti-is/?p=all (accessed September 1, 2013).

onegshabbat.blogspot.com/2012/06/blog-post_19.html, (accessed December 2, 2013).

www.jpost.com/Opinion/Columnists/The-impending-haredi-implosion (accessed in April 8, 2014).

www.telegraph.co.uk/news/worldnews/middleeast/israel/7919501/Israeli-rabbis-clamp-down-on-burka.html (accessed September 1, 2013)

www.yoel-ab.com/data/upload_images/docs/4581bc19075add6b.jpg (accessed September 1, 2013).

tsotar.com/zofar/see_article.asp?id=4720 (accessed in April 8, 2014).

www.youtube.com/watch?v=rp1OeIfoDow&hl=iw (accessed in July 23, 2014).

www.yadvashem.org/odot_pdf/Microsoft%20Word%20-%207459.pdf (accessed in December 24, 2012)

www.yadvashem.org/yv/en/exhibitions/communities/munkacs/between_two_wars.asp (accessed May 9, 2012).

www.yadvashem.org/yv/en/exhibitions/communities/munkacs/rabbi_shapira.asp (accessed in April 8, 2014).

Idel, Moshe. *Hasidism: Between Ecstasy and Magic*. Albany: State University of New York Press, 1995.

Messianic Mystics. New Haven & London: Yale University Press, 1998.

Inbari, Motti. "Religious Zionism and the Temple Mount Dilemma: Key Trends." *Israel Studies* 12(2), (2007), 29–47.

Jewish Fundamentalism and the Temple Mount – Who Will Build the Third Temple? Albany: SUNY, 2009.

Messianic Religious Zionism Confronts Israeli Territorial Compromises. New York: Cambridge University Press, 2012.

Jacobson, Yoram. "Exile and Redemption in the Ger Hassidic Dynasty." *Da'at* 2/3 (5738/9–1978), 175–216 (in Hebrew).

"Truth and Faith in Ger Hassidic Dynasty." In: Dan, Joseph and Joseph Hakar (eds.), *Studies in Kabbalah, Jewish Philosophy, and Ethics and Contemplation Literature*. Jerusalem: Magnes Press, 5746–1985, pp. 593–616 (in Hebrew).

Kadosh, Refael. *Extremist Religious Philosophy: The Radical Religious Doctrines of the Satmar Rebbe*. PhD Dissertation, The University of Cape Town, 2011 (in Hebrew)

Kahane, David. *A History of Our Rabbi*. Brooklyn, NY: Emet – Or Torah Munkacs, 5758 – 1998 (in Hebrew).

Kaplan, Zvi Jonathan. "Rabbi Teitelbaum, Zionism, and Hungarian Ultra-Orthodoxy." *Modern Judaism* 24(2), (2004), 165–178.

Katz, Jacob. "Orthodoxy in Historical Perspective." In: Medding, Peter (ed.), *Studies in Contemporary Jewry 2; The Challenge of Modernity and Jewish Orthodoxy*. Bloomington: Indiana University Press, 1986, pp. 3–17.

"Towards a Biography of the Hatam Sofer." *Divine Law in Human Hands: Case Studies in Halakhic Flexibility*. Jerusalem: Magness Press, 1998, pp. 403–443.

A House Divided: Orthodoxy and Schism in Nineteenth-century Central European Jewry. Hanover, NH: Brandeis University Press, 1998.

Kazemzadeh, Masoud. *Islamic Fundamentalism, Feminism, and Gender Inequality in Iran under Khomeini*. Lanham, MD: University Press of America, 2002.

Keren-Kartz, Menachem, "Maharitz Dushinsky: 'A Guard for the Guard,' – Thwarting the Rapprochement of Agudat Yisrael to Zionism." In: Brown, Benjamin and Nissim Leon (eds.), *Hagdolim: The People who Shaped Haredi*

Judaism in Israel: A collection of Essays in Honor of Professor Menachem Friedman. Jerusalem: Van Leer, (forthcoming) (in Hebrew).

Marmaros-Sziget: "Extreme Orthodoxy" and Secular Jewish Culture at the Foothills of the Carpathian Mountains. Jerusalem: Carmel, 2013 (in Hebrew).

"Hast Thou Escaped, and also Taken Possession? The Satmar Rebbe – Rabbi Yoel Teitelbaum and his Followers' Response to Criticism of his Conduct during and After the Holocaust." *Dapim: Studies on the Holocaust* 28(2), 97–120.

"Marmaros – The Cradle of Extreme Orthodoxy." *Modern Judaism* 35(2), 147–174.

R' Yoel Teitelbaum – The Satmar Rabbi (1887–1979): Biography, Tel Aviv: PhD dissertation, Tel Aviv University, 2013 (in Hebrew).

Kluger, Binyamin. *All of Rabbi Moshe Blau's Writings*. Jeruslaem: Hotzaat Mashabim, 1983 (in Hebrew).

The Neighborhoods Surrounding Jerusalem. Jerusalem: Self-publication, 1979 (in Hebrew).

Kook, Zvi Yehuda. "The Nation of Israel Stand up and Live." In: Melamed, Zalman (ed.), *Eretz Hatsvi-Our Rabbi in the Battle over Our Entire Land*. Bet El: Netivei Or, 1994 (in Hebrew).

Kraus, Itzhak. "The Theological Responses to the Balfour Declaration." *Bar Ilan* 28–9 (5761 – 2000), 81–104 (in Hebrew).

Lamm, Norman. "The Ideology of the Neturei Karta: According to the Satmarer Version." *Tradition* 12(2), (1971), 38–53.

Landau, Shlomo Zalman and Yosef Rabinowitz. *Or Liyesharim*. Warsaw: R. Meir Yechiel Alter Publications, 1900.

Levi, Dalya. "'Or Liyesharim' – An Anti-Zionist Manifesto – And Several Responses." *HaTziyonut* 19, (1998), 31–65 (in Hebrew).

Liebes, Yehuda. "HaEda HaHaredit in Jerusalem and the Judea Desert Sect." *Jerusalem Research in Judaic Studies* 3, (1981), 135–152 (in Hebrew).

"The Messiah of the Zohar – On the Messianic Image of Rabbi Shimon Bar Yochai." In: Zakowitz, Yair (ed.), *The Messianic Idea in Israel*. Jerusalem: Israel National Academy of Sciences, 5742 – 1982, pp. 87–236 (in Hebrew).

Liebman, Charles. "Extremism as a Religious Norm." *Journal of the Scientific Study of Religion* 22(1), (1983), 75–86.

Luz, Ehud. "The Limits of Toleration: The Challenge of Cooperation between the Observant and the Nonobservant during the Hibbat Zion Period, 1882–1895." In: Almog, Shmuel, Jehuda Reinharz, and Anita Shapira (eds.), *Zionism and Religion*. Hanover, NH: Brandeis University Press, 1998, pp. 44–54.

Maciejko, Pawel. *The Mixed Multitude: Jacob Frank and the Frankist Movement, 1755–1816*. Philadelphia: University of Pennsylvania Press, 2011.

Magid, Shaul. "The Politics of (un)Conversion: The 'Mixed Multitude' (erev rav) as Conversos in Rabbi Hayyim Vital's Ets ha-da'at tov." *Jewish Quarterly Review* 95(4), (2005), 625–666.

Marcus, Joel. "Modern and Ancient Jewish Apocalypticism." *Journal of Religion* 76 (1), 1996, 1–27.

Margaliot, Shimon. *Azamer bi-Shvahin: The Life of the Hasidic Kabbalistic Rabbi Yeshayah Asher Zelig Margaliot, May a Sage's Memory Be a Blessing*. Jerusalem: self-publication, 5763 – 2003 (Hebrew).

Margaliot, Yeshayah Asher Zelig. *Ashrei Ha'Aish*. Jerusalem: Breslav Press, 5681 – 1921 (in Hebrew).

Amudei Arazim. Jerusalem: Maarav Print, 5692 – 1931/2 (in Hebrew).

Mark, Zvi. "Messianic Hopes in Ger Hasidic Dynasty." *Tarbitz* 87(2), (5768 – 2007), 295–324 (in Hebrew).

The Hidden Scroll – the Secret Messianic Vision of Rabbi Nachman of Breslov. Ramat Gan: Bar Ilan University Press, 2006 (in Hebrew).

Meir, Yonatan. *Rehovot ha-Nahar: Kabbalah and Esotericism in Jerusalem (1896–1948)*. Jerusalem: Ben Zvi Institute, 2011 (in Hebrew).

Meisels, Dovid. *The Rebbe – The Extraordinary Life and Worldview of Rabbeinu Yoel Teitelbaum the Satmar Rebbe*. Lakewood, NJ: Israel Book Shop, 2011.

Melton, Gordon. "Spiritualization and Reaffirmation: What Really Happens When Prophecy Fails." *American Studies* 26(2), (1985), 17–29.

Mendels, Doron. *The Rise and Fall of Jewish Nationalism*. New York: Doubleday, 1992.

Meshi Zahav, Zvi and Yehuda Meshi Zahav. *The Martyr Rabbi Yaacov Yisrael de Haan, May G-d Avenge His Blood: The First Zionist Murder in the Land of Israel*. Jerusalem: Institute of Haredi Judaism, 5746 – 1986 (in Hebrew).

Mintz, Jerome. *Hassidic People: A Place in the New World*. Cambridge: Harvard University Press, 1992.

Mintzburg, Mordechai. *From the Diary of Rabbi Amram – Chapters from the Memoirs of the Rabbi and Tzaddik Amram Barsh"i Blau, May the Memory of a Tzaddik Be for a Blessing*. Jerusalem: self-publication, 5767 – 2007 (in Hebrew).

Myers, David. "'Commanded War': Three Chapters in the 'Military' History of Satmar Hasidism." *Journal of the American Academy of Religion* 81(2), (2013), 1–46.

Nadler, Allan. "Piety and Politics: The Case of the Satmar Rebbe." *Judaism* 31(2), (1982), 135–152.

"The War on Modernity of R. Hayyim Elazar Shapira of Munkacz." *Modern Judaism* 14(3), (1994), 233–264.

Nakdimon, Shlomo and Shaul Mayzlish. *De Haan: The First Political Assassination in the Land of Israel*. Tel Aviv: Modan, 1985 (Hebrew).

Neturei Karta, "To Our Brothers in Exile." *HaHomah* 42 (29 Adar 5708 – 1948), 1 (in Hebrew).

Oleszak, Agnieszka. "The Beit Ya'akov School in Krakow as an Encounter between East and West." *Polin* 23, (2010), 277–290.

Pedaya, Haviva. "Eretz: Time and Place – Apocalypse of End and Apocalypse of Beginning." In: Ravitzky, Aviezer (ed.), *The Land of Israel in 20th Century Jewish Thought*. Jerusalem: Ben-Zvi Institute, 2004, pp. 560–623 (in Hebrew).

Pedhazur, Ami. *The Triumph of Israel's Radical Right*. New York: Oxford University Press, 2012.

Peek, Charles, George D. Lowe, and Susan Williams. "Gender and God's Word: Another Look at Religious Fundamentalism and Sexism." *Social Forces* 69(4), (1991), 1205–21.

Piekarz, Mendel. *Ideological Trends in Poland during the Interwar Period and the Holocaust.* Jerusalem: Bialik Institute, 1990 (in Hebrew).

Poll, Solomon. *The Hassidic Community of Williamsburg* (2nd edition). New Brunswick: Transaction Publishers, 2006.

Ratzbi, Shalom. "Anti-Zionism and Messianic Tension in the Thought of Rabbi Shalom Dover." *HaTziyonut* 20, (5756 – 1996) 77–101 (in Hebrew).

Ravitzky, Aviezer. "'Forcing the End:' Zionism and the State of Israel as Antimessianic Undertakings." In: Frankel, Jonathan (ed.), *Studies in Contemporary Jewry 7: Jews and Messianism in the Modern Era: Metaphor and Meaning.* New York: Oxford University Press, 1991, pp. 34–67.

"The Messianism of Success in Contemporary Judaism." In: Stein, Stephen (ed.), *The Encyclopedia of Apocalypticism, 3: Apocalypticism in the Modern Period and the Contemporary Age.* New York and London: Continuum, 1998, pp. 204–29.

Messianism, Zionism, and Religious Radicalism. Chicago & London: University of Chicago Press, 1993.

Ross, Tamar. "Orthodoxy, Halakhah and the Challenge of Feminism." In: Salmon, Yosef, Aviezer Ravitzky, and Adam Praziger (eds.), *Jewish Orthodoxy: New Aspects.* Jerusalem: Yad Ben Zvi, 2006, pp. 255–96 (in Hebrew).

Roth, Aharon. *Shomrei Emunim 2.* Jerusalem: unspecified publisher, 5719 – 1959 (in Hebrew).

Rubin, Israel. *Two Generations of Urban Island* (2nd edition). New York: Peter Lang, 1997.

Rugh, Andrea B. "Reshaping Personal Relations in Egypt." In: Marty, Martin and Scott Appleby (eds.), *Fundamentalisms and Society: Reclaiming the Sciences, the Family and Education.* Chicago: University of Chicago Press, 1993, pp. 151–80.

Samet, Moshe. *Chapters in the History of Orthodoxy.* Jerusalem: Carmel, 2005 (in Hebrew).

"The Beginnings of Orthodoxy." *Modern Judaism* 8(3), (1988), 249–69.

Scharfer, Caroline. "Sarah Schenirer, Founder of the Beit Ya'akov Movement: Her Vision and Her Legacy." *Polin* 23, (2010), 269–275.

Schlesinger, Akiva Yosef. *Lev Ha'ivri.* Jerusalem: Zuckerman, 5784 – 1924.

Schochman, I. "From inside the Walls." *Davar,* November 29, 1938, 5 (in Hebrew).

Scholem, Gershom. *Sabbatai Sevi: The Mystical Messiah, 1626–1676,* Princeton: Princeton University Press, 1973.

The Messianic Idea in Judaism. New York: Schocken Books, 1972.

Schwartz, Dov. *Faith at a Crossroads – A Theological Profile of Religious Zionism.* Leiden, Boston & Koln: Brill, 2002.

Religious Zionism: History and Ideology. Boston: Academic Press, 2009.

Segal, Eliezer. "Disarming Phineas: Rabbinic Confrontations with Biblical Militancy." In: Hawkin, David J. (ed.), *The Twenty-first Century Confronts Its Gods: Globalization, Technology, and War.* Albany: SUNY, 2004, pp. 141–56.

Shabbtai, K. "At the Gates of Mass Hysteria." *Davar*, May 25, 1962, 2 (in Hebrew).

Salmon, Yosef. *Religion and Zionism – Early Conflicts*. Jerusalem: The Zionist Library, 5750 – 1990 (in Hebrew).

Shapira, Chaim Elazar. *Mashmia Yeshua*. New York: Emet – Or Torah Munkacs, 5751 – 1990 (originally published in 1919) (in Hebrew).

  Minchat Elazar 5. Jerusalem: Emet – Or Torah Munkacs, 5756 – 1995 (in Hebrew).

Shapira, Zvi Elimelech. *Maayan Ganim*. Zolkeiw: S. Meyerhoffer, 1848 (in Hebrew).

Shen, David. *Lovers of G-d in the Carpathian Mountains*. Jerusalem: Shem publishers, 5765 – 2004 (in Hebrew).

Shilo, Margalit. *Princess or Prisoner? Jewish Women in Jerusalem, 1840–1914*. Waltham MA: Brandeis University Press, 2005.

Shneler, Raphael. *The Educational System of the Jewish Radical Haredim in Jerusalem as their Main Contributor to Continuity and Change*. Ramat Gan: PhD Dissertation, Bar Ilan University, 1977 (in Hebrew).

Shuchtman, Eliav. "Jewish Government Cannot Be a 'Pursuer'." *Tehumin* 19 (5759 – 1999) 40–8 (in Hebrew).

Sievers, Joseph. "Hasmoneans." In: Collins John J. and Daniel C. Harlow (eds.), *The Eerdmans Dictionary of Early Judaism*. Grand Rapids, Mich.: William B. Eerdmans, 2010, pp. 705–9.

Silber, Michael K. "Akiva Yosef Shlesinger-The First Zionist?" *Cathedra* 73, (1994), 78–105 (in Hebrew).

  "A Hebrew Heart Beats in Hungary: Rabbi Akiva Yosef Schlesinger – Between Ultra-Orthodoxy and Jewish Nationalism." In: Sagi, Avi and Dov Schwartz (eds.), *One Hundred Years of Zionism 1*. Ramat Gan: Bar Ilan University Press, 5763 – 2003, pp. 225–254 (Hebrew).

  "Alliance of the Hebrew, 1863–1875: The Diaspora Roots of an Ultra-Orthodox Proto-Zionist Utopia in Palestine." *The Journal of Israeli History* 27(2), (2008), 119–47.

  "Schlesinger, Akiva Yosef." *YIVO Encyclopedia of Jews in Eastern Europe*, 2010. www.yivoencyclopedia.org/article.aspx/Schlesinger_Akiva_Yosef, (accessed March 4, 2013).

  "The Emergence of Ultra-Orthodoxy: The Invention of Tradition." In: Werthei-mer, Jack (ed.), *The Uses of Tradition: Jewish Continuity in the Modern Era*. New York: Jewish Theological Seminary, 1992, pp. 23–84.

Smith, Morton. "Zealots and Sicarii, Their Origins and Relation." *Harvard Theological Review* 64(1), (1971), 1–19.

Sorkin, David. *Moses Mendelssohn and the Religious Enlightenment*. Berkeley: University of California Press, 1996.

Sorotzkin, David. "Building the Earthly and Destroying the Heavenly: The Satmar Rebbe and Radical Orthodox School of Thought." In: Ravitzky, Aviezer (ed.), *The Land of Israel in 20th Century Jewish Thought*. Jerusalem: Ben-Zvi Institute, 2004, pp. 133–67 (in Hebrew).

  Orthodoxy and Modern Disciplination: The Production of Jewish Tradition in Europe in Modern Times. Tel Aviv: HaKibbutz HaMeuchad, 2011 (in Hebrew).

The Supra-Temporal Community in the Era of Change: The Emergency of Perceptions of Time and Collective as the Basis for Defining the Development of Jewish Orthodoxy in Modern Times. PhD Dissertation, The Hebrew University of Jerusalem, 2007 (in Hebrew).

Special correspondent, "Satmar Hasidim Who Demonstrated with Fatah in New York Expelled by the Rebbe, but Defended by Neturei Karta." *Ma'ariv*, March 13, 1970, 20 (in Hebrew).

Spiro, Abram. "The Ascension of Phinehas." *Proceedings of the American Academy for Jewish Research* 22, (1953), 91–114.

Sprinzak, Ehud. *Brother against Brother: Violence and Extremism in Israeli Politics from Altalena to the Rabin Assassination*. New York: The Free Press, 1999.

Sukrallah, Hala. "The Impact of the Islamic Movement in Egypt." In: Juschka, Darlene M. (ed.), *Feminism and the Study of Religion: A Reader*. London: Continuum, 2001, pp. 180–97.

Tau, Zvi. *On the Faith of Our Times – Guidelines for Understanding the Period*, 1. Jerusalem: Hosen Yeshuot, 5754 – 1994 (in Hebrew).

Teitelbaum, Yoel. *Divrei Yoel 1: Correspondence* (3rd edition), New York: Jerusalem Book Store Inc., 1982 (in Hebrew).

Sefer VeYoel Moshe: Kolel Shelosha Maamarim (5th edition), Brooklyn, NY: Bet Mishar Yerushalayim, 1981 (in Hebrew).

Tikochinski, Shlomo. "The Transfer of Lithuanian Yeshivot to the Land of Israel: The Story of the Hebron and Ponivez Yeshivot." In: Immanuel Etkes (ed.), *Yeshivot and Batei Midrash*. Jerusalem: Zalman Shazar Center Press, 2006, pp. 273–314 (in Hebrew).

Tishbi, Yeshayahu. "The Messianic Idea and Messianic Tendencies in the Rise of Hasidism," *Zion* 22, (5727 – 1967), 1–45 (in Hebrew).

The Teaching of the Zohar, 2. Jerusalem: Bialik Institute, 1949 (in Hebrew).

Tudor-Baumel, Judith and Jacob J. Schacter. "The Ninety-Three Bais Yaakov Girls of Cracow: History or Typology?" In: Schacter, Jacob J. (ed.), *Reverence, Righteousness, and Rahmanut: Essays in Memory of Rabbi Dr. Leo Jung*. Northvale, N.J.: Jason Aronson, 1992, pp. 93–130.

Ukeles, Jacob B., Steven M. Cohen, and Ron Miller. *Jewish Community Study of New York: 2011 Special Report on Poverty*. New York: UJA-Federation of New York, 2012.

Uni, Assaf. "Neturei Karta Delegate to Iranian Holocaust Conference: I Pray for Israel's Destruction 'in Peaceful Ways.'" *Ha'aretz*, January 24, 2007 (accessed: September 1, 2013). www.haaretz.com/hasen/spages/810100.html.

Unsigned. "Where are We Coming?" *HaHomah* 26 (2nd edition), (20 Kislev 5708) 1 (in Hebrew).

Unsigned. "Children of Amram Blau Elected as Leaders of Neturei Karta." *Ma'ariv*, July 17, 1974, 4 (Hebrew).

Unsigned. "Fervent Ceremonies against the Beach were Given in Synagogues in Tiberias." *Heruth*, January 27, 1962, 4 (in Hebrew).

Unsigned. "For Those Who Believe in God." *HaHomah* 27 (11 Shevat 5708 – 1948), 1 (in Hebrew).

Unsigned. "HaEdah HaHaredit is splitting." *Davar*, August 19, 1965, 14 (in Hebrew).

Unsigned. "Jerusalem." *Davar*, September 17, 1946, 4 (in Hebrew).

Unsigned. "Jerusalem." *Hatzofeh*, July 25, 1945, 4 (in Hebrew).

Unsigned. "Ministry of Finance is willing to Loan 100 Pounds to Agudah for Purchasing the Pool." *Heruth*, May 29, 1958, 8 (in Hebrew).

Unsigned. "Neturei Karta." *Hatzofeh*, August 7, 1945, 2 (in Hebrew).

Unsigned. "On the Outrage Regarding the Education Danger." *HaHomah* 58, (21 Kislev 5709 – 1949), 1 (in Hebrew).

Unsigned. "Protest March against Galei-Gil." *HaHomah* 23, (28 Iyar 5707 – 1946), 4 (In Hebrew).

Unsigned. "Rabbi Hirsch Gave Arafat an Amulet to Prevent Harm." *Davar*, July 7, 1994, 4 (Hebrew).

Unsigned. "Radical Haredi Leaders Demand Equal Status to Their Community as the National Community." *HaMashkif*, July 16, 1947, 4 (in Hebrew).

Unsigned. "Radical Netuei Karta." *Hatzofeh*, July 26, 1945, 8 (in Hebrew).

Unsigned. "Sabbath Demonstrations Continued the Entire Sabbath." *Heruth*, November 27, 1954, 4 (in Hebrew).

Unsigned. "The Club in Dispute in Jerusalem – Institution under State Supervision." *Davar*, November 25, 1954, 8 (in Hebrew).

Unsigned. "The Demonstration of Haredi Jewry against the Zionist Leadership." *HaHomah* 43 (Sivan 5708 – 1948), 4 (in Hebrew).

Unsigned. "The Discussion on the 'Club Affair' was Transferred to the Interior Committee." *Hatzofeh*, December 15, 1954, 1 (in Hebrew)

Unsigned. "The Insolent Smear Me With Lies, but With My Whole Heart I Keep Your Precepts." *HaHomah* 26 (2nd edition), (20 Kislev 5708 – 1948), 1 (in Hebrew).

Unsigned. "Two Yeshivah Students Were Convicted of Torching Eros." *Ma'ariv*, August 5, 1972, 5 (in Hebrew).

Unsigned. *Booklet of Holy Utterances*. London: Self-publication, 5734 – 1974 (Hebrew).

Urbach, Ephraim. *The Sages: Their Concepts and Beliefs*. Jerusalem: Magnes Press, 1975 (in Hebrew).

Van Henten, Jan Willem. "Martyrdom." In: Collins, John J. and Daniel C. Harlow (eds.), *The Eerdmans Dictionary of Early Judaism*. Grand Rapids, MI: William B. Eerdmans, 2010, pp. 917–9.

Vitlin, M. "Also Neturei Karta's Rabbi is willing to Move to the Patronage of Abdullah." *Heruth*, August 15, 1949, 1 (in Hebrew).

Weitzman, Steve. "He That Cometh Out: On the Disclosure of Messianic Secrets." In: Morgan, Michael and Steve Weitzman (eds.), *Rethinking the Messianic Idea: New Perspectives on Jewish Messianism*. Bloomington: Indiana University Press, pp. 63–92.

Wessinger, Catherine. "Catastrophic Millennialism." In: Landes, Richard (ed.), *Encyclopedia of Millennialism and Millennial Movements*. New York: Routledge, 2000, pp. 61–3.

Wilste, Jeff. *Contested Waters: A Social History of Swimming Pools in America*. Chapel Hill, NC: UNC Press, 2007.

Wolf, Michal. "The Halachic Attitude to Din Rodef and Din Moser." In: Arad, Moshe and Yuval Wolf (eds.), *Delinquency and Social Deviation: Theory and Practice*. Ramat Gan: Bar Ilan University Press, 2002, pp. 215–49 (Hebrew).

Yehoshua, B. "Reb Amram Refuses to Break his Engagement to the Convert." *Ma'ariv*, July 14, 1965, 18 (in Hebrew).

Yoval, Yisrael. "Vengeance and Curse, Blood and Libel." *Zion* 58, (5753 – 1993), 33–90 (in Hebrew).

Zameret, Zvi. *Education during the First Decade*. Tel Aviv: Open University Press, 2003 (in Hebrew).

ARCHIVES

Boston University, Gottleib Archival Research Center, Amram Blau, 1731, boxes 1–3 (hereafter cited as "Blau Archive").

Index